Revelation

Revelation

From Metaphor to Analogy

Richard Swinburne

CLARENDON PRESS · OXFORD

Oxford University Press, Walton Street, Oxford OX2 6DP
Oxford New York
Athens Auckland Bangkok Bombay
Calcutta Cape Town Dar es Salaam Delhi
Florence Hong Kong Istanbul Karachi
Kuala Lumpur Madras Madrid Melbourne
Mexico City Nairobi Paris Singapore
Taipei Tokyo Toronto
and associated companies in
Berlin Ibadan

Oxford is a trade mark of Oxford University Press

Published in the United States by
Oxford University Press Inc., New York

British Library Cataloguing in Publication Data
Data available

Library of Congress Cataloging in Publication Data
Swinburne, Richard.
Revelation : from metaphor to analogy / Richard Swinburne.
Includes index.
1. Revelation.   2. Metaphor—Religious aspects.   3. Analogy
(Religion).   I. Title.
BT127.2.S85   1992   231.7'4—dc20   91-18222
ISBN 0-19-823969-6
ISBN 0-19-823968-8 (pbk.)

Printed in Great Britain
on acid-free paper by
Biddles Ltd
Guildford and King's Lynn

Acknowledgements

Much of the material of four papers of mine published elsewhere is scattered throughout the book. These are 'Analogy and Metaphor', in G. J. Hughes (ed.), *The Philosophical Assessment of Theology* (Search Press, 1987); 'Meaning in the Bible', in T. A. Roberts and S. Sutherland (eds.), *Reason, Religion and the Self* (University of Wales Press, 1989); 'Interpreting the New Testament', in T. P. Flint and E. Stump (eds.), *Philosophical Theology and Biblical Exegesis* (University of Notre Dame Press, 1992); and 'Revelation', to be published in K. J. Clark (ed.), *Natural Theology*. I thank the editors and publishers of these volumes for their permission to reuse the material and the Oxford University Press for permission to reuse some short passages first published in previous books of mine. I am most grateful to Mrs Alicia Loreto-Gardner for her patient typing and retyping of many versions of this book; and to Tom Wright and John Barton for most helpful comments on earlier versions of Chapters 7 and 10 respectively. I have been conscious in writing this book of an intellectual debt to various former members of the University of Oxford who have argued that the claims of the Christian revelation stand up well before the tribunal of an impartial reason—to Duns Scotus and John Locke; and especially to two former members of Oriel College, Joseph Butler and John Henry Newman.

Oriel College, Oxford   R. S.
December 1990.

Contents

Introduction

There are various ways in which one person can communicate a message, a claim that something is so. The obvious way is to use sentences of normal grammatical forms containing words having their literal senses. But there are other ways: we may use words analogically and metaphorically, and use models, parables, and poems. And words are not the only vehicle by which a message may be communicated. Parables may be acted (e.g. in liturgy), and moral instruction may be conveyed by example. All of these latter ways for conveying a message are more prominent in less scientifically orientated cultures. Not that models and metaphors lack importance in scientific discourse; one cannot do without them anywhere, but they are less prominent there than elsewhere. Cultures very different from our own, such as the cultures in which the great religions arose, may employ a variety of methods to convey a message; and it requires some sensitivity to the culture to recognize the job which words (or other devices) are being used to do, for instance when they are being used to convey a historical claim, when they are being used to make a philosophical claim, and when they are being used simply to encourage and inspire. The first part of this book will analyse these different ways of conveying a message. I hope that this discussion will be of general philosophical interest, as well as of interest to those concerned with the topic which is the ultimate focus of the book. That topic is the topic of revelation. Some religions claim that God has revealed certain truths which it matters that humans believe. Both Christianity and Islam claim this, and so to a lesser extent does Judaism. The focus of this book is: what are the grounds for believing some claim of this kind, that some book or creed or act conveys revealed truth? Part I is a necessary prolegomenon to this enquiry, because we need to be clear about the criteria for determining what the message of the purported revelation is before we can set about assessing its credibility. I apologize to those readers, presumably the majority, whose interest in this book is an interest in the credibility of claims of revelation, for the rigour of the philosophical

Criteria to determine what the message is

discussions and distinctions of Part I; and ask them to take on trust their relevance to what is to come.

Part II considers the central issue of the tests by which one can recognize something as revealed truth. I shall consider whether humans have reason for expecting a revelation and what kind of revelation we might expect a God (if there is a God) to provide. In so far as there is good reason to expect a revelation, we need less strong detailed historical evidence to show that it has occurred. If a well-established scientific theory leads you to expect that stars will sometimes explode, then some debris in the sky of a kind which could have been caused by an exploding star, but which (though improbably) just might have some other cause, may nevertheless be reasonably interpreted as debris left by an exploding star. But if a well-established theory says that stars cannot explode, you will need very strong evidence that the debris could not have had another cause before interpreting it as debris of an exploding star. Similarly, how strong we need our historical evidence to be depends on how likely it is a priori that God will give us a revelation. But we do need historical evidence, and that, I shall argue, must take the form of evidence of a miraculous intervention into the natural order, reasonably interpreted as God's authentication of a purported revelation. Also some elements of that revelation must seem probable on other grounds and no elements must seem highly improbable—for example, the moral claims of the revelation cannot clash violently with our understanding of what is morally good.

Part III then seeks to apply the results of Part I to assessing the documents (Bible and creeds) and institutions (the Church) of the purported Christian revelation, to see what its message is; and to apply the results of Part II to see what factors are relevant to assessing its truth. It will turn out that the degree of prior probability of the central doctrines of Christianity, and the extent of historical evidence for the Resurrection, are the crucial factors. The former are matters for philosophical investigation; but in other books, not in this one. The latter is a matter for historical investigation, by other writers.

Divine revelation may be either of God, or by God of propositional truth. Christianity has claimed that the Christian revelation has involved both; God became incarnate and was in some degree made manifest on Earth, and through that incarnate life various propositional truths were announced.[1] My concern in this book is with revelation in

---

[1] The First Vatican Council declared that God revealed 'himself and the eternal decrees of his will' (Denzinger, *Enchiridion symbolorum* (henceforth 'Denzinger'), 3004); and the Second Vatican Council said much the same in *Dei Verbum*, 2.

Revelation – by God of propositional truth

the secondary sense of revelation of propositional truth. I am not concerned with all knowledge which God makes available to us, nor with all knowledge about himself, but with that knowledge which he communicates directly only to certain individuals, and they communicate to the rest of the world—when the grounds for the belief in these items of knowledge available to the first recipients are not available to the rest of the world, but the latter have to accept them, in the traditional phrase, 'upon the credit of the proposer, as coming from God in some extraordinary way of communication'.[2] Knowledge of God and his purposes, obtained by this route, is the concern of revealed as opposed to natural theology (which is knowledge of God and his purposes available from the study of publicly available evidence of the natural world). However, the division between natural and revealed theology cannot be a sharp one. Although a study of the natural world provides, I believe, good reason for believing that there is a God, further reason for that belief would be provided by the fact (if it is a fact) that there are creeds and books of purported revelation of a kind which is to be expected if there is a God. Conversely, evidence from the natural world that there is a God provides part of the grounds for supposing that creeds and books are his revelation. (If you already know that Shakespeare existed you need less in the way of internal evidence from plays purportedly written by him, to show that they were really written by him.)

Religions often claim to have minor as well as major revelations. The former are purported particular messages to individuals about matters of mere immediate concern; the latter are big messages of world-shaking significance for the practice of religion. My concern will be only with the latter. I wish to examine whether we have reason to expect a revelation of this kind, and what would show that we had got it.

Some modern theologians have denied that Christianity involves any propositional revelation,[3] but there can be little doubt that from the

---

[2] John Locke, *An Essay Concerning Human Understanding*, IV. 18. 2.

[3] David Kelsey wrote in 1975 of 'a wide-spread consensus in Protestant theology in the past four decades that the "revelation" to which scripture attests is a self-manifestation by God in historical events, not information about God stated in divinely communicated doctrines or concepts' (*The Uses of Scripture in Recent Theology* (SCM Press, 1975), 32). This 'wide-spread consensus' was hardly heard of before this century. For the major writers of this century who championed accounts of revelation which they saw as involving no propositional element, and the difficulties of such accounts, see A. Dulles, *Models of Revelation* (Gill & Macmillan, 1983).

second century (and in my view from the first century) until the eighteenth century Christians and non-Christians were virtually unanimous in supposing that it claimed to have such a revelation, and so it is worthwhile investigating its traditional claim. It is in any case very hard to see how God could reveal himself in history (e.g. in the Exodus or the life, death, and resurrection of Jesus) without at the same time revealing some propositional truth about himself. For events are not self-interpreting. Either God provides with the historical event its interpretation, in which case there is a propositional revelation; or he does not, in which case how can anyone know that a revelatory event has occurred? Events can only be recognized as revelatory by a community who do not witness them with their eyes if they can inherit a true description of what has occurred. If God really did reveal himself to us in Christ, then he must have revealed some propositional truth, minimally the truth that Christ's acts were his acts. (Though God could reveal through some prophet a truth about himself, without in any interesting sense revealing himself.)

This book is intended as the second of four books, a tetralogy, planned on the philosophical issues arising in connection with Christian doctrines. The first book, *Responsibility and Atonement*,[4] after analysing the notion of moral responsibility, applied that analysis to the Christian doctrines of man's moral status and possible destiny which crucially involve that notion—the doctrines of sin, original sin, the Atonement, corruption and sanctification, Heaven and Hell. It argued that, given that there is a God, man needs to make atonement to God for his sins and to be helped on the road to Heaven; and that as no ordinary human can do that for himself, let alone for others, there is reason to suppose that God himself might become incarnate (i.e. become human) in order to make atonement for us and assist our sanctification. Issues arise as to whether intelligible sense can be given to God becoming incarnate, and to the associated Christian doctrine of the Holy Trinity (God as three persons in one substance); and whether there is any a priori reason to suppose these doctrines true. These issues will be considered in the third volume of this tetralogy, which will explore the peculiarly Christian understanding of the divine nature. But, although I have argued, and shall argue further there, that there are some a priori grounds for supposing all these doctrines true, clearly a major ground is provided by revelation. Christians claim that these doctrines have been

[4] Clarendon Press, 1989.

revealed. How to assess such a claim is the theme of this volume. The final volume of the tetralogy will be concerned with the Christian doctrine of Providence (God's government of and purpose for the world and its human inhabitants during their life on Earth) and the resources which it contributes to a resolution of the problem of evil. The order of these volumes is one natural order of enquiry into the issues covered, for one who already has some reason for believing that there is a God, confronted with the phenomenon of Christianity. He first hears its message of sin, atonement, and sanctification; and needs to understand this. He then enquires why he should believe this message, and, hearing the answer, 'It is revealed', needs to probe that answer. He then finds that, lying behind the doctrines of atonement and revelation, there is a peculiarly Christian doctrine of God which is needed to make sense of the earlier doctrines and which purports to give a fuller understanding of the divine goodness and the goodness at which humans should aim. He then comes to investigate whether all these doctrines provide more resources than does natural theology on its own for understanding God's purpose in creating a universe, and allowing evil to occur in it.

Although I am writing four books which make a tetralogy, I emphasize that each book is intended to be fully comprehensible on its own. However I do sometimes make explicit assumptions for which I have argued elsewhere; philosophy is such an integrated subject that it is inevitable that the writer of a philosophical work makes assumptions about some matter in another area of philosophy. The crucial assumptions which I am making in the tetralogy as a whole are the existence of God, for which I argued in my earlier trilogy on the philosophy of theism;[5] and substance dualism, the view that man consists of two substantial parts, body and soul, for which I argued in *The Evolution of the Soul*.[6]

---

[5] *The Coherence of Theism* (Clarendon Press, 1977); *The Existence of God* (Clarendon Press, 1979); and *Faith and Reason* (Clarendon Press, 1981). See esp. *The Existence of God*.

[6] Clarendon Press, 1986.

PART I

Meaning

I

Terminology

Part I is concerned with the different ways of communicating a message that something is so. In this chapter I introduce a precise vocabulary for talking about these matters. Let us call a claim, a message which someone might try to convey to someone else, and which has a permanent truth-value (is eternally either true or false), a statement. A statement says that something is so. If it is so, the statement is true; if it is not so, the statement is false.

A statement is often expressed by a token declarative sentence. By a _token sentence_ I mean a sentence uttered (written, or otherwise given forth) on a particular occasion by a particular person in particular circumstances, for example, 'It is raining now', uttered by me in Oxford at 6 p.m. yesterday, 1 March 1990; or 'you look tired', uttered by me at 2 p.m. today, 2 March 1990, to John. Any utterance of the same words is a token of a type; the _type sentence_ 'you are tired' may be uttered by different speakers on different occasions. Each such utterance is the utterance of a different token of the same type. By a _declarative_ sentence I mean one which expresses a claim that something is so, independently of the sentence being uttered, as opposed to asking a question, or issuing a command. Indicative sentences are normally declarative. Different token sentences may say the same thing, make the same claim about the world, convey the same information. Hence philosophers wish to introduce a notion of a statement or proposition or thought, as that which token sentences mean or express, and which may remain the same while the token sentence changes. But there are different ways of understanding 'say the same thing' which generate different notions of statement, proposition, or whatever. Because the philosophical terminology for what sentences express is not standard, I make my own distinction between two different ways of understanding what a sentence expresses.

I distinguish in future between <u>statement</u> and <u>proposition</u> as follows. The _proposition_ which a token sentence _s_ expresses is that element of claim in what is said which is also made by any other token sentence (whether of the same type or not) which is synonymous with *s*. Two sentences express the same proposition if and only if they are synonymous.[1] 'Rex mortuus est', uttered by a Latin speaker of the fourteenth century, 'Le roi est mort', uttered by a French speaker of the eighteenth century, and 'The king is dead', uttered by an English speaker of the twentieth century, express the same proposition. If you take into account only what dictionaries would tell you that the words mean, and forget the context of utterance, the three sentences mean the same. By contrast, the *statement* which a token sentence expresses is that element of claim in what is said which is made by any other token sentence *r* which would be synonymous with *s* if you substitute in both *s* and *r* the same rigid designators (see below) of any individuals referred to.

A *referring expression* is a word or words which pick out an individual thing in order to say something about it. Referring expressions include indexicals, definite descriptions, and proper names. *Indexicals* are devices which pick out different individuals in different contexts; their meaning determines how to use them in different contexts. Thus 'I' is an indexical; it refers to the speaker or writer of the sentence containing it, whoever that is. So too are 'you', 'he', 'this', 'today', 'tomorrow', 'the place over there', and so on. *Definite descriptions* are expressions of the form 'the so-and-so', which pick out the one and only individual which is so-and-so—for example 'The king of Spain' or 'The oldest living human being'. *Proper names* are names which have no meaning determining which individuals they pick out (i.e. do not like definite descriptions pick out some individual in virtue of his possessing some property), but have conventions associated with them in a given context of use determining this. 'Aristotle' is a proper name; who it picks out (the philosopher or the shipowner) is determined by the conventions of the context in which it is used. A *rigid designator* is a referring expression which (in virtue of its meaning and the context of its use) picks out the individual it does quite independently of whether the individual gains or loses properties during its existence. Proper names are rigid designators; definite descriptions are (normally) not. 'The president of the USA' picks out George Bush, but only while he continues to be president of the USA. Hence it is not a rigid designator. But 'George Bush' is a rigid designator, because it will pick out the

---

[1] I assume, contrary to Quine, that the notion of synonymy is sufficiently clear to be used in such a definition. On this see my 'Analytic/Synthetic', *American Philosophical Quarterly*, 21 (1984), 31–42. See esp. 39–40.

same individual whatever happens to him in life. An individual is any thing. But the most evident kinds of thing to which reference is made are substances, places, and times. By a *substance* I understand a thing, such as a desk or planet or person, which causally interacts with other things.

Substances are contrasted with the (monadic) *properties* they possess, such as being brown or square; and the *relations* which they possess to other substances, such as being-to-the-left-of, or caused-to-exist-by. *Predicates* are words designating properties or relations, such as 'brown' or 'to the left of'. A given individual may be picked out by, referred to by, different referring expressions—'George Bush' and 'the president of the USA' both (now) pick out the same individual. The way by which an individual is picked out is often called its *mode of presentation*.

These definitions should now clarify my account of what a statement is. With normal subject-predicate sentences (i.e. sentences attributing a property to an individual at some time and place) my account boils down to: the statement which a token sentence *s* expresses is that element of claim in what is said which is made by any other token sentence *r* which predicates the same properties of the same individuals, at the same times and places (however the individuals, times, and places are picked out); when properties are the same if and only if the predicates which designate them are synonymous. So two sentences express the same statement if and only if they attribute the same property to the same individuals at the same place and time, whatever the mode of presentation by which those individuals, places, and times are picked out. The three token sentences cited on p. 10 did not express the same statement, for (we may reasonably suppose) they concern different kings. Whereas 'I am ill', spoken by me, 'you are ill', addressed to me, and 'he is ill', spoken of me, all uttered at the same time do all express the same statement (although not the same proposition). So do 'I will go to London tomorrow', uttered by me on 1 January, 'I am going to London today', uttered by me on 2 January, and 'I went to London yesterday', uttered by me on 3 January (given that the referent of 'London' remains the same).

Both token sentences and the propositions and statements which they express may be said to be true or false. Whether a given token sentence is true or false depends on three facets of the world: (1) the conventions of the language in which the sentence is uttered, (2) the referential context—that is, those circumstances of its utterance which determine the reference of its expressions referring to individuals, places, and times (e.g. by whom it is uttered, when, to whom, in the presence of which objects, in which community)—and (3) other features of the world, which I shall call the remaining truth-relevant conditions. Whether 'you are ill' is true depends on (1) what the words mean, (2) who is being addressed and when, and (3) whether that person is ill. (1) determines which proposition is uttered, (1) and (2) together determine which statement is uttered, and the other features (i.e. (2) and (3) for a proposition, (3) for a statement) determine whether that proposition or statement is true. The conventions of language determine the meaning of general terms, connectives, and so forth. They lay down how, in the circumstances of utterance, to determine the referent of indexical expressions: for instance, they state that 'you' refers to the person to whom the speaker is talking. It is then those circumstances (i.e. (2)) which determine what the referent is (e.g. what 'you' is). The conventions of language however contain no rules for determining the reference of proper names such as 'George Bush' or 'Margaret Thatcher'; that is not a matter of language, but of community practice (i.e. (2)).

It follows that the truth-value of a statement is invariant: if true, it is true always and everywhere, by whoever and to whomever it is uttered. This will be because its truth depends on the properties possessed by individuals at places and times, independently of how those individuals, places, and times are picked out. The proposition expressed by a token sentence has a content independent of the who, where, and when of utterance; but these latter come in to determine its truth. So the proposition expressed by 'I am cold' may be true today, false tomorrow, true when uttered by me but false when uttered by you—just as it may be funny or irrelevant or contradict what has been said before, today but not tomorrow, when uttered by you but not when uttered by me. Propositions are, as it were, meaning-involved expressions waiting to be pinned down to who, where, and when, before they have a definite truth-value. Statements are meaning-involved expressions already so pinned down. The truth of statements is absolute, of propositions relative. For propositions, truth is a relation between a proposition and a referential context. In my terminology a token sentence expresses both a proposition and a statement.[2] The truth-conditions of a proposition are those combinations of referential contexts and remaining truth-relevant conditions under which the proposition would be true;

[2] See Additional Note 1.

the truth-conditions of a statement are those truth-relevant conditions under which it would be true.

In so far as statements affirm the possession of properties by substances at places and times, they make no reference to the mode of presentation of those substances, places, and times. The mode of presentation contained in the sentence in virtue of the linguistic conventions is, as it were, cancelled out by the referential context. We get to the same things via different modes of presentation which are then dismissed as irrelevant. Yet since the linguistic conventions alone determine which proposition is expressed by a sentence, propositions retain within them the mode of presentation. Token sentences are the primary truth-bearers; but there is a point in distinguishing a notion of what is said from the notion of the sentence by means of which it is said. Yet if we do that in terms of statements, we need to bear in mind that the statement ignores certain aspects of what is said; and we need some other understanding of 'what is said', such as the proposition, in order to be able to talk about them.[3] My concern with what is expressed by a sentence will in general in Parts II and III be a concern with the statement rather than the proposition expressed—for my concern is with messages which one author may convey to many hearers over many years about how things are independently of the 'mode of presentation' to particular hearers (e.g. in terms of the temporal and spatial distance of events reported, from those hearers). However, despite this technical though important philosophical point, since statements are expressed by sentences via the propositions which the sentences express, I shall follow theological terminology in describing my concern with the revelation which can be expressed by sentences as a concern with 'propositional revelation'. Also, henceforward, in talking of what is expressed by a token sentence or what such a sentence means, I shall not distinguish between the proposition and the statement expressed, except where it is important to do so for the point which I am making; otherwise either it will be obvious which I intend or my point will apply to both the proposition and the statement.

I earlier defined a token sentence as 'a sentence uttered (written, or otherwise given forth) on a particular occasion'. Each new utterance of the same type sentence is an utterance of a new token sentence; and

---

[3] That we need propositions as well as statements in order to express certain important truths about the world is argued in my 'Tensed Facts', *American Philosophical Quarterly*, 27 (1990), 117–30.

each new inscription in writing of the same type sentence is an inscription of a new token sentence. I now make one qualification. Where the sentence is embedded in a large repeatable context, as a sentence of a book of which there may be many copies or of a play of which there may be many performances, I count all tokens of the sentence in that context as the same token as long as the context remains qualitatively identical in all respects which affect the meaning of the token utterance; for instance, as long as the sentence remains part of the play and is not used for some other purpose. Each utterance by Hamlet of 'To be or not to be; that is the question' in a new performance of *Hamlet*, or inscription of the sentence in a new copy of the play, is to count as the same token. I count it thus, because the context which determines meaning is not the theatre in which the play is produced, nor the paper on which it is printed, but the surrounding sentences; and because the latter remain the same in those respects which determine the meaning of our sentence, I shall count the context as the same and so the tokens as the same.

I must now add a further qualification to something which I wrote above. I wrote that the conventions of the language determined which proposition was expressed by a token sentence, and I implied that the context of utterance was relevant only in determining the reference of referring expressions, and so which statement was expressed. Context can however also come in to determine in what language the sentence was uttered. For there are combinations of noises or written marks which constitute sentences with quite different meanings in different languages. The sentence can only be a sentence of a language spoken by the speaker; if it is a sentence of two languages spoken by the speaker its relevance to the discussion and its being believed to be understood by the hearer if it is a sentence of one language rather than another are the factors which determine of which language the sentence is a sentence. I do not speak Japanese. If I utter noises which constitute either some Japanese sentence or some English sentence equally well, what I have uttered is the English sentence. But if I do speak Japanese, but all the same the previous conversation was all in English, I have no reason to suppose my hearers to speak Japanese, and the sentence is only relevant to the discussion if taken as having the meaning of the English sentence, then also I have uttered the English sentence. Even when it is clear in which language the sentence was uttered, context can also come in to determine which proposition is expressed, where what is said might have two quite different meanings (in the sense that it could be translated into another language by sentences with quite different meanings). Although linguistic conventions are the main factor in determining which proposition is expressed, and so each token of the same type sentence normally expresses the same proposition, type sentences may have more than one meaning in the sense that different tokens of that type may express different propositions, and then we need to know the context of the token sentence in order to disambiguate. So we must add to (1) on p. 11 'and those circumstances of utterance which disambiguate among possible propositions'.

'There is a crook in the next room' will in a context of discussion about sheep or fell-walking mean (i.e. express the proposition) that there is a stick or staff with a curved end in the next room; in most other contexts it will express the proposition that there is a criminal in the next room. However, type sentences often have what I call a normal meaning, that is, a meaning which speakers of the language with no knowledge of the particular context of their utterance presume them to have in a context unless special features of that context come to their attention. The proposition normally expressed by 'The king is in the castle' is the proposition that there is a hereditary ruler of a country in a large fortified building with thick walls and strong gates. Context alone will reveal which king and which castle. That what I have just laid out is meant is rightly presumed in the absence of special features of context—for example, that the local Town Hall is called 'the castle', although it is nothing like what is normally called a 'castle'. Type sentences may sometimes have more than one normal meaning, in that independently of context there is no presumption that among several possible meanings they have one rather than the other.

However, despite these two additional roles for context, it remains the case that the normal role of context is not to determine in which language the sentence was expressed, nor to disambiguate among possible translations, but to add the reference of referring expressions.

A contrast is often made between *sentence-meaning* and *speaker's meaning*. However, discussions do not always make it clear what contrast is being drawn. Sometimes 'sentence-meaning' is used to mean the meaning(s) of the type sentence, that is, the proposition(s) which any token of the type expresses, while 'speaker's meaning' is used to mean the statement which a given token expresses. I shall not use the expressions in these senses. I shall use 'sentence-meaning' in this context to mean the statement expressed by a given token sentence and contrast it with 'speaker's meaning', the 'meaning' of the speaker in uttering it, in one or other of two useful senses in which this term has been used.

The first clear and useful thing which may be meant by 'speaker's meaning' is the meaning which the speaker meant the sentence uttered by him to have. Although speaker's meaning will then of course in general coincide with sentence-meaning, it will not do so in those few cases where the meaning which the speaker meant the sentence uttered by him to have is not the meaning it actually has. There are two possibilities under this heading. First, the speaker may not utter the sentence he intended ('meant') to utter, through a slip of the tongue. I say, 'He mumbles a lot', meaning to say, 'He grumbles a lot', because I do not take trouble to articulate my words. Secondly, the speaker may utter the sentence he intended to utter, but in the false belief that the sentence had a different meaning, that is, expressed a different statement. A student may say when discussing Hume, 'There are no casual connections between events', meaning that there are no causal connections, through a belief that 'casual' means causal.[4]

The second clear and useful thing which may be meant by 'speaker's meaning' is the information, question, or command which the speaker intends to convey by what he says. In this sense too speaker's meaning will normally coincide with sentence-meaning, but sometimes it will not. First, the speaker may intend to convey not merely what he actually says, but something further. I say, 'It's cold', and thereby hint that I would like you to close the window. I say to a student who arrives late at a morning class, 'Obviously your alarm clock wasn't working this morning', as a way of pointing out to him that he is late. The token sentence which I utter means one thing (expresses a certain proposition and statement) and by uttering it I say and intend to say that thing; but I say it in order to suggest or hint at something else.

---

[4] Under this heading comes any case where the sentence makes a reference other than that which the speaker intended it to make. Intuitions differ about when a sentence does make such a reference. But an obvious example would seem to be a case such as when a speaker says, 'Her husband is kind to her', believing falsely and without the public context suggesting this that Jones is her husband and intending to make a comment about him. Here, as Kripke suggests, the token sentence refers to someone other than Jones, although the speaker referred to Jones (see Saul Kripke, 'Speaker's Reference and Semantic Reference', in P. A. French *et al.* (eds.), *Contemporary Perspectives in the Philosophy of Language* University of Minnesota Press, 1979)). There may, however, be cases where the context makes it so clear in a way understood by all participants in the conversation that an object a is the intended referent of 'the ϕ' that the fact that a is not in fact ϕ does not have the consequence that a token sentence 'The ϕ is ψ' does not refer to a.

Secondly, there are cases where the speaker intends to convey something other than he says and not what he intentionally says. I utter and mean to utter a token sentence which I know has a certain meaning but I do not intend to convey to you the information (command or question) contained in that sentence, but something else. One uncontroversial example would be where I intentionally utter a false sentence, intending thereby to convey to you the opposite of what I say, and believing that my sentence will have that effect because I believe that you think I am a liar. Another uncontroversial example would be where there is a private understanding between speaker and hearer (a code, say, for use between secret agents) that a certain sentence will be used to convey information other than that which it contains.

Many examples however which are cited under this heading, of alleged cases where speaker's meaning diverges from sentence-meaning, seem to me not to be cases thereof, but rather to be cases where the meaning of the token sentence diverges from the normal meaning of the type sentence. They are cases where the conventions for understanding the sentence as being used to convey information other than that contained by a sentence of that type uttered in most other circumstances are public ones (not, as above, private ones for use between secret agents). But then the token sentence uttered in the particular circumstances does contain that information, because it has the meaning (of expressing that information) which is other than the normal meaning possessed by sentences of that type. For what public conventions about how a sentence is to be interpreted do is to determine what the sentence means.

Metonymy, for example, does not exemplify the required speaker's meaning/sentence-meaning contrast. Metonymy involves referring to an object by using the name or description of some adjunct. Instead of saying, 'a presidential spokesman said', I say, 'the White House said'. Here it is not that I say one thing, that a white house talked, in order to convey some other suggestion. I do not say that a white house talked. I use a sentence which, independent of context, would mean that a white house talked (that is the normal meaning of the type sentence), but in the context of political discussion my token sentence has quite another meaning. I do not mean to convey any information other than I do convey, that is, the statement expressed by the token sentence which I utter.

Henceforth I shall use 'speaker's meaning' to denote either of the two useful senses distinguished earlier.[5] In cases where speaker's meaning (in one or other of these senses) is contrasted with sentence-meaning, truth or falsity belong to the token sentence in virtue of its meaning; and what the speaker meant by uttering it does not affect its truth-value.

Not all indicative sentences are declarative. There are sentences which have the grammatical form of an indicative sentence, but which do not claim that things are so, but purport to make them so, and do make them so if the circumstances of utterance are right. Thus 'I promise to pay you $10' does not purport to report something which is so independently of the utterance of the words, but purports to make something the case—it purports to set up a commitment which did not exist before the words were uttered, and it does set up that commitment, unless circumstances are unusual in that it is uttered in the course of a stage play or a translation exercise or something similar. Such sentences are called 'performative utterances'.[6]

To return to declarative sentences—the proposition expressed by the token sentence is a function of the meanings of the type sentence and of the context. The meanings of the type sentence are a function of the senses of the component words, and the way in which they are combined.

Words of the language have each some one (or sometimes more than one) logico-grammatical status—as noun, adverb, verb, or whatever of different kinds (proper name, common name, mass noun, etc.) which logicians have classified. Certain combinations of words are well-formed sentences, that is, ones which have a meaning, and among them are declarative sentences, ones which express propositions as opposed to interrogative sentences or commands. Whether a combination of words is a well-formed declarative sentence depends on the order in which

---

[5] The source of the sentence-meaning/speaker's meaning distinction is the writings of H. P. Grice: 'Meaning', Philosophical Review, 66 (1957), 377–88, 'Utterer's Meaning, Sentence-Meaning, and Word-Meaning', *Foundations of Language*, 4 (1968), 1–18, and 'Logic and Conversation', in P. Cole and J. L. Morgan (eds.), *Syntax and Semantics*, iii (Academic Press, 1975); all these are now republished in Paul Grice, *Studies in the Way of Words* (Harvard University Press, 1989). Grice is well aware of the token sentence/ type sentence meaning distinction and the difference between it and a sentence-meaning/speaker's meaning distinction, but the way in which he uses the latter distinction seems to me not always satisfactory. For example, like Searle (as we shall see), Grice regards metaphorical meaning as speaker's meaning.

[6] This terminology was introduced by J. L. Austin—see his 'Performative Utterances', in his *Philosophical Papers* (Oxford University Press, 1961).

words of different grammatical status follow each other. Logicians have codified many of the possible forms of such sentences. They may for example be subject-predicate sentences (sentences attributing a property to an individual or stating a relation to hold between two or more individuals—e.g. 'this door has a mass of 10 lbs.' or 'this door is to the left of that door') or universal sentences (sentences attributing some property to all individuals possessing some other property—e.g. 'all emeralds are green') or existential sentences (sentences stating that there exists an individual having a certain property or combination of properties, or related by a certain relation to some other individual— e.g. 'There is someone somewhere taller than John'). So 'John this desk square' is not a well-formed sentence at all, whereas 'John opens this desk' is a well-formed declarative sentence.

Some words have more than one grammatical status (e.g. 'smiles' as a plural noun or a verb). Where the resulting sentence is well formed only on one interpretation, that is the interpretation. Otherwise it is left to considerations of making sense in the context, as opposed to grammar, to disambiguate.

Words have not merely a grammatical status but (within that status) one (or more) senses. Its *sense* is its context-independent contribution to the meanings of the type sentence to which a word belongs. Many words have more than one sense: 'lock' as of a door and 'lock' of hair, 'pen' for animals and 'pen' to write with. The frame of the rest of the type sentence often makes clear how an ambiguous word is to be taken. In the absence of special information about the context words are to be taken in the sense which gives the type sentence its normal meaning. In 'I shut the sheep in the pen', 'pen' is to be taken as an animal pen rather than pen for writing with, because that is the meaning the type sentence is presumed to have independent of context, since writing pens are not normally the sort of thing which can contain sheep. However, a token sentence 'I shut the sheep in the pen' could have a meaning other than the normal meaning of the type sentence: for example, in a fairy story about sheep being shut in a giant fountain-pen. Context (of paragraph, speaker, hearer, and environment) selects among the normal meanings of type sentences and may give to a token sentence a meaning other than a normal meaning. A token sentence must be presumed to have among its possible meanings the one which makes it a natural thing to say in the context, if with all other meanings it is not. This may be because only so would it be relevant to the subject of the conversation; or because otherwise it would be obviously (to the speaker and hearer) false. If with two or more meanings the sentence is a natural thing to say in the context, whereas with all other meanings it is not, then it is ambiguous between interpretations with the former senses. In a conversation about money hidden in various places including the sides of rivers, 'I put the money in the bank' will be ambiguous (whereas it will not be if the conversation has had no reference to hiding money by the sides of rivers). If with no sense is the sentence a natural thing to say in the context, then the sentence must be taken to have that meaning and the words that sense which makes the sentence the least unnatural thing to say (or, if there is more than one such meaning, to be ambiguous between them).

Among the senses of a word there is often one which it is presumed to have in the absence of information about the sentence frame into which it fits or the context of its utterance. This is the contribution which we presume that it will make to the meaning of any type—and so token—sentence in which it occurs in the absence of information that it does not make that contribution (because with a different possible sense the resulting token sentence would be a more appropriate thing to say in the context). This presumed sense is naturally called the *literal* sense. Thus the literal sense of 'cold' is that to say that something is cold is to say that it has a relatively low temperature on a scale such as the Centigrade or Fahrenheit scale. But when people and social environments are said to be 'cold', something different is meant. To say that the sense of low temperature is the literal sense is to say that the presumption with respect to '*x* is cold' is that this is what is being said. If there is no presumption between two or more senses or in favour of another sense, then, I shall say, the two or more senses are all literal senses. I distinguish my sense of 'literal sense' from that sense of 'literal sense' in which the literal sense is the historically prior sense; historical priority is not a consideration relevant to philosophical analysis of kinds of meaning.

The sentence frame selects among the senses of words to yield the *normal meaning* of the sentence type, that is, the proposition normally expressed by a sentence of that type.[7] Context of utterance then adds the reference in order to determine which statement is expressed. It indicates about whom a claim is being made in 'I am old'. Context may reveal as inappropriate the normal meaning or meanings of the type

[7] On how the sentence frame selects the sense of a word within it, see James F. Ross, *Portraying Analogy* (Cambridge University Press, 1981), chs. 2 and 3.

sentence, and so force it to be understood in a less usual way, and in the process it may force a less usual sense on the component words. Normally it is right to suppose that the senses of words are there, sentence frame selects among them to yield possible sentence-meanings, and context selects among these. But, as we shall see in Chapter 3, sometimes it is the other way round. Context may force a token sentence to acquire a meaning, that is, express a proposition, which no one would previously have supposed to be a possible meaning of the type sentence; and that in turn forces a sense on the component words which no dictionary would have listed as a possible sense thereof.

The sense of a word, I wrote earlier, is its context-independent contribution to the meanings of the type sentences into which it can slot. The sense of a word is picked out by the verification conditions of sentences in which it occurs, or the verification conditions of sentences in which there occur words to which it is logically related. Verification conditions are circumstances in which sentences containing the word at issue are confirmed or disconfirmed. (To confirm a sentence in the sense in which I shall use the term is to adduce some evidence which supports, counts for, in favour of, adds somehow to the probability of the sentence being true. To disconfirm a sentence is to adduce some evidence which counts against it. Confirmation is thus the weakest way of understanding 'verification'; disconfirmation the weakest way of understanding 'falsification'.) Thus the sense of 'red' is given by examples of objects which confirm and examples of objects which disconfirm 'this is red', for example by objects which are clear examples of red things and objects which are clear examples of non-red things. Like all words, even a word so closely related to observation as 'red' also has logical relations to other words, and these also help to give a sense to the word. It is true of logical necessity, 'if it is red, it is coloured' and so 'if it is not coloured, it is not red', and 'if it is green all over, it is not red'; and since 'green' and 'coloured' are also pinned down by examples, these logical relations also help to give a sharp sense to 'red'. If a word can contribute in two quite distinct ways to the meanings of the type sentences into which it can slot, then it has two senses. A form of sentence is the form of a declarative sentence if many sentences of that form are confirmable or disconfirmable by experience.

The distinctions made earlier in the chapter relied on the understanding that the meaning of a sentence is a public thing, determined by the publicly accessible criteria of the meanings of words and sentence forms in the language and how context selects among those meanings; not a private thing, determined by the intention of the speaker. I may say, 'you are gauche', intending thereby to say that you are left-wing; but what I actually say is that you are clumsy. Whether a sentence is a well-formed declarative sentence and so expresses a proposition, and what that proposition is, is a matter of whether there are *publicly agreed criteria* for what makes it true and what those criteria are. There are such criteria if (on the whole) speakers agree about which observations or experiences (described in words or pointed to) confirm or disconfirm the sentence; and which other sentences are entailed by, or entail, are compatible or incompatible with, synonymous or not-synonymous with, etc., the sentence in question. The existence of agreement on the truth-conditions of 'once upon a time, before there were humans, the Earth was covered by sea' is shown by the fact that everyone says that it entails 'if there were humans as long as 2 million years ago, then the Earth was covered by sea more than 2 million years ago'; and that the sentence would be verified conclusively if a non-human observer could have hovered above the Earth before there were humans and seen it covered by sea, and would be confirmed if in all parts of the Earth were found remains of sea-living creatures dating from a certain period of history, and no human remains dating from as early a period. And so on.

Since the meaning of a sentence is a function of the senses of the words which occur in it and the ways in which they are combined, alternative criteria for a sentence having a meaning are provided by speakers showing in other ways that they understand the senses of the component words and the significance of the form in which they are put together. That will be shown if the speakers show that they understand other sentences in which those words occur or which have the same form as the given sentence; which in turn will be shown by their agreement about when such sentences would be confirmed or disconfirmed by experience, and what their logical relations are to other sentences. Such agreement will be shown either by showing (e.g. pointing to) the circumstances in which they are purportedly verified, and so on, or by describing them in sentences, and all agreeing that those circumstances do verify, or those descriptions do describe. Thus agreement on the meaning of 'The lawn is green' is shown by agreement as to what sorts of things are 'lawns' are, what sorts of objects are 'green', and when sentences of the form 'a is ϕ' are true. Agreement in much judgement is necessary for words to have senses and sentences to have meaning. A declarative sentence is well formed (its words have sense and are properly put together) and thus *meaningful*, that is, expresses a proposition, if there are conditions (even if ones logically impossible of realization) under which it would be true. There are such conditions if speakers agree in what they say on matters described above. To the extent to which such agreement is lacking sentences and words lack a clear meaning. And two declarative sentences have different meanings in so far as speakers agree as to how their truth-conditions differ.

While one speaker disagreeing with almost all the other speakers of a language does not damage clarity of meaning—the former speaker simply has not grasped the meaning—substantial disagreement among speakers with respect to the conditions under which a sentence would be true or a word applicable makes the sentence or word to that extent vague in meaning—its use does not then discriminate with respect to those different conditions. If some speakers said, 'the lawn is green', when any patch of grass with which they were confronted was green, and others said, 'The lawn is green', only when a smooth well-cut extensive patch in a garden was green, and there was a continuum of usage between the groups in that there were speakers who used it in various intermediate ways, then the sense of the word 'lawn' would be *vague*. Contrast this with the situation where there are only the two extreme sharply defined groups. Here we can say that each group is using the word 'lawn' in a different clear sense; and that the language contains these two senses, and that unless context disambiguates, the sentence 'the lawn is green' is *ambiguous*, that is, it expresses the disjunction of the two propositions which a sentence of that type can express—that either the 'lawn' in one sense is green or that the 'lawn' in the other sense is green.

There would however only be total agreement about the truth-conditions of a sentence in so far as there is agreement about *all* the consequences, confirming experiences, and so forth of that sentence and other sentences of the same form and of other sentences in which the words which compose the original sentence appear. But all that some speaker can tell us is that he agrees with us about *some* of what follows from such sentences, would confirm them, and so on. But as there is no end of consequences, confirming experiences, and so on, agreement over some of these does not guarantee agreement over all. Thus two speakers may agree so far with respect to everything observed whether or not it is 'green'. That is good evidence that they mean the same by 'this is green'. But the evidence is fallible, because their subsequent judgements may yet diverge. All the time they may have different

concepts of greenness, but this has not come to light because the only
instances about which they have made judgements are ones for which
their concepts overlap.

This latter point can also be illustrated by Wittgenstein's example[8] of
teaching a pupil '+ 2'. We think that he has understood when he gives
the right answers for the value 'x + 2' up to the value of x = 1,000, but
then he surprises us by giving the answers for '1,000 + 2' as '1,004',
'1,004 + 2' as '1,008', '1,008 + 2' as '1,012', and so on. We say that he is
now performing the different operation of adding 4 instead of the operation of adding 2, but he claims, 'But I went on in the same way.'
Wittgenstein comments, 'In such a case we might say perhaps: It comes
natural to this person to understand our order with our explanations as
we should understand the order: "Add 2 up to 1,000, 4 up to 2,000, 6
up to 3,000 and so on." The example shows, on my interpretation of it,
that while it looked by his initial responses that he understood '+ 2' in
our way really he didn't.

A case as extreme as Wittgenstein's of someone who has been taught
a word in similar circumstances to those in which the rest of us have
learnt it, and who diverges so radically in his subsequent practice, is not
very likely to occur in practice. Humans have such a similar psychology
and neurophysiology to each other that similar procedures of teaching
the use of a word are likely to lead to agreement in subsequent
judgements in not too dissimilar circumstances as to its applicability
and the consequences which follow in sentences in which it occurs.

What is however not unlikely is that while similarity in training gives
to most or all learners a common understanding of the right way to use
a word when it is applied in circumstances similar to the circumstances
of training, learners will diverge in their application of the word (to
which objects they apply it, which conclusions they derive from it being
predicated of an object) when the question arises of its application in
circumstances very different from the circumstances of training. To the
extent to which that is so, the word has no clear sense when applied
beyond circumstances of the kind in which it was originally learnt. I
shall have more to say on this point in the next chapter.

I should add that, in saying that for sentences to have meaning there
needs to be agreement about (among other things) what would verify
them, I am not committing myself to any form of *verificationism*—the

[8] L. Wittgenstein, *Philosophical Investigations*, trans. G. E. M. Anscombe (Basil
Blackwell, 1953), § 185.

doctrine that a declarative sentence is meaningful if and only if it is possible in some sense or other to verify *it*. For a sentence to be meaningful there needs to be some agreement about what would verify it *or* other sentences of the same form or sentences in which the same words appear, but I am not claiming that there need always be agreement about the former, let alone that the circumstances which would verify it need be ones in any way capable of realization. I have claimed that the words which occur in a sentence must themselves occur in sentences confirmable or disconfirmable by experience, or be logically related to other words thus related to experience. We could not understand 'photons are particles with zero rest mass' unless we could understand 'zero' and 'rest mass' and so the latter words must be related to experience by occurring in confirmable or disconfirmable sentences or being logically related to ones that are. And likewise the sentence form, the way in which the words fit together—in this case a subject-predicate sentence—must be one of which there are instances which can be confirmed or disconfirmed. But it does not follow from all that that a declarative sentence is meaningful only if it itself can in some way be confirmed or disconfirmed. It does seem that we understand a sentence in virtue of understanding the words and how they are put together, without bothering to consider whether that sentence can in any way be verified. And sometimes, while it is obvious to us that we understand what a sentence means—for example the sentence 'once upon a time, before there were humans, the Earth was covered by sea'—it is not initially obvious to us how it can be verified. And so, often, we wonder how or whether a sentence can be verified and we work out the answer by considering the meaning which we already suppose the sentence to have in virtue of the way in which it is built up. If we could not determine the meaning of a sentence before we knew how it could be verified, we could not go through the routine of asking what kind of procedures would verify some scientific theory, as scientists often do. There is however no need for me to take a stance on whether some very weak form of verificationism is true. If a sentence does need in some sense itself to be verifiable in order to be meaningful, we can suppose this added as an additional criterion for meaningfulness.[9]

The meaningfulness of a sentence, that is, its expressing a proposition, is to be distinguished from the *coherence* (i.e. logical possibility or

[9] There are many different forms of verificationism, varying from the strong form that for a declarative sentence to be meaningful it must be capable in practice of being verified

self-consistency) of the proposition which it expresses.[10] 'He is under 5 ft. and also over 6 ft. tall' is meaningful; we know what it is saying. But the proposition which it expresses is incoherent, that is, necessarily false. The contrast becomes more obvious in the case of many sentences of mathematics (e.g. '5 + 7 = 13' or 'every even number is the sum of two prime numbers'); they express propositions which are comprehensible, but the issue arises whether they are ones which are necessarily false (i.e. whether they have buried in them an inconsistency which some piece of mathematical reasoning could draw to the surface). But only if a sentence expresses a proposition at all can it express one which is necessarily false. My concern in this chapter is only with meaningfulness, not with coherence.

Non-verbal Communication

Our understanding of a statement as a claim about how things are is an understanding of something which could be expressed by a sentence if we had a language rich enough to do the job. For a claim that something is so is a claim that the world is this way rather than that way, and so something which could be expressed by a sentence if we had words for 'this way' and 'that way'. We may nevertheless not have a language rich enough to express some statement in a sentence, and yet have other ways in which to express it.

A natural gesture or symbolic act may (without using words) express a claim that something is so, or express a command or question, or constitute a performative action—if either because of our inborn psychology, or because of a convention established in a society, many in the society recognize it as doing so.

Natural gestures are such things as kisses, embraces, smiles, grimaces of repulsion, stances of aggression, which, for psychological reasons (without needing a convention to establish them), naturally go with

conclusively by anyone at any time, to the weak form that for a declarative sentence to be meaningful it must be logically possible for someone or other at some time or other to get evidence which gives some support to the claim that it is true or to the claim that it is false. For further discussion of verificationism, see pp. 63–70 of my 'Verificationism and Theories of Space–Time', in R. Swinburne (ed.), *Space, Time, and Causality* (D. Reidel, 1983).

[10] For criteria of coherence, see my *The Coherence of Theism* (Clarendon Press, 1977), chs. 2 and 3.

likes or dislikes, joy or sadness. They typically express one's own state, and may also express attitudes towards others, and in so far as intentionally performed in order to do so, may intentionally communicate those attitudes. It is not always clear where the border between the natural and conventional is to be drawn—some ways of showing affection or repulsion may seem natural, while really being established not by nature but by very early training; but I suspect that some gestures do really go naturally with affection or repulsion. However convention is more important than nature in fixing the significance of communicative actions. To spit at someone is to express dislike and contempt. To hit a child in certain circumstances (e.g. after he has been caught in the act of stealing) constitutes the hitting as punishment, and communicates without words, 'what I am doing to you is punishing'. To take off one's hat or keep silence as a funeral procession passes is to show respect to the dead. If a group of soldiers run up the flag of their country on an unoccupied piece of land, they thereby (performatively) declare the land to belong to their country. And so on.

Our society however has relatively few symbolic actions with recognized significance. One reason for that is that it is rich in words, and uses those for all purposes. But a deeper reason is that it is much less conscious than were older societies of its role in an ongoing historical tradition of deep significance. So often in other societies symbolic actions are those which re-enact acts of earlier agents, with whom the agent identifies himself in a common role. To sit at the head of the table is, in some societies, to declare yourself head of the family. To put on the crown of the dead king is to announce yourself as his successor. To put on the mantle of Elijah is to announce that you are the new Elijah, in the sense of the successor who will fulfil the same role towards Israel and God as did Elijah.[11]

I doubt if there are any totally natural gestures which express a claim that something is so, as opposed to expressing an attitude or issuing a command. Even something as primitive as shaking your head horizontally can mean 'no' in some societies, and, I believe, 'yes' in others. Convention is necessary to give to symbolic acts declarative force. Earlier societies have had a rich understanding moulded by their histories of the significance of acts of various kinds, ready to interpret particular token acts.

[11] 2 Kgs. 2: 13–14.

2

Presupposition

Presupposition and Statement

When you use words to convey information or express a belief or attitude, it is often easier to do so (you need to use a shorter sentence, and the hearer is more likely to understand it) if you express it in terms of shared presuppositions. Believing that the New York office in which I am conducting a conversation is on the eighty-first floor, and hearing the wind howl outside, I may say, 'The eighty-first floor feels the wind.' But my point is not really about the eighty-first floor, but about the floor on which I believe the office to be situated. Believing that the person to whom you are talking is your cousin, I may say, 'I see you agree with your cousin'; my point is that you agree with the person to whom you are talking, his being your cousin is not an aspect of the situation on which I am commenting, but my belief that your collocutor is your cousin gives me a short way of referring to him.

Sometimes one speaker makes use of the presuppositions of his audience, even when he does not share them, in order to express his belief or whatever. This too is because he can express his belief more briefly and intelligibly and make it more acceptable to his audience if he uses such a presupposition in terms of which to clothe his message. Your son is no longer employed at the job he held some months ago with a bank—you think that he resigned, but I suspect that he was dismissed. He looks happier since the change. I seek to say this, and I do so by saying, 'He looks happier since he resigned from the bank.' Because of the irrelevance of such presuppositions to the job which the speaker is trying to do with his sentence, it is natural to understand the sentence as expressing a statement which does not state the presuppositions in terms of which it is cast, and to whose truth-value the truth or falsity of the presuppositions is irrelevant.

Philosophers have most usually discussed this question in connection with referring expressions, that is, expressions such as proper names ('John') or definite descriptions ('the Prime Minister') which purport to pick out individual objects in order to say something about them, for example, 'John is old.' It is the presupposition of sentences containing referring expressions that there exists an object picked out by that expression. Now suppose, to use an example much discussed in the philosophical literature, that I am at a party and note a man in the corner, drinking what I take to be Martini, being very cheerful. I seek to comment on his cheerfulness and do so by saying to my companions, 'The man drinking Martini is very cheerful.' However the man to whom I was intending to refer was drinking not Martini, but sherry. Is what I have said true, false, or neither? Contemporary philosophers are divided on this issue. Some, following Russell,[1] claim that what I have said is false. For what I have said is analysable as 'There is a man drinking Martini and he is very cheerful', and since the first conjunct ('There is a man drinking Martini') is false the whole is false. Others, following Strawson,[2] claim that it is neither true or false, for since the referring expression fails to refer there is nothing for what I say to be true or false about. Yet others may plausibly claim that if the context makes clear to whom I am intending to refer and what I say applies to him, then what I have said is true.[3]

Our ordinary usage with respect to 'true' and 'false' is not clear enough for us to settle this issue by a simple appeal to that.[4] However there seems to me reason for adopting a version of the third position, that where public criteria make it clear to what reference is being made—in the sense that others in that context would agree on which object is being referred to (even if the speaker himself did not have the intention of referring to that object), the fact that the reference is made by means of a false description does not affect the truth-value of what is said—does not therefore make it false or neither-true-nor-false. The reason is, I suggest, compelling where it is a presupposition, not just of the speaker or one or two of those to whom he was talking, but of the whole culture that the false description applies to the object in question, and that is why the public criteria (i.e. those of the culture) pick it out. We of our culture can see what those criteria pick out, and then pick out the object in question by a route which does not use their presuppositions.

---

[1] 'On Denoting', repr. in Bertrand Russell, *Logic and Knowledge*, (ed. Robert C. Marsh) (Allen & Unwin, 1956).
[2] 'On Referring', in P. F. Strawson, *Logico-Linguistic Papers* (Methuen & Co., 1971).
[3] See Additional Note 2.
[4] See S. A. Kripke, 'Speaker's Reference and Semantic Reference', in P. A. French *et al.* (eds.), *Contemporary Perspectives in the Philosophy of Language* (University of Minnesota Press, 1979), on this.

Roman historians may record the deeds of 'the divine Augustus'. Must we judge all the details of his life which they give not to be true just because we think that no Augustus was 'divine'? Biographers tell us mundane details of the life of Gautama ('the Buddha'); if they tell us that 'the enlightened one' did this or that, do we judge what they say false (or neither-true-nor-false) if we think that Gautama was not at all 'enlightened'. The answer in these cases, intuitively, is surely 'No'.

The reason for saying that the falsity of the description in a referring expression does not, so long as there is public agreement about what is the referent, which arises from agreement in the culture that that description applies to a certain individual, affect the truth-value of the sentence, is this. Although speakers may use declarative sentences for many different purposes (e.g. to express their beliefs or attitudes), their paradigm job is to convey information, to add to the hearer's stock of beliefs. By a sentence such as 'The divine Augustus travelled to Brindisi', written in the course of conveying other detailed historical information, a Roman historian is seeking to add to his readers' stock of information. He would regard himself as having succeeded if they then came to believe that Augustus travelled to Brindisi, whether or not they shared his view that Augustus was divine. That that is what is crucial in the utterance of the sentence would be a view held not merely by the individual speaker but by others of his culture; they would see that as the job of the sentence in that location. The writer and his hearers would see the sentence as false if Augustus did not travel to Brindisi. If we judge it as false (or neither-true-nor-false) if either Augustus was not divine or he did not travel to Brindisi, we would be taking into account in judging its truth-value an aspect quite other than the writer and immediate readers would have judged as part of his message; we would have imposed our categories of 'true' and 'false' upon the sentence in virtue of truth-conditions which the speaker and his culture would not have regarded as relevant to the information which the sentence was being used to convey. We would thus be ignoring the close tie between the meaning of a sentence (and so what makes it true or false) and the belief which, other things equal, speakers in a culture use the sentence to instil. Our account of what made the sentence true or false would not be one sensitive to the normal role of the sentence in the circumstances of its utterance.[5]

---

[5] See Additional Note 3.

But if falsity of description of a referent does not destroy the reference or the truth of what is said about it, so long as there are public criteria for what the referent is, the same should apply to any other false assumptions used in a sentence by means of which a speaker seeks to do a job quite other than convey those assumptions in terms of which its message is cast. I say, pointing to some water, 'That is a very beautiful river', but what I point to is not a river, it is a lake. It is nevertheless a beautiful stretch of water. Is what I have said true, false, or neither? I say, in the course of commenting on what Jane (picked out by the referring expression 'Jane') did on some day, 'Jane cooked a meal for her father.' I say that because I believe that the man in whose house Jane lived was her father; but he is not, he is only her stepfather. She nevertheless cooked a meal for him. Is what I have said true, false, or neither?

The answer may not be obvious in these cases. But where not merely the assumptions of speaker and hearer, but the presuppositions of a whole culture, are what lead a typical speaker to convey information by means of a sentence which encapsulates those presuppositions (information quite other than that those presuppositions are true), then we ought, I suggest, to regard truth and falsity as belonging to a statement which does not contain those presuppositions, although it has been expressed by means of them. This is because the criteria for truth, falsity, and so on of public utterances are those of the whole culture which uses the language, and not those of an individual speaker or hearer who may misuse the language; and those criteria must be ones which pick out the sentence as true if the belief which it would be used to instil by a typical speaker of the language in the context in question is a true one. In order to separate statement from presupposition, we must ask, whatever the speaker's actual beliefs, what were the common beliefs of the culture which they could reasonably presuppose that the speaker shared with them; and whatever the actual purpose of his utterance, can any such presupposed beliefs be siphoned off, leaving what the culture would naturally suppose to be the main message intact? If they can, we must then judge the truth-value of the utterance by criteria to which the falsity of the presuppositions is irrelevant. I end my biography of Brown by saying that he 'fell asleep' or 'joined the spirits of his ancestors'. The point of my remark is not to make a theological claim, but to make a biographical one about the date of Brown's death. To assess the remark for truth-value it is not necessary to have a view about the afterlife. What determines the truth or falsity of 'Brown fell asleep in AD 1650', as uttered in seventeenth-century England, is not whether death is a temporary sleep, but only whether Brown died in 1650.

The statement is whatever the speaker, by public criteria, is seeking to add to the existing beliefs of the hearers. This may be expressed in terms of beliefs peculiar to the culture, but must be separable from them, by the above criteria. In that case, even within that culture, the statement could be expressed (albeit clumsily and at length) in ways that do not use the presuppositions of the culture. If the culture has a way of talking about death which picks it out as an end of life on this Earth without making any assumptions about whether or not there is life after death and of what kind it is, I can express the statement which I attempt to convey by 'Brown fell asleep in AD 1650' without the presupposition that death is a temporary sleep, by writing, 'Brown died in AD 1650.' But such a distinction between statement and presupposition cannot be made if a culture does not have any way of describing the objects or properties at stake other than in ways which encapsulate its peculiar beliefs. If (implausibly) the culture could not distinguish between death and normal falling asleep, then the above distinction between the statement and the presupposition could not be made.

To take another example: someone in the eighteenth century might claim (r): 'All mammals need to breathe dephlogisticated air in order to stay alive.' He might make this comment in the course of a work on mammals, sharing the belief of his culture that what we call oxygen was air with the phlogiston removed. Now if he has other ways of referring to the gas which we call oxygen than as 'dephlogisticated air'—for example as the gas which is produced by such-and-such a process, or found in a fairly pure form in such-and-such circumstances—then even if he does not refer to that gas as 'oxygen', he may be said to have the belief that (s) 'oxygen' (identified by him and ourselves in many similar ways) 'is dephlogisticated air', a presupposition which can be separated off from r to yield a claim more clumsily expressed (namely without our word 'oxygen') which was what he was trying to convey by his original sentence, that is, was his original claim. But if he has no other way of referring to oxygen except as 'dephlogisticated air', then r does not presuppose s—because the writer does not have a belief that s. r is not then about oxygen, but simply about air from which phlogiston has been removed. As there is no such thing, mammals do not need to breathe it in order to stay alive and r is then false. But if the writer shares with his culture the belief s, then r is true. The presuppositions of a culture must thus be expressible within the culture, if they are to be disregarded for the purpose of judging the truth or falsity of sentences which encapsulate them.

Presupposition and Vagueness

The presuppositions of a culture have also a more general influence on the truth-values of its sentences, even when they do not serve *as* presuppositions. Our language contains words and sentence forms which allow us to describe facts of the world and distinctions between them of which we are aware. And the 'we' has to be more than one; for, as I have emphasized, words and sentence forms can only belong to a public language in so far as there are public criteria for their correct application. I showed in Chapter 1 how speakers share a common understanding of how words and sentence forms come together to form meaningful sentences, an understanding derived from observing how sentences of those forms and containing those words are confirmed in familiar situations. In virtue of this they know what sentences of familiar forms using familiar words mean when they are formed to describe situations purportedly not very different from the paradigm ones from which we learn their meaning. But, I commented there, such procedures may give only a vague meaning to sentences formed to describe situations purportedly rather different from the paradigm situations of learning, especially if the possibility of the latter situations was not even envisaged when the words and sentence forms acquired currency in the language. The presuppositions of the culture, about which situations are possible, demarcate the area within which its sentences have clear meaning.

Thus, to take a simple example, suppose a world where all objects are similar in colour either to the sky (coloured as now), or to tree leaves in spring (coloured as now). The culture therefore has only two colour words 'blue' and 'green'. Members of the culture might then make a general claim *s*: 'everything coloured is either blue or green.' Suppose now that the world changes. Objects appear which are—clearly, by our standards of similarity—intermediate in colour between blue and green, but some of them nearer in colour to standard blue things and the others nearer in colour to standard green things. Has *s* been shown false? That depends on whether the intermediate objects which are more blue than green are correctly described as 'blue', and the objects which are more green than blue are correctly described as 'green'. What determines whether they are so describable?

There are two possible facets of the situation under which there would be clear answers to the question. The first is that the original culture may have explicitly considered the possibility of intermediate objects, and explicitly laid down (in a dictionary, say) a rule for what is to be said in these circumstances, conceived but not then realized. It may have laid down either that an object is 'blue' if and only if it resembles the so far observed standard blue objects as much as they resemble each other; or that an object is blue if and only if it resembles standard blue objects more than it resembles standard green objects. On the latter definition such an intermediate half-blue object would count as blue, on the former it would not. And similar definitions could have been laid down for 'green'. The culture would thus have deliberately prepared itself for new possibilities. And according to which definitions it had laid down, *s* might or might not have been falsified.

The other possible facet of the situation which could lead to clear answers to the question is that, although the possibility of the new situation had not been considered in advance and explicit definitions of 'blue' and 'green' were not available in advance to deal with it, nevertheless, when the new situation occurred, (almost) every member of the culture might agree with each other in their spontaneous judgements as to how to describe the new objects—for instance, that objects nearer in colour to blue than green objects were 'blue'. The original learning situation might have inculcated in the learners concepts of 'blue' and 'green' with much more extensive rules for their application than we would ordinarily suppose. In consequence of how the concepts were applied, *s* might or might not have been falsified.

The new situation might however be more radically different from the old one than what I have described. I have so far imagined a situation where all objects were by our standards of similarity clearly more similar to standard blue objects than to standard green objects, or conversely. But now suppose that red objects appear. Would *s* have been falsified, or not? If a definition of 'blue' and 'green' had been provided in advance, everything would turn on how the definition was interpreted. Are red objects more similar to blue objects than to green objects or not? Again, (almost) all members of the culture might agree in their judgements one way or the other—which would show that the concepts they had acquired had certain boundaries. If they all judged that red objects were very similar to blue objects, and so to be called 'blue', that would show that (despite its initial apparent similarity to our concept) their concept of 'blue' was really very different from ours. And if there was no definition of 'blue' or 'green' in advance, but nevertheless agreement in judgement as to whether red objects were or were not blue, that would settle whether *s* had been falsified and thereby show us more precisely how they understood 'blue' and so, more precisely, which statement was being expressed by the sentence *s*.

However, given rational creatures not very different from us human beings, neither of these possibilities is likely to arise. There is a narrow limit to the worlds very different from their own which humans are equipped (either via a definition or not) to describe. For the most likely scenario when the world changed colour in the first respect is that humans would differ with respect to how to describe the new objects and so with respect to the truth-value of *s*. And while the more likely scenario, when red objects appeared, is that they would judge *s* false, it is not at all unlikely that some of them might detect a sufficient similarity between (e.g.) blue objects and red ones for them to affirm *s* as true. These situations thus reveal that the meaning (that is, the public meaning) of *s* is vague, because there is no public agreement about what constitutes its truth-conditions in certain situations.

The learning situation of humans typically equips them with capacities for judgement about the applicability of concepts in many situations, but not in yet other situations. The reason for this is that humans are not clones of each other; and in consequence they have slightly diverse psychological and physiological make-up from each other which limits sharply the extent to which they will agree spontaneously, without using an explicit definition, on how words are to be used in new situations. And explicit definitions will only be provided as to how words should be applied for those situations which the culture regards as possible. For those situations are the only ones for which the culture will have 'thought through' how its words are to be applied. Since humans have finite imagination, there are limits to their abilities to conceive of possible and especially logically possible situations; and hence the presuppositions of the culture about which situations are likely or possible delimit the area of situations for which there are clear criteria for when their sentences are true or false.[6]

---

[6] Whatever the presuppositions of the culture, there will always be *some* possible cases on the border between being instances and non-instances of a concept—some possible object on the border in colour between clearly blue and clearly non-blue; between being

What applies to my simple colour example applies completely generally. Consider a quite different kind of word: 'adultery'. Learners may
be introduced to this word by example, but definition by other words is
surely more central for conveying the meaning. So they may be told
that 'adultery is having sexual intercourse with someone else's spouse'.
But the culture will have a certain limited conception of the possibilities
of intercourse and of marriage. It might only know of 'normal' sexual
intercourse between male and female, and marriage as a state brought
about by pledges of one male and one female of lifelong fidelity to each
other. In that case, the teaching *r* 'adultery is always wrong' would have
clear consequences for many situations conceivable by the members of
that culture—for example that, if John is married to Mary, it would be
wrong for him to have sexual intercourse with Jane. But neighbouring
societies might have thought of ways of familiarity very similar to
'sexual intercourse', ways which can be practised between male and
male; and of pledges of fidelity with various qualifications attached to
them (e.g. pledges to be faithful if the woman is capable of child-
bearing, etc.). The question then arises as to which kinds of familiarity
are, given *r*, forbidden by which kinds of pledge? Our original society
may or may not have thought through some of these possibilities
explicitly, or be so uniformly conditioned by nature and nurture as to
have no hesitation in its judgements on which kinds of relationship of
the kinds mentioned constitute 'adultery'. But of course there are
further even stranger situations conceivable, such as societies in which
the most intensely derived kind of intimacy has no connection at all
with child-bearing, or societies in which there are three sexes (and of
course what that amounts to depends on how the concept of a 'sex' is
understood). Given that we are not clones of each other, we have natural inclinations to apply words slightly differently in new situations
unless we have a definition to provide guidance. But we will not have
definitions of any use unless society has taken account of possible
situations and devised definitions of how words should be used in those

less than 6 cm. long and 6 cm. or more long. For any concept one can conceive of objects
further and further away from standard cases of its applicability until we come to cases on
the border between applicability and non-applicability. In this respect no concept can be
perfectly exact. (On this see my 'Vagueness, Inexactness, and Imprecision', *British
Journal for the Philosophy of Science*, 14 (1969), 281–99). My point in the text is that the
border between the applicability and non-applicability of a concept may be a vast area of
uncertainty, not a mere point of transition, because human learning (contingently) does
not provide humans with sufficiently exact concepts.

situations; and whether it has will depend on its presuppositions as to what is possible or likely. So the presuppositions of the society limit how it understands 'adultery is always wrong' and the extent to which that gives clear guidance for conduct.

One writer who stressed the influence on our thought of presuppositions was Collingwood.[7] All propositions, he claimed, presuppose things. These presuppositions can be stated and, if 'relative' rather than 'absolute', can be argued about. But he did not bring out how presuppositions can act so as to limit the clarity of sentences for unconceived circumstances. A writer who did do this was Waismann.[8] He claimed that many 'empirical concepts' (i.e. ones applied to objects in virtue of observable features) have what he called 'open texture'. He claimed that 'no definition of an empirical term will cover all the possibilities'. Any attempt to lay down the conditions of use of some term will never be able to cater for every possibility, because it is always possible that I might have some totally new experience 'such as at present I cannot even imagine' or some new discovery may affect our whole interpretation of facts. Now Waismann does not claim that such inexactness is a feature of all empirical concepts, yet he seems to claim that it is an essential feature of most.

I cannot see that he has given any argument that this is essential to concepts as such. But his point remains a very important point about the concepts picked out by words of a language used by creatures of finite imagination who are not clones of each other; and hence a very important contingent truth about human beings or similar rational creatures.

Context and Standard of Accuracy

A final connected point is that sentences are normally uttered to convey information in certain particular contexts of enquiry, which have their own standard of the kind of accuracy required. To convey information to guide conduct quickly and easily, it is often best to do so by means of a sentence which is, if we speak strictly, inaccurate and ignores

---

[7] R. G. Collingwood, *An Essay on Metaphysics* (Clarendon Press, 1940), § 47.

[8] F. Waismann, 'Verifiability', *Proceedings of the Aristotelian Society*, Supplementary Volume, 19 (1945), 119–50, repr. in A. G. N. Flew (ed.), *Logic and Language* (1st series) (Blackwell, 1951). The quotations are from 121–4 of the reprinted version.

qualifications and exceptions. We may describe an object as 'round' even if it is not of a shape which satisfies the geometer's definition of 'round' in the sense of being a shape each of the points of whose bounding line is equidistant from a central point. We may do so if the context of discussion is such that objects quite similar to such geometrically 'round' objects count as 'round'. The context of discussion will have that character if the accuracy of the information in that respect is not important for behaviour, and the words being used are sufficiently accurate to suggest to the hearers the discrimination important for behaviour. If the only objects within range are either roughly square or roughly round, and I am giving instructions to a hearer as to which objects to pick up, I will say, 'pick up the round one to your left', so long as only one object to the hearer's left is approximately round.

A statement being true is a matter of its truth-conditions being satisfied to the degree of accuracy appropriate in the context. If I say, 'all the objects are either round or square', the context of discussion (in the respect of the level of accuracy in which it is interested) is crucial for assessing the truth or falsity of what I have said. It is crucial in the respect already noted, of what is to count as 'round' or 'square'; it is also crucial for what we are to say if there is just one exception. Is one exception to 'all *A*s are *B*' enough to render the statement false? All depends on the context. If 'all *A*s are *B*' is a suggested scientific law of nature, a (repeatable) exception renders the sentence false; but if it is a sentence in a guidebook describing a terrain, then maybe the sentence is true (to the limits of accuracy appropriate in the context).[9]

---

[9] These points derive from J. L. Austin's discussions of similar examples in his *How to Do Things with Words* (Clarendon Press, 1962), 142–6. See also his *Sense and Sensibility* (Clarendon Press, 1962), 124–31.

3
Analogy and Metaphor

I argued in Chapter 1 that the sense of a word is a matter of its semantic relations to the world (which states of affairs identified ostensively confirm or disconfirm sentences containing it), and the syntactic relations of sentences which contain it to other sentences (which other sentences confirm or disconfirm the former, and in the extreme entail it or its negation).

Now words may have more than one sense, as I have commented in Chapter 1: 'bank' may mean edge of a river, or place where money is kept. A use of a given token word 'φ' on one occasion and a use of another token of the same type on another occasion are uses of the word in the same sense if the two words have the same synonyms, same antonyms, are determinates of the same determinable, and have the same determinates. For then the contribution of each word to the meanings of the sentences in which they occur will be the same.

Analogy

It seems a natural use of the terms 'univocal', 'analogical', and 'equivocal', consonant with their role in the history of comment on language, to mark cases where a given token word 'φ' is used in the same sense as, in a similar sense to, and in a quite unrelated sense from another token 'φ' of the same type. I shall say that a word 'φ' is used on two occasions in a univocal sense if it is used in the same sense, in an analogical sense if it is used in a similar sense, in an equivocal sense if it is used in an unrelated sense. (Distinctions between the 'univocal', the 'analogical', and the 'equivocal' can be made in more than one way. What I would claim for my way of making the distinction is that it is a fairly natural and useful one and gives these terms a use similar to those which many others have given them in the history of thought. But it needs to be kept in mind that some writers use these words, as also the words 'literal' and 'metaphorical', in very different ways from other writers.

We shall see that in due course with respect to Aquinas's use of 'analogical'.) A word has the same sense if it has all the same synonyms, contraries, determinates, and so on; similar sense if it has many of the synonyms, and so on; unrelated sense if it has none of the same synonyms, and so on. These relations between senses have been analysed in a careful and sophisticated way by James F. Ross in his *Portraying Analogy*.[1] Ross introduces his category of a predicate scheme. Consider the words which can be substituted for a given word 'ϕ' in some sentence, while leaving the sentence, in Ross's terminology, 'acceptable', which I shall simply read as 'well formed'.[2] Thus you can replace 'boy' in 'The boy asked for a job' by 'girl', 'old man', 'plumber', or 'carpenter'. But only some of the substitutes are meaning-relevant, that is, have with the original word such connections of meaning as being synonyms,[3] antonyms, contraries, determinates of the same determinable, determinates of the other, and so on (p. 69); as in this example do 'girl' and 'old man', but not 'plumber' or 'carpenter'. The meaning-relevant substitutes for a word form its predicate scheme. Words have the same meaning, are being used univocally, if they have the same predicate scheme (namely the same synonyms, contraries, determinables, etc.); similar meaning, are being used analogically with respect to each other, if they have overlapping predicate schemes; and are equivocal with respect to each other if their predicate schemes do not overlap.

Thus in 'All bachelors are lonely', uttered on a certain occasion, 'bachelor' has the same sense as when it is used in a large number of other contexts, for in each it has the same synonyms (e.g. 'man who has never married'), contraries ('married man', 'widower', 'divorced man', 'unmarried woman' ...), is a determinate of the determinable 'man', and has as its determinates such sets as ('bachelor under 20 years old', 'bachelor between 20 and 30 years old' ..., etc.) and ('bachelor who wishes to be married', 'bachelor who does not wish to be married').

---

[1] Cambridge University Press, 1981.

[2] Although Ross does not define an 'acceptable' sentence, he suggests that it is at least a well-formed sentence of the language which preserves the consistency or inconsistency of the original sentence (ibid. 58); it seems to me that this understanding of 'acceptable sentence' makes for unnecessary complication and that we should understand by 'acceptable' simply 'well formed'.

[3] Ross prefers to talk of 'near-synonyms'. However, in view of there being a satisfactory test (see below) for the more precise notion of 'synonym' itself, it seems to me preferable to use the latter.

The token 'ϕ' in a token sentence p (e.g. 'a is ϕ) is synonymous with 'ψ' if the substitution of 'ψ' for 'ϕ' would yield a token sentence q (namely 'a is ψ') synonymous with p. p and q are synonymous sentences if (for all A) 'A believes that p' (uttered in the same context as p) is logically equivalent to 'A believes that q (and if all other replacements of p by q in belief-contexts yield logically equivalent sentences—e.g. 'A believes that B believes that p' is logically equivalent to 'A believes that B believes that q'.[4] So by this test in most token sentences of the type 'John is a bachelor' 'bachelor' is synonymous with 'unmarried man'. For 'I believe that John is a bachelor', said in a context of discussing John's personal relationships, is logically equivalent to 'I believe that John is an unmarried man' said in that context. These are logically equivalent in the sense that each entails the other. Hence 'John is a bachelor' is synonymous with 'John is an unmarried man', uttered in the same context.

Ross's account of univocity goes back to that given by Aristotle.[5] Ross however has applied these notions in a more detailed way to analogy than did either Aristotle or any of his successors. Among the hundreds of examples which he discusses, he considers eighteen examples of different senses of the word 'charged'. Some of these are equivocal with each other, and some analogous (and the extent of analogy varies). Thus (pp. 100 f.) there is analogy between 'He charged his assistants to watch the financial markets' (in the sense of instructed them) and 'He charged her with information as to her opponents' (in the sense of mentally burdened or loaded her with it). 'For', writes Ross (p. 101), 'the former allows as near-synonyms "instructed", "informed", "ordered", "commanded", and "directed", but [the latter] does not allow "ordered", "commanded" or "directed" yet does allow "instructed", "informed" and the like.'

An important case of analogy is where a word with its predicate scheme is removed from one context and applied in another—which

---

[4] This further clause is a requirement for sentence-synonymy additional to that contained in my 'Analytic/Synthetic', *American Philosophical Quarterly*, 21 (1984), 31–42, where I gave only the simpler requirement that p and q are synonymous if 'A believes that p' is logically equivalent to 'A believes that q'. It was pointed out to me by Roy Sorenson that it is open to counter-examples, such as that although 'A believes that someone exists' is logically equivalent to 'A believes that A exists', 'A exists' is not synonymous with 'someone exists'. The additional clause rules out counter-examples of this kind. See 'Analytic/Synthetic' also for an account of the meaning of and tests for entailment and so for logical equivalence (mutual entailment).

[5] *Topics*, 106[a]–107[b].

occurs, for example when the word comes to be used in an abstract sense (p. 108):

> Thus in 'the arch *carries* the weight of the roof', we could substitute 'bears', 'holds', 'sustains', or 'supports'. So too in 'the first premiss *carries* the weight of the argument'. The first mentioned near-synonyms for the first occurrence are also near-synonyms for the second.

Yet one set of words (with their contraries, determinates, etc.) is 'a contrast in modes by which one physical object is said to impede the gravitational pull on another', while the other does 'not presuppose physical activity at all'. Hence the implications of the two 'carries' are different, and this will emerge with them or their synonyms having some different contraries, determinates, and so forth. One 'carries' is a species of 'exerts a physical force on'; the other is a species of 'gives logical support to'.

Analogy is a matter of degree. Uses of words are analogous to the extent to which they have the same synonyms, antonyms, and so on; and so some uses of words are more closely analogous than others. When uses of tokens of the same type have none of the same synonyms, antonyms, and so on, they are straightforwardly equivocal.

Tokens of 'bank' meaning river bank are straightforwardly equivocal with tokens of 'bank' meaning money-shop. Among cases of the equivocal in my sense are words related by what Ross calls denominative analogy (Aquinas's 'analogy of attribution'[6]). Here the token word is used because of a relation to objects, situations, and so on to which types of the same word standardly apply. We call things Victorian if they resemble things typically current in the Victorian period.[7] One instance of this is where the relation is causal or significative, namely an object is called 'ϕ' because it is the cause of things being 'ϕ' or shows them to be 'ϕ'. To use the example used by Aquinas, a diet is 'healthy' if it causes a man to be 'healthy' and urine is 'healthy' if it is a sign of a man being 'healthy'. But although there is a connection of meanings, one is not saying something similar of urine and the diet in describing them both as 'healthy'.

---

[6] This is Aquinas's 'analogy of attribution' according to Cajetan's simple account of Aquinas's system. See B. Mondin, *The Principle of Analogy in Protestant and Catholic Theology* (Martinus Nijhoff, 1968), 37–8. Aquinas seems to have classified kinds of analogy differently at different stages of his thought. On this see ibid. ch. 2.

[7] Ross, *Portraying Analogy*, 123.

Metaphor

When a word is being used in an already existing sense, then mere knowledge of the language in which a token sentence containing it is uttered shows the possible contributions which it can make to the meaning of that sentence. Context of utterance may be needed to discriminate between possible meanings; but that context is not needed for the purpose of generating a possible meaning to start with. Metaphor arises when a word or words are not used in any pre-existing senses, nor in any new sense given an explicit definition, but where knowledge of a wide context—a lot of information about where the token sentence containing the word was uttered, by whom, in what circumstances, against what background of common assumptions—will reveal what is being said. The sense is a new one, generated by the context and by the previous established senses of the word together.[8] The new sense may be analogical with the old one or it may not. (It might, for example, on the contrary exemplify denominative analogy.) If similar metaphors are used frequently, the sense becomes an established one, and the use in that sense is no longer metaphorical. (The metaphor is dead.) When words are used metaphorically the token sentence has a meaning other than a normal meaning of sentences of its type.

I illustrate:

1. Wittgenstein paints in oils rather than water-colour.
2. Cynthia proved to be a hedgehog.
3. Eliot took poetry off the gold standard.
4. Jane was not so much the last rose of summer, but the first winter jasmine.
5. No iceberg melts in winter.
6. Computer failure will often lead to your take-off being aborted.
7. If you open up a can of worms, you should be able to catch quite a lot of fish.
8. Here comes Ronald Reagan.

---

[8] The joint generation of new sense by prior sense and context is the theme of Josef Stern, 'Metaphor as Demonstrative', *Journal of Philosophy*, 82 (1985), 677–710. He compares this process to the process of the generation of the reference of a demonstrative (e.g. 'I') by the sense of the demonstrative (e.g. to refer to the speaker of the utterance containing it) and the context (showing by whom the utterance containing 'I' was spoken).

All of these sentences, except perhaps (3), have a normal meaning with words used in normal senses, which can be supposed to be the meaning of a token of these types in the absence of information about the context of their utterance. But information about the context of a given token (e.g. that 'Jane' and 'Cynthia' were used to denote female humans; or that (8) was spoken about my friend John) may rule out all normal meanings. Each of these sentences could acquire a whole variety of new meanings and so some of their words have a whole variety of new senses according to the context; no dictionary could list the possible senses. (2), for example, may be a description of how Cynthia looks, or how she behaves in her personal relations, and in the latter case it could utilize different features believed to be true of hedgehogs to make different comparisons. It could be saying that in her sexual relationships, or in her relationships with employers, or in her relationships with friends, she 'clams up' unless approached with extreme gentleness and tact; or alternatively that she is very 'prickly', takes remarks the wrong way if that is possible, is quick to resent the slightest suggestion that there is anything wrong with her. (6) could be used in the course of a description of a whole variety of human activities; and what corresponds to 'computer failure', 'take-off', and 'abortion' will vary in each case. One use, but obviously only one use, is to make the point that getting to know a certain person is difficult, you seem to be beginning to exchange confidences and talk readily when some irrelevant accident outside your control makes your relationship much more formal.

One comes to understand what is being said by noting its obvious inappropriateness,[9] that is, its obvious (to speaker and hearers) irrelevance or falsity in the context if the words are taken in pre-existing senses. However, we then look for the distinctive features of the objects, activities, or whatever denoted by the words in their pre-existing senses (features which belong necessarily to those objects, etc., or contingently, or are generally believed to belong, or are suggested by the objects).

---

[9] H. P. Grice classically elucidated the maxims of normal conversation. To conform to these the speaker has to say what is neither more nor less than an appropriate response to previous remarks, what is true, backed up by evidence, unambiguous, etc. See H. P. Grice, 'Logic and Conversation', in P. Cole and J. L. Morgan (eds.), *Syntax and Semantics*, iii (Academic Press, 1975). My account in these chapters of how context determines the sense of an expression, put in his terms, is that, if we can, we construe an expression in that sense in which the speaker would be obeying the maxims of normal conversation.

Different contents will often make different features distinctive.[10] We then consider the statements which would be made by the sentence if the words are taken to denote such features instead of having a pre-existing sense. Words which in their pre-existing senses denote aspects of the discussion in which the sentence occurs are, however, other things being equal, to be retained in those senses. All of this will throw up many possible meanings for the sentence. If with only one of these is the sentence a natural, relevant thing to say in the context, that is the meaning the sentence has. If on no interpretation is the sentence a natural, relevant thing to say in the context, it must be understood as having the meaning (whether a pre-existing meaning, or one thrown up by the context) which makes it the least unnatural thing to say, and that might sometimes be just the normal meaning. If on more than one interpretation it is natural and relevant, then the sentence is ambiguous and may be true on one interpretation and false on another.[11]

For example, take (1). Suppose it occurs in a context when Wittgenstein or philosophers generally are being discussed. Then 'Wittgenstein' has to be taken to refer, in accord with normal conventions of reference, to the philosopher Wittgenstein. If the discussion were about which philosophers painted and how they painted, then the sentence could be supposed to have its normal meaning. But suppose, more plausibly, that it occurs in a discussion of Wittgenstein's style of argument. Then it would not be a natural relevant thing to say, and we must look for some other meaning. One distinctive feature of painting in oils as opposed to water-colours is that you dab the paint on to points rather than stroke it on with flowing strokes over a wide area. The work of art is constructed by many separate contributions rather than by fewer connected contributions. What this suggests in the case of writing philosophy is making many separate points which produce a total integrated view, rather than a number of connected arguments in which there is a flow of thought; and that of course is characteristic of Wittgenstein's style. There are, no doubt, also other distinctive features of oil painting as opposed to water-colour painting, but in the absence

[10] See Additional Note 4.

[11] My account of how one determines the meaning of a metaphorical utterance owes quite a lot to John R. Searle, 'Metaphor', in A. Ortony (ed.), *Metaphor and Thought* (Cambridge University Press, 1979), esp. 113–20. But for Searle, as we shall see shortly, such factors as those described in the text do not determine the meaning of the sentence, but rather what the speaker meant to convey by uttering the sentence; the former has only a normal meaning.

of any of them having obvious relevance to philosophical style, we take the one suggested. The sentence says that Wittgenstein wrote philosophy by making a large number of separate points which give a total view, rather than a number of longer connected arguments. The sentence can now be assessed for truth or falsity.

Or take (8). These are of course plenty of contexts where it will have its normal meaning. But suppose it to be uttered when a man, John, known not to be Ronald Reagan, comes into the room, then the beliefs of speaker and hearer about John and Ronald Reagan may be such as to give it a new meaning which makes it relevant to the context. If the surrounding conversation has been about the fact that, although John is a friendly man, he has recently made a speech advocating reintroduction of the death penalty, then the common belief of society that Reagan is a popular, friendly conservative, an actor who appeals to gut old-fashioned attitudes with no sensitivity to liberal values or the subtleties of issues, shows what I mean when I say, 'Here comes Ronald Reagan'; I mean that John is like Reagan in these respects.

Metaphorical sentences are often very vague; there is often a wide border area of possible states of affairs which are such that in them there is no true answer as to whether the metaphorical sentence is true or false. In a conversation about Cynthia touching both on her appearance and her personal relations, it may be quite unclear just how hedgehog-looking and clamming-up or prickly in her behaviour she has to be in order for 'Cynthia proved to be a hedgehog' to be true. If the conversation has been long and detailed and the assumptions of its participants (about Cynthia and hedgehogs) are detailed and evident, that would make the truth-conditions sharper than they would otherwise be; but there might still be quite a wide border area, in which it would be as near to the truth to say 'Cynthia proved to be a hedgehog' was true as to say that it was false. However, all sentences have border areas for their truth—when the curtains are blue-green, it is in many contexts as near to the truth to say that 'The curtains are green' is true as to say that it is false. Metaphorical sentences simply have wider border areas than most other sentences, in that there are wider areas in which there is not the kind of agreement in application described in the last chapter, if a sentence is to have a truth-value. Sometimes, however, it must be acknowledged, it is just so unclear what kind of comparison is being made by a metaphorical sentence that it cannot be said to have a truth-value. However, I would claim, given that the sentence occurs in the course of a conversation or a passage of writing with a clear subject-matter, a metaphorical sentence is normally such as to be true under some conditions of the world and false under others.

Metaphorical sentences may or may not be paraphrasable by other non-metaphorical sentences. Thus some distinctive feature of the objects picked out by the word 'φ' which is being used metaphorically may be one for which the community lacks a word or words; 'φ' may then be used metaphorically in that context as a name for that feature. Then a metaphorical sentence containing 'φ' used in that sense will not be paraphrasable by a non-metaphorical sentence. Such a metaphor is a 'creative' metaphor, in that it enables us to 'see' things which we had not seen before.[12]

The account of metaphor which I have given is in some ways a very considerable elaboration of what is known as the comparison theory of metaphor. This holds that when '*S* is *P*' makes a metaphorical assertion it means the same as the simile '*S* is like *P* ', and similarly for sentences of other forms. But this will not do as it stands. In a metaphorical assertion some words are to be taken in their normal sense, some are not. We need a context to show which words are and which are not to be so taken. Also, everything is like everything else in some respect, and one could not say that either 'man is a wolf' or 'man is like a wolf' is either true or false, without taking account of a lot of context to show the kinds of respect in which comparison is being made. Also the comparison is sometimes not with the object or property or activity apparently referred to, but with something associated with it. To reveal what comparison is being made we need, once again, context. Black's 'interaction' account of metaphor claims that a metaphorical assertion forces a system of commonplaces associated with one subject ('wolf') on to another ('man'): 'the metaphor selects, emphasizes, suppresses and organizes features of the principal subject ["man"] by implying statements about it that normally apply to the subsidiary subject ["wolf"].'[13] Again, this seems on the right lines, but needs to be elaborated to apply to sentences other than subject-predicate sentences, to show how context picks the features for comparison, and so forth.

Both Black and comparison theory[14] allow that metaphor yields

---

[12] On how metaphors can be 'creative' see Stern, 'Metaphor as Demonstrative', 703–4.

[13] M. Black, 'Metaphor', in his *Models and Metaphors* (Cornell University Press, 1962), 44–5.

[14] Especially as elaborated by Robert J. Fogelin, *Figuratively Speaking* (Yale University Press, 1986).

claims which can be assessed for truth or falsity. But Searle[15] and Davidson[16] have both claimed that the only meaning which metaphorical assertions have is their normal ('literal') meaning; yet by uttering a sentence with that meaning, the speaker manages to convey to the hearer a quite different idea. Man is not a wolf, but saying that he is helps the hearer to see man as a wolf.[17] Searle expresses this view by distinguishing speaker's meaning from sentence-meaning and claiming that metaphorical meaning is speaker's meaning.

The difficulty with this way of putting things is that, as Soskice well illustrates[18] and as Searle explicitly points out, the metaphorical statement 'a is ϕ' and the simile 'a is like ϕ' will have totally different truth-conditions, and that seems very odd when we take a complicated metaphor like: 'Human language is a cracked kettle on which we beat out tunes for bears to dance to, when all the time we are longing to move the stars to pity', and compare it with Flaubert's actual simile: 'Human language is like a cracked kettle on which we beat out tunes for bears to dance to, when all the time we are longing to move the stars to pity.' Surely the truth-conditions of the two statements are the same.[19]

If my account in Chapter 1 of what constitutes the distinction between speaker's meaning and sentence-meaning is correct, Searle has misapplied it. Metaphor does not involve the speaker saying something other than he means to say; nor does it involve the speaker meaning what he says (in a normal sense) but hinting at something further or hoping that the speaker will come to believe something other than what was said as a result of having private criteria for interpreting it. It is rather, as with metonymy, that the speaker uses a sentence which independent of context would mean one thing but which in the context (as shown by public criteria) means something else.

There is a wide unclear border between metaphor and analogy as I have defined them. Not all metaphors force analogical senses on words. For a word may be used metaphorically to designate a property contingently associated with the property which it normally designates, with-

---

[15] 'Metaphor'.

[16] D. Davidson, 'What Metaphors Mean', in his *Inquiries into Truth and Interpretation* (Oxford University Press, 1984).

[17] Ibid. 262–3.

[18] Janet Martin Soskice, *Metaphor and Religious Language* (Clarendon Press, 1985), 92. Aristotle held that the difference between simile and metaphor is 'but slight'. 'The simile is also a metaphor: the difference is but slight' between calling Achilles a lion and describing him as being like a lion (*Rhetorica*, 1406^{b}).

[19] See Additional Note 5.

out there being any similarity of meaning between the two uses—as does 'is a wolf' when it is used to designate the property of selfish ferocity which wolves are believed to exhibit, but which is not a defining criterion of being a wolf. And when an analogical sense created by a metaphor passes into established use, that use is no longer (on my definition) metaphorical; but it is vague (on that definition) how frequently and in what circumstances a word needs to be used in a sense for that sense to become established.

Declarative sentences are sometimes uttered, not in order ultimately to get us to believe them but simply in order to get us to think along the lines which they suggest. This is especially the case with sentences in poetry. Barring the case of fiction, the sentences nevertheless do have a truth-value, even if it is not important for the writer or speaker what that is. If what is said seems odd and outlandish when taken literally, either context will force a metaphorical meaning upon it, and then that can be assessed for truth or falsity; or it will not, and in that case what is said must be taken literally, at its face value. Either way, the sentence has a truth-value. But just as context is crucial for clarifying what the meaning of the sentence is, so context will often also make clear whether the speaker is trying to get us to believe what the sentence says, or whether his sentence has some other purpose. Even if the writer is trying to convey a belief, the way he does it, the style of his writing, may be at least of equal importance to him. In that case the role of metaphor is more to stimulate imagination than to convey truth—as far as expressing the statement is concerned, the job might be done equally well by a non-metaphorical sentence. But the use of metaphor may enable the speaker to get his message home to the speaker, who might pay no attention to some dry sentence containing words used in literal senses.[20]

Developing Language

So then humans have available for transmitting a statement words with various established senses, and sentence forms into which words can be

---

[20] Fogelin (*Figuratively Speaking*) points out that metaphors may vary along two dimensions—that of incongruity, and that of richness of comparison. If incongruity dominates we have metaphors of wit, initially puzzling, and, when we see them, striking but often far-fetched. These are of less value, perhaps, for conveying information than metaphors which can be developed into a rich system of comparisons.

put together, which make sentences which express those statements. And if speaker and hearer both have available to them words with the requisite senses, senses as clear and as precise as the speaker needs to transmit his message, the use of sentences written or spoken is the obvious way to transmit the statement: it is the way made for the job. But the words which humans have most readily available to them are words whose meaning is learnt from their primary use in connection with fairly down-to-earth human activities. Such words may not be immediately suitable for talk about abstract philosophical concepts, subatomic entities, infinite space and time, or God. They may need to have their meanings stretched, and to be used in odd ways, if they are to be used for talk about such fundamental matters.

However humans have thought about deep matters for many millenniums, and in sophisticated societies they have developed some vocabulary appropriate for this purpose. Mundane words have been given analogical senses, which continued use has made clear and precise. The analogical senses in which neutrons are 'particles' or light is a 'wave', a desk is a 'substance', time is 'composed of' many periods of time, and so on, are fairly clear and precise senses used within the literature which discusses such matters. If there is not available such an analogical sense, a statement may be expressed by a sentence using language metaphorically. But metaphors, as we have seen, have very vague meanings, and to make new precise statements with deep meanings we may need to introduce new words, or give new senses to old words. One way to do this is to use a word in a metaphorical sense and then let that metaphorical sense become established, become a dead metaphor. As the word becomes used with a metaphorical sense in similar contexts, speakers begin to explain its use to others, illustrate by example when it would and when it would not be correct to use it in this sense. Thereby they implicitly lay down the semantic and syntactic rules for its use in this sense; and continued use in different contexts can lead, via a growing understanding of the correct use of the word in the new sense, to its sense being a precise sense.

The alternative way to introduce a new word or an old word with a new sense is explicitly, by giving examples of its correct application and/or defining its relations to other words.

When words which have a sense in the language are combined into a well-formed declarative sentence, and the context gives its referring terms a reference, then, by the argument of Chapter 1, that sentence will express a statement and in that sense have meaning. But note that it may not have one clear unambiguous meaning. Sometimes it will be indeterminate which of two or more meanings the sentence has—though that will become less likely in so far as more context comes in to disambiguate.

4

Genre

Genre

To convey information of any detail and complexity, we need to use more than one sentence, to make a lengthy speech or (if the information is to have any permanence) write a work of some length. Written works fall into different genres. Genres differ from each other in many respects, of which I draw attention to three.[1] They differ first on their subject-matter. The work may be about history or philosophy, or simply tell a story. Secondly they differ in style. They may be written in prose or poetry; and there are different forms of each. There are novels and short stories and prose poems. There are sonnets and limericks and trochaic hendecasyllables. And thirdly genres differ in the amount of metaphor, the kinds of background knowledge, and the conventions of reference which they use. Works of certain genres are expected to use many words in metaphorical senses, whereas the expectation for other genres is that this is not so. The expectation is that most genres of poetry available today will use a lot of metaphor whereas works of history or science fiction are expected to use very little. There are genres with their own conventions for referring to individuals. (Pastoral poetry had a stock of names for referring to individuals who were known outside the genre by quite different names.[2]) Some genres are distinguished by the kinds of literature they take for granted as known; and works make their points by the way they diverge from paradigm examples of the genre. Many a Greek tragedy concerned the same series of events as many another (e.g. the Oedipus story, or the fall of Troy). The message of the work is carried by the way it diverges

[1] Alistair Fowler (*Kinds of Literature* (Clarendon Press, 1982), 60–74) finds at least 15 feature differences which form a basis for classifying works of literature into genres. He points out that works may belong to more than one genre. Fowler's illuminating work is concerned only with literary genres.

[2] Ibid. 79.

from its predecessors. The common theme simply forms a framework in which to express this message.

Arising out of these differences is a central difference that genres differ in respect of whether the work has truth-value; and if so whether and how that value is a function of the truth-values of the component sentences. For works of most non-literary genres (be they works of history, philosophy, or physics) the whole is true if and only if each constituent declarative (unquoted) sentence is true; to the extent to which it contains false sentences, it is not completely true. (If a sentence is quoted, its truth-value is of course irrelevant to the truth-value of the whole. What is relevant is whether the speaker (writer) said to have uttered (written) that sentence did so.) Even here however some sentences matter a lot more than others. There is often a main point or points of works of history, philosophy, physics, or whatever; and the work is said to be 'in essence' or 'fundamentally' true if that point is correct, even if the work contains false sentences. By contrast however in a work of fiction, such as a novel or short story, and in many (but not all) kinds of poetry, most of the sentences which it contains do not have a truth-value. The major reason for this is that the referring terms do not have and (unlike the cases considered in Chapter 2) are not supposed to have a reference. There never was a Mr Pickwick, and so sentences purporting to be about him are neither true nor false. Even if some sentences in such a work do have a truth-value (as when a historical novel includes some sentences about a person who actually lived) their truth-value is not relevant to the truth-value of the whole. In general works of fiction or poetry are not true or false; but if they have any evident message detectable by public criteria, they may be described as 'true' in so far as that message is true. Thus parables or poems commending some sort of conduct or depicting a typical feature of the world, or describing a situation as bad or good, may be described as true if that conduct is indeed good (even if the hero described as doing the actions never existed), or the situation is typical or bad or good (even if the particular one described never occurred).[3] In these cases the truth-value of the whole does not derive from that of the individual sentences; the whole is not true in virtue of all (or almost all) the individual sentences being true. One very simple example which

---

[3] For similar points, see R. W. Hepburn, *Wonder and Other Essays* (Edinburgh University Press, 1984), ch. 3, 'Poetry and "Concrete Imagination": Problems of Truth and Illusion'.

brings this out is worth quoting in full—Leigh Hunt's poem, 'Abou Ben Adhem':

> Abou Ben Adhem (may his tribe increase!)
> Awoke one night from a deep dream of peace,
> And saw, within the moonlight in his room,
> Making it rich, and like a lily in bloom,
> An angel writing in a book of gold:—
> Exceeding peace had made Ben Adhem bold,
> And to the presence in the room he said,
> 'What writest thou?'—The vision rais'd its head,
> And with a look made of all sweet accord,
> Answer'd, 'The names of those who love the Lord.'
> 'And is mine one?' said Abou. 'Nay, not so,'
> Replied the angel. Abou spoke more low,
> But cheerly still; and said, 'I pray thee, then,
> Write me as one that loves his fellow men'.
> The angel wrote, and vanish'd. The next night
> It came again with a great wakening light,
> And show'd the names whom love of God had blest,
> And lo! Ben Adhem's name led all the rest.

The message is evident: love of one's fellow-men matters greatly, those who love their fellow-men love God. Put like that, of course, the message sounds banal. Hence the need to put it in poetic form to make it come alive. In so far as the poem is true, its truth consists in that message being a true one. Its truth does not have anything to do with whether or not there was really a man called 'Abou Ben Adhem', whether he really awoke one night and saw an angel, and so on.

If works of literature have one clear message in the way that 'Abou Ben Adhem' does, the appellations 'true' or 'false' seem to have application. I have, alas, no general theory as to how to pick out the message of a work of literature in such a way as to assess it for truth,[4] but clearly some works do have such a message. Otherwise parables and plays, dialogues, novels, and poems are more properly assessed as 'illuminating', 'inspiring', 'profound', and so forth, rather than as 'true' or 'false'. Indeed whole works of philosophy or history, while assessable as 'basi-

---

[4] J. R. Searle, 'The Logical Status of Fictional Discourse', repr. in P. A. French *et al.* (eds.), *Contemporary Perspectives in the Philosophy of Language* (University of Minnesota Press, 1979), comments on the lack of a general theory of this matter. See his p. 242. See this article generally on the differences between genres.

cally' 'true' or 'false' ('essentially' 'correct' or 'incorrect') are often more naturally assessed, with respect to their truth-content, by a range of similar adjectives. In the case of such works, the main 'message' is often more obvious than it is for a work of literature; it is often in fact provided in a 'synopsis'. Further, even for individual sentences, assessment by means of such adjectives as 'fair', 'accurate', 'roughly correct', and so on sometimes seems more in place than 'true' or 'false'. This is so even where the sentence is of a type which can have a very precise interpretation. And, as I commented in Chapter 2, only where it is clear what standard of accuracy is required does the true/false dichotomy seem in place—those sentences are true which are accurate to that standard, false which are not. J. L. Austin discusses such sentences, and comments with regard to the sentence 'France is hexagonal', 'it is a rough description; it is not a true or false one'.[5]

We need to know to which genre a literary work belongs in order to be able to assess its truth-value or the truth-value of any sentence within it. And if the genre is unfamiliar, we cannot do this. Just as the context of the sentence is crucial for understanding the sense of a word, so the context of (a speech or) a literary work is crucial for understanding the meaning of a sentence. And conventions of the genre determine how that context affects the meaning of a sentence. Thus if 'Larry is an elephant' occurs in a children's story, it has no truth-value. If it occurs in a guidebook to the London Zoo, it does and is to be taken literally; the genre rules out the possibility of metaphor. But if it occurs in a poem, metaphorical meaning is always a serious possibility, to be adopted if a literal meaning is in any way unlikely. The context of the society in which the work is written determines the available kinds of genre. Familiarity with that context will show us which statements (if any) the sentence of that work express. Genre is not a restriction on an author. Rather it provides him with a set of conventions, all ready to use, to express his message.

Models and Allegories

Two kinds of genre are of especial relevance to my present purposes. The first is the genre of the prose parts of articles or books of physics or chemistry, when the author explains to us by means of models the

[5] J. L. Austin, *How to Do Thing with Words* (Clarendon Press, 1962), 139–48. See 142.

nature of the reality which lies behind our observations—the composition of the atom, the nature of light, the structure of space. Models in the sense which I shall elucidate are systems of literal and metaphorical comparison. I still find the account given in Mary Hesse's *Models and Analogies in Science*[6] by far the most satisfactory account of scientific models, and I shall simply describe this. Some familiar observable system is found to bear certain similarities to a scientific process under investigation. Let us call the former the model, and the latter the process. There are certain properties found to be in common to the two—we call these the 'positive analogy'; some are found not to be common—ones possessed by the model and not by the process—we call these the 'negative analogy'. There are other properties possessed by the model, such that we do not know whether or not the process possesses these; we call these the 'neutral analogy'. If there are a considerable number of 'positive analogies', that gives reason for supposing that the properties of the "neutral analogy" are in fact possessed by the process, and the model proves fruitful to the extent to which we find that they are. Thus water waves exhibit properties of diffraction interference, and reflection. So too do sound and light—'positive analogy'. Also like water waves, sound is produced by motion of a source (stick vibrated in pond, vibration of string or gong). Sound like water is transmitted by a medium—air—whereas light (despite initial hypotheses to the contrary) is not. All this suggests that we shall find analogies for elements in the wave equation $y = a \sin 2\pi (x / \lambda - ft)$, applying to water ($y$ is height or amplitude of the water at a point x measured horizontally; a is the maximum amplitude of waves; λ is the wavelength, the distance between two maximum amplitudes; f is their frequency, the number of waves passing an observer in unit time; and t the time elapsed since an initial instant) in a similar equation for sound and light, and these we find. A similar equation applies if we read the amplitude as loudness for sound and brightness for light (these being the properties of 'more of' the process at a place as it were), frequency as pitch or hue (the varied quality of the process, produced by increasing the speed of its production), and wavelength as the velocity of propagation divided by the frequency.

There are however two different ways of construing what is going on in Hesse's particular example, according to what you think the meaning of the word 'wave' is. What is it to say that something is a wave? Is it

[6] Sheed & Ward, 1963.

just to say that it propagates in accordance with the wave equation—in which case water waves, sound waves, and light waves are all literally waves. Or is it perhaps rather to say that it propagates by the propagation of a vertical disturbance in an observable medium (i.e. as a ripple)? In that case, of the three, only water waves are really waves. Sound waves and light waves are only waves (in my sense) analogically. For sound waves are not observable, and their disturbance is in the direction of propagation, and the disturbance of light rays is in all directions perpendicular to the direction of propagation and not in a medium. But 'analogies' in my sense there are; and these form a system. There are analogies between various features of the process and various features of the model and these suggest further ones. (The analogue term may originally have been introduced as a metaphor, and in that case we have a system of metaphorical comparison.)

Models (in Hesse's sense of 'model$_2$') are systems of detailed comparison, whether systems of objects with many of the same properties or only systems of objects with many similar properties. It may be that sometimes we need more than one model, where each makes a quite different comparison from the other, and they cannot with the normal senses of words be fitted together—in that if you take the words in each in their literal or other established senses, you would contradict yourself by affirming both together. The two models can only be coaffirmed if you take the words in each analogically, and then just what the analogical sense amounts to may be unclear. It is fixed partly by the need for compatibility with the other analogical sense. What the extent of the comparison amounts to is fixed by the other semantic and syntactic rules which govern the use of the words involved.

Thus, according to quantum theory small subatomic entities, such as photons, are said to be both waves and particles. But in literal senses of 'wave' and 'particle', photons cannot be both. A particle is a small chunk of something material or quasi-material which passes through space. A 'wave', as we have seen, is a disturbance in a medium or at any rate something which spreads out over space in accordance with the wave equation—in a way that a particle could not. A wave spreading from a point affects a three-dimensional sphere around the point, whereas a particle could only pass along a narrow path through that space. Physicists have observed phenomena most plausibly explained by supposing that photons are waves, and other phenomena most plausibly explained by supposing that photons are particles. So they must, if they are to say what a photon really is and not merely describe and predict phenomena, say that it is something both wavelike and particle-like; and further meaning is given to the claim by saying which phenomena are caused by photons and explaining what are the consequences of a photon being a wave (e.g. that it spreads in accord with the wave equation) and it being a particle (e.g. that a photon can be found only at one point on a wave front). When such a two-model claim is spelled out, it becomes an issue whether what is being claimed is coherent.[7] My concern now however is simply to explain how models function in conveying meaning, not whether the claim conveyed is coherent.

Somewhat similar to the genre of model is that of allegory. The basic idea of an allegory is of a fictional story in which the persons or things 'correspond' to the real persons or things, and their relations and properties (including actions) 'correspond' to those of the real persons or things. A simple and obvious modern example of an allegory is George Orwell's *Animal Farm*, first published in 1945. This is the story of a farm whose animals, inspired by the socialist teaching of a pig called Major, expel the human farmer Mr Jones. Major dies before the revolution, but it is led by two pigs, Snowball and Napoleon. Napoleon however eventually drives out Snowball and establishes a tyrannical rule. The farm clearly corresponds to Russia, which became the Soviet Union. Major is Marx. Snowball is Trotsky, and Napoleon is Stalin. The correspondences of words and actions of the fictional characters to the real historical figures and groups thereof who dominated the history of the Soviet Union are very detailed and very obvious to many readers of 1945. The correspondences are not total—for example there is no animal corresponding to Lenin—but so many of the details are similar that it remains very obvious what corresponds to what. An older example of an allegory is John Bunyan's *Pilgrim's Progress*. This is the story of a pilgrim named 'Christian' journeying to 'the Heavenly City', and this journey clearly corresponds to the gradual formation of a Christian's character by doing actions so as to make him fitted for Heaven. There are obstacles and diversions making the journey a difficult one, and these (in view of the similarities between physical obstacles on a path and temptations making it difficult for someone to pursue a goal with constancy) correspond to the temptations which beset the Christian in his life. Thus, after beginning his journey,

---

[7] For fuller discussion of the two-model situation of Quantum Theory, see my *The Coherence of Theism* (Clarendon Press, 1977), ch. 4; and for discussion of how coherence or incoherence of claims can be shown, see ibid. chs. 2 and 3.

Christian comes to a mire, 'The Slow of Dispond' through which he must pass. Struggling in the mire at the beginning of his journey corresponds to the situation of the sinner when 'awakened about his lost condition, there ariseth in his soul many fears, and doubts, and discouraging apprehensions'.[8] For the first part of his journey Christian has to bear on his back a heavy burden, of which he cannot rid himself, but which falls from his back when he comes to a cross. The guilt of our sin is thus compared to a burden of which Christ rids us through his Passion, though we cannot rid ourselves. And so on. The comparisons are so well worn as to be obvious.

Some of the parables of Jesus look like allegories, and indeed are interpreted in the New Testament itself as such. The parable of the sower is so interpreted in St Mark's Gospel.[9] The sower 'soweth the word'; he is an evangelist (maybe the Evangelist, Christ) who proclaims the Gospel. Some seed 'falls by the way side'; but this seed is immediately removed by Satan. The ground on which this seed falls is compared to a group of hearers who do not even start to respond to the Gospel. Other seed 'falls upon rocky places'. These rocky places are like a group of hearers who receive the Gospel 'with joy' but abandon it 'when tribulation or persecution ariseth'. It is characteristic of allegory that to many separate items of the real world there correspond separate items of the allegorical story (persons, their actions, etc.). New Testament scholars have disputed whether all or any of the parables were originally intended as allegories, and suggested that instead each parable, as originally told by Jesus, perhaps has only one or two main points in the way that 'Abou Ben Adhem' does.[10]

In a scientific model, the comparison being made (e.g. of light to a water wave) is stated explicitly. That is sometimes also the case with allegories; but here it is more usual for the context to suggest—in

[8] John Bunyan, *The Pilgrim's Progress*, ed. R. Sharrock (2nd edn., Clarendon Press, 1968), 15.

[9] The parable is told in Mark 4: 3–8, and the interpretation provided in Mark 4: 14–20. I have slightly rephrased the 'interpretation' so as to make it consistent with itself and, I suspect, the intentions of its author. St Mark, after providing the interpretation that 'the sower soweth the seed', goes on to compare the seed, instead of the ground on which it falls, to different groups of hearers. I can only read this as a mistake which is so obviously such that readers normally ignore it and unthinkingly read the interpretation in the way in which I have expounded it.

[10] On this contrast J. Jeremias, *The Parables of Jesus*, rev. edn. trans. S. H. Hooke (SCM Press, 1953), with John Drury, *The Parables in the Gospels* (SPCK, 1985), and G. B. Caird, *The Language and Imagery of the Bible* (Duckworth, 1980), ch. 9. See p. 166 of Caird for his comment on the parable of the sower.

accordance with the rules for metaphor elucidated earlier—which comparison is being made. The longer an allegory the easier it is to interpret. Clearly an allegory referring to two individuals and two of their interactions might be similar enough to various goings-on in the real world relevant to the context; but the more individuals referred to and the more details provided of their interactions, the fewer will be the candidates for plausible comparisons. In many prose allegories the system of comparisons is a neat one (e.g. each country in a war is compared to each person or animal in a short story), but in poems any system of metaphors is often less clear-cut, in fact often too vague to deserve the name of 'allegory'.[11] Here the metaphorical sentences on their own might be interpreted in many different ways. But only some of those interpretations, and perhaps only one, will give the sentences senses in which they fit naturally together to form a poem making connected claims, relevant to the context of its production. Fogelin has analysed such a poem as a system of 'interacting metaphors', which 'establishes the level of specificity at which the metaphor is to be read'.[12]

Once the context makes clear, of some of the individuals and their characteristics in the fictional allegory, to which real-life individuals and characteristics they correspond, further correspondences will be more obvious and the comparisons being made then make claims (which can be assessed for truth-value) about the real-life situation. Thus the parable of the sower ends with the claim that some seed 'fell into the good ground, and yielded fruit, growing up and increasing; and brought forth thirtyfold, and sixtyfold, and a hundredfold'. Once we interpret the sower as the evangelist and his seed as the Gospel, the claim being made is that often the Gospel message is heard and taken seriously and makes a great difference to the lives of those who take it seriously.

Biblical commentators have often interpreted biblical passages allegorically, when they were not originally so intended. In doing this, they followed in the steps of the commentators of classical and later Greece who interpreted the narrative poems of Homer allegorically. Thus Metrodorus of Lampsacus 'allegorized away the very existence of Homer's gods and goddesses. He said that Agamemnon was the *aether*, Achilles the Sun, Helen the earth, Paris the air, Demeter the liver, Dionysus the spleen, and Apollo the gall',[13] and so read the *Iliad* as a

---

[11] For a brief history of allegory, see John MacQueen, *Allegory* (Methuen, 1970).
[12] Robert J. Fogelin, *Figuratively Speaking* (Yale University Press, 1986), 106–12.
[13] R. P. C. Hanson, *Allegory and Event* (SCM Press, 1959), 56.

scientific treatise! Biblical commentators, as we shall see in Chapter 10, were not as extreme in their allegorizing as that. Modern writers sometimes distinguish between typology and allegory. Thus R. P. C. Hanson defines typology as 'interpreting an event of the present or recent past as the fulfilment of a similar situation recorded or prophesied in Scripture'; and he distinguishes this from allegory, which he defines as interpreting 'an object or person as in reality an object or person of a later time',[14] no attempt being made to trace any 'similarity of situation' between them. This is not as sharp a distinction as Hanson would like, since there is always going to be some similarity between any two objects—Metrodorus no doubt found similarities, however extravagant, between Demeter and the liver, and so on. A distinction can however be made between past events (believed historical, at any rate in some aspect) interpreted as predictions or prototypes of present events in which people are interpreted as people, what they did being similar in respects which were important for the original story of the past event, as originally recounted (which we may call typological interpretations), and allegorical interpretations, in a narrower sense, where the comparisons are more remote. Thus to interpret Elijah feeding the 100 as a prophecy or prototype of Christ feeding the 4,000 or 5,000 is typological interpretation. Elijah is seen as the type of Christ, who is seen as the new Elijah. In such cases the later person—for instance Christ—may perform the act deliberately in order to fulfil the prophecy, and thus declare himself (by a non-verbal action) to be the new such-and-such.

Double Meaning

There are works which have two distinct meanings—they are histories (or historical works or poems) and purport to tell what happened; but they are also allegories of something else (e.g. the spiritual state of man). It is not easy to find crystal clear cases where the author has both a precise historical message and a definite figurative message, from periods and kinds of literature far from the biblical, but the modern genre which often produces examples not too far away from the clear biblical cases is narrative poetry. Tennyson's *Idylls of the King* tell the story of King Arthur. He derived the framework of his narrative from

---

[14] Ibid. 7. For a similar distinction, see G. W. H. Lampe and K. J. Woolcombe, *Essays in Typology* (SCM Press, 1957), *passim*.

Malory's *Morte d'Arthur*, which was supposed to contain some history. But also, as J. T. Knowles wrote:

King Arthur, as he has always been treated by Mr Tennyson, stands obviously for no mere individual prince or hero, but for the 'King within us'—our highest nature, by whatsoever name it may be called—conscience; spirit; the moral soul; the religious sense; the noble resolve. His story and adventures become the story of the battle and preeminence of the soul and of the perpetual warfare between the spirit and the flesh.[15]

Why should we accept this interpretation? First, it is a general rule that poetry often contains a 'deeper meaning' than the surface one. Secondly, legend pictured Arthur as a perfect man. As Knowles goes on to write: 'For so exalting him there is almost abundant warrant in the language of many old compilers, by whom "all human perfection was collected in Arthur".'

Thirdly, a perfect man is a fairly unlikely occurrence and so are quite a number of other things in the *Idylls*, and so the story suggests looking for another interpretation; though Tennyson's attempt to be faithful to Malory suggests that that is not the only meaning. The forming and the triumph of conscience amid adversity was a very Victorian idea. As Knowles went on to say:

Nothing is more remarkable than the way in which so much symbolic truth is given without the slightest forcing of the narrative itself. Indeed, so subtle are the touches and so consummately refined the art employed, that quite possibly many readers may hold there is no parable at all intended.

And fourthly, this letter of Knowles from which I have been quoting elicited from Tennyson a letter to Knowles praising his interpretation as 'the best, and indeed...the only true critique of the Idylls'.[16] Though he later emphasized that there was no exact 'spiritual equivalent' for each person or place mentioned, he still claimed 'there is an allegorical or perhaps rather a parabolic drift in the poem'. Yet 'I hate to be tied down to say "*this* means *that*", because the thought within the image is much more than any one interpretation'.[17]

So the conventions of the genre, backed up in this case by author's affirmation, indicate a double meaning. (Although, since meaning is a

[15] J. T. Knowles, letter to the *Spectator*, 1 Jan. 1870, reprinted in J. J. Jump (ed.), *Tennyson: The Critical Heritage* (Routledge & Kegan Paul, 1967), 312–17.

[16] Quoted in Jump, *Tennyson*, 11.

[17] Quoted in C. Ricks (ed.), *The Poems of Tennyson*, iii (Longman, 2nd edn., 1987), p. 258.

public matter, an author cannot declare his sentences to have a meaning of which they are not susceptible; his later interpretation can choose among possible interpretations, and that interpretation together with the original can form a message as a whole.) Modern conventions for double meaning are not very clear ones, but when we come to biblical genres, the conventions are often much clearer. The world of the biblical writers from the second century BC onward was full of terms having standard symbolic meanings, which I shall illustrate in Chapter 10; and they often use those terms to describe events which they clearly believe to be historical (e.g. because they report events which others in the community believe to have occurred).

Insertion into a Larger Context

One work may be used to form part of a larger work. The larger context may change the meaning of the shorter work radically. First, of course, speeches and documents may be quoted verbatim. The original production of the speech expressed certain views; its quotation merely claims that those words were uttered.

Secondly a preface or appendix may be added in which explicitly or by implication the author states that he no longer affirms some of the contents, or that he wishes them to be understood in some unusual way. The most usual modern example of this is where one author puts a number of previously published papers together under one cover, and adds a preface explaining that while he republishes the papers in the form in which they were originally published, he now wishes some of them to be understood with certain qualifications; or, more radically, that he does not now agree with the argument of some of the earlier ones but republishes them in order to show what is wrong with them. In such a context the author is not stating the views contained in the papers but rather quoting them; and the meaning of the whole is what the author says it is in the preface, with the qualifications which he makes there—even if that was not the meaning of the papers as originally published. For an example of a preface which changed the whole meaning of a work, albeit covertly, consider Osiander's preface to Copernicus' *De revolutionibus*, saying that this detailed work, which asserted that the Earth went round the sun and thereby enabled detailed calculations of planetary positions to be made, was to be read not as claiming that the Earth did go round the sun but simply as saying that this assumption was useful for making predictions. The meaning of the work with the preface is now very different from its meaning without it.

Thirdly a footnote may correct something in the text, saying that it is to be understood in some unusual way.

Context

One thing which should be very clear, as a result of the discussions of the last four chapters, is the very large role played by the context of utterance or inscription in determining the meaning of an individual sentence. Let us summarize the various ways in which context determines meaning, distinguishing, in the case of a written sentence, between the immediate context of the surrounding sentences (which I shall call the literary context), the authorship and intended audience (which I shall call the social context), and the context of the wider culture within which the sentence appears (which I shall call the cultural context). The literary context determines the language in which the sentence is written—one sentence on its own could be a sentence of more than one language or at any rate dialect. The surrounding sentences will show to which language the sentence belongs, and so the meaning of some of its words. Likewise it will remove ambiguities in the senses of words of a given language. Also, the literary context helps to determine the genre to which the sentence belongs—the context, in showing whether 'Larry is an elephant' comes from a zoo guide or a children's story, helps to show whether it is supposed to have a truth-value on its own. (I write 'helps to show', for the wider cultural context is also necessary; it determines which genres there are and the rules for different genres for how the truth-value of an individual sentence is a function of the truth-value of the whole.) The social context determines the reference of referring expressions. Who wrote the sentence to whom, when, and where determines the reference of 'I', 'you', 'now', 'here', and connected indexical expressions. It also determines the reference of proper names. Which 'John' or 'Aristotle' is being referred to is a function of how speaker and hearer usually use these names (and the literary context may disambiguate if they use them in more than one way.) Social context also helps to determine which sentences are to be understood literally and which metaphorically. Knowledge of the author's beliefs and those of his intended audience will pick out an expression as metaphorical. Finally social context determines the standard of accuracy relevant to determining the truth of a sentence.

As I have already noted, the cultural context of literary practice helps to determine the genre of the work to which a sentence belongs. Genre also helps to distinguish the literal from the metaphorical. Cultural context also crucially determines how the distinction between statement and presupposition is to be made.

I wrote above that 'knowledge of an author's beliefs and those of his intended audience will pick out an expression as metaphorical'. If he says something obviously (to himself and his audience) false or irrelevant if taken literally, we read what he says metaphorically. But of course not all of an audience may have the same beliefs about what is false; in that case I suggest that our conventions are such that if an author says something false, and obviously so both to himself and to many of his intended audience, that suffices to force a metaphorical meaning on the passage; clearly not everyone can understand everything that is said to them. Sometimes the intended audience may fail to understand what is being said because they lack any beliefs about the field which will enable them to recognize the falsity (or irrelevance) of what is being said. The obviousness of the falsity (or irrelevance) must be understood as its obviousness to those who have some familiarity with the field. Poems are not always understood by those who read them, and that is because they lack a certain background of belief which the author has which makes possible the recognition of metaphor. A poet may write a poem about distant islands, which may not be understood except by those who visit the islands and acquire enough true beliefs about them to share with the author a recognition of manifest falsity, which enables them to see which passages are to be taken metaphorically and which literally, and to understand the metaphors involved. Fortunately poets sometimes help us by telling us where to find the background knowledge, or even by providing it for us. T. S. Eliot provided a series of notes on *The Waste Land* which he hoped would provide the knowledge which would enable his readers to understand the poem.

PART II

Evidence of a Revelation

5

The Need for Revelation

Part I was concerned with the means by which a message can be communicated. A whole range of devices from using words in a literal sense, through using words in a metaphorical sense, to using symbolic acts, is available; and how they are to be interpreted depends crucially on the context—by whom the message is announced, to whom, against what background of shared assumptions. We now proceed to the central question of how we could recognize a message from God.

The Kind of Revelation Needed

As I emphasized in the Introduction, with all claims about particular occurrences which are to be expected on one world-view but not on another, it is crucial to take into account the other evidence for that world-view. Reports of observations are rightly viewed very sceptically when the phenomena purportedly observed are ruled out by a well-established scientific theory, but believed when they are to be expected in the light of such a theory. If you have a well-established theory which says that change does not occur in the heavenly regions (regions of the sky more distant from Earth than the moon), you will rightly discount reports of observers on a particular occasion who claim to have observed a new star appear where there was no star before, or to have observed a comet pass through those regions (as opposed to being a mere sublunary phenomenon). When that theory has been shown not to be well established, you require a lot less in the way of detailed observational evidence to show the flare-up of new stars or the routes of comets through the heavens. So if there is other evidence which makes it quite likely that there is a God, all powerful and all good, who made the Earth and its inhabitants, then perhaps it becomes to some extent likely that he would intervene in human history to reveal things to them; and claims that he has done so require a lot less in the way of historical evidence than they would do otherwise. I am assuming here

established that the probability of God exists

as I have argued elsewhere[1] that there is much evidence from other sources that there is an all-powerful and all-good God. If so, does that give us reason to suppose that he would intervene in human history to reveal things to us? I believe that it does.

A God who made human beings with capacities to do actions of supererogatory goodness and to make themselves saints would think it good that they should do so, and might well help them to do so. If they do become saints, he would think that that was such a good thing that it was worth preserving them after this life to pursue the supremely worthwhile life of Heaven, centred on the worship of God.[2] Although God could from the start have made humans fitted for Heaven, it is obviously a good thing that they should have the opportunity to choose for themselves whether or not to make themselves fitted for Heaven; and so that he should make them with a character largely unformed but one which they could choose, by deliberate action (or negligence) over a period of time, to mould for good or ill. And it is good too that we should be able to help each other in forming our characters. A very generous God would allow to men the privilege of sharing in his work of determining how the world is to be; and the most important such privilege which he could give us is to allow us to share in the work of forming for good or ill the characters of others. As a good parent may give to an elder child, as a generous gift to that elder child, a share of the responsibility in bringing up a younger child, so a good God may allow to humans a share in the responsibility of educating other humans. And of course our world is a world which, if God has made it, he has made like this. It is a world where, through our choices, we form our own characters. As Aristotle famously remarked, 'We become just by doing just acts, prudent by doing prudent acts, brave by doing brave acts'[3]. That is, by doing just, prudent, and so on acts, when they do not come naturally, we make ourselves the kind of people who do them naturally. Conversely, by omitting to do such acts again and again, we make ourselves naturally unjust, cowardly, and so on. And it is also a world where we can help others to form their characters; we can tell them, and show them, what is good; and by example influence them to do good and become naturally good. Or we can, through negligence or deliberately, influence others so that they become bad.[4]

---

[1] *The Existence of God* (Clarendon Press, 1979).

[2] For argument that that life would be supremely worthwhile, see my *Faith and Reason* (Clarendon Press, 1981).

[3] *Nicomachean Ethics*, 1103^b.

[4] For more detailed analysis of the process of sanctification and corruption, see my *Responsibility and Atonement* (Clarendon Press, 1989), ch. 11.

But if, in such a world where they can form characters for good or ill, humans are to have the opportunity to make themselves saints, they need to have some information available as to what life is worth living, and how to take steps to live that life. The information which they need is of four kinds. First, they need to know such general moral truths as that benefactors deserve gratitude, wrongdoers need to make atonement (by way of repentance, apology, reparation, and penance) to those whom they have wronged, holy beings deserve worship, and so on. Secondly, they need factual information which will enable them to apply those moral truths, in seeing which particular actions are good or bad, obligatory or wrong. If there is a God, the crucial factual information will be that there is a God, holy and all good, who made us and keeps us in being with the many blessings of life on Earth.

Objections to supposing that there is a God may need to have their force blunted. Thus the revelation may give grounds for supposing that there are reasons why God might allow evil to occur, without telling us in detail what those reasons are—for example any evidence that our omniscient and perfectly free creator allowed himself to suffer some of the evil which we suffer on Earth would be evidence that that evil had a good purpose, even if it did not show us what that purpose is. From the fact that there is a God it will follow that he is to be worshipped, and thanked, and that man must make atonement to him for wrongs against him (that is, sins). But it will also follow, as I have argued elsewhere,[5] that it is very difficult for man to make atonement for his sins and to help his fellows to make their atonement as he should. For in order to have a significant choice between what we believe good and what we believe evil, we must have bad natural inclinations. For to believe something good is already to recognize it as worth doing and so to be inclined to do it, in the absence of contrary inclinations. Those contrary inclinations, of sloth, lust, greed, pride, and such like, with which we are born, give us a significant choice as to whether or not to do the good; but they make it difficult for us to make atonement for our sins, and to help others to whom we have obligations to make atonement for their sins. In that situation, just as a good parent might provide for a child unable to pay his debts the money to do so, so God might provide for men a perfect life which they could offer back to God instead of the life they ought to have lived themselves. God could become man and live on man's behalf a perfect human life culminating in a death arising from its perfection; and, in order to allow the men whom he has created

---

[5] On all this, see *Responsibility and Atonement, passim.*

access to himself, he has reason to do so. If he has done so, it must be among the items of information which men need to have—that and how he has done so. For an atonement which another makes available for us can only be something through which we secure forgiveness and reconciliation if we offer it on our own behalf to him whom we have wronged. Unless I offer to someone whom I have wronged compensation for the wrongdoing (wherever I get the compensation from), I take no part in the process of making atonement for my wrongdoing; and it is good that I should be a voluntary party thereto.

So humans need, thirdly, the information of how, if at all, God became incarnate and provided any atonement for their sins; and the information of how to plead that atonement. God needs to have revealed himself in the primary sense, and to have made available information as to how in detail he has done this. And, finally, men need to know that there is a Heaven to be had after this life for those who have obtained forgiveness for their sins and made themselves fitted for Heaven; and (if that is how it is) that there is a Hell, for those who ignore God, to be avoided. That there is a Heaven will provide encouragement in pursuit of the good. For while it is good that good acts be done for their own sake, it is also good that men should pursue Heaven: it is good that men should make the best of themselves, and to have for eternity the Beatific Vision of God is the best thing that could happen to a human.

If there is a God who wills men's eternal well-being and chooses to allow men the choice of whether to seek it or not, there is reason to expect that he will take steps to ensure that they acquire information as to how to attain that well-being of the kinds which I have set out. Cannot man's natural reason find out some, at least, of these things, without God needing to intervene in history to provide information in propositional form? Certainly natural reason can discover unaided the general moral truths, and there is perhaps enough evidence that there is a God without God needing to tell us so by a verbal communication. But even in these cases revelation helps—if an apparently knowledgeable person tells us basic moral truths, and assures us that he is there, and makes it fairly clear to us that he is telling us these things, our confidence in their truth justifiably increases. I have claimed that we have some a priori reason to suppose that God will become incarnate and provide an atonement for us. But it is by no means certain that, if there is a God, he will do this. (Maybe, despite the difficulty of man making his own atonement, God judges it no better to make atonement for him than to leave him to try to make his own atonement.) And, anyway, mere a priori reasoning cannot tell us how and where the atonement will be made. Only if God provides historical information as to where and when it happened, and a mechanism whereby we are allowed to appropriate that atonement for our use, can we participate in the process of atonement. If we are to pay our debts (albeit with money provided by another) rather than the creditor just forget about them, our benefactor has to provide a formal means whereby we can appropriate recognizable sums of money and transfer them. So too if God makes available an atonement for us to use, instead of merely ignoring our sins, he needs to show us what the atonement is (e.g. how in Christ he lived a perfect life, culminating in allowing himself to be killed unjustly), and how we can use it (e.g. by pleading that sacrifice by participating in the eucharist which regularly re-presents it). So we need historical information about how God provided an atonement, and practical information about how we can plead it. It is hard to see how we could get the historical information without God, either himself or through another, telling us what was happening; or the practical information without further divine instruction—for he who provides something for us has the right to lay down the conditions under which it becomes ours. And, finally, the goal of Heaven and the danger of Hell are things at which we can only guess without God telling us more. To strengthen some of these beliefs needed for our salvation, and to provide others of them, we need propositional revelation.

It is good to have true beliefs on important matters, quite independently of the use to which we can put them. It is very good that we should have true beliefs about the matters which I have listed, quite apart from the fact that we need those beliefs to get to Heaven. And, although our natural reason can make some progress in big matters, if there is a God, the truth about the universe is a very deep one, well removed from ordinary human experience. We need help from above, in order to understand the deepest reality.[6]

So there is some a priori reason to suppose that God will reveal to us

---

[6] 'God destines us for an end beyond the grasp of reason. Now we have to recognize an end before we can stretch out and exert ourselves for it. Hence the necessity for our welfare that divine truths surpassing reason should be signified to us though divine revelation' (St Thomas Aquinas, *Summa theologiae*, 1.1.1, trans. T. Gilby (Blackfriars, 1964), i). It is for this reason, of course, that we cannot predict in advance the content of Revelation. See J. Butler, *The Analogy of Religion*, (George Bell & Sons, 1902), pt. II, ch. 3, part of the heading of which is 'Of our Incapacity of Judging What were to be expected in a Revelation'.

those things needed for our salvation.[7] How will he reveal them? If, as I have urged, a major purpose of such revelation is to enable us, by showing us what it is, to choose whether to pursue the way to Heaven or to neglect to do so, it would be consonant with that purpose that we should also have the opportunity to choose whether to find out by investigation what the way to Heaven is or to neglect to do so—and so that the revelation should not be too open, but something to be looked for and found. Also, since it is good that men should have the opportunity to help each other towards material and spiritual well-being, it is good that the revelation be something which they can help each other to find. In a free society we have recognized great value in people working out for themselves their moral views, not having them forced down their throats from above. That is because our moral beliefs are a crucial part of our character, and in the absence of contrary desires, we will conform to them. To acknowledge the good of men working out their own moral views is not to deny that there are moral truths. These are matters for discovery, not invention; but it is good that each should have the opportunity to discover them for himself; and that men should have the opportunity to help others to discover moral truths for themselves. This procedure involves the inevitable risk that the enquirer may at some stage think that he has found moral truth when he has not—something which may be the enquirer's fault, the result of idleness or self-deception on his part. The risk is inevitable, because if there were not that risk, then there would be no disagreement among those who think that they have discovered moral truth, and in that case everyone else would rightly believe, without seeing any need for painful enquiry, that moral truth was as agreed by those who thought that they had found it.

It might be expected that the availability of revelation in part or more fully only to some should reinforce the opportunity of helping others to discover the revelation: two could co-operate in discovering the revelation, or one could tell another about it. However, while it is good that revelation should be available and discoverable, it is good that it should not be too evident, even to those who have discovered it, that

---

[7] For one writer, among many, who does not expect a God to intervene in history to give us a revelation, and clearly thinks that (at any rate, given many reincarnations) we are well enough equipped to 'respond to the transcendent' given only our natural powers, see John Hick, *An Interpretation of Religion* (Macmillan, 1989), esp. pt. IV. For him the authority of a religion derives only from its moral and spiritual content, which we humans judge on its merits, without needing to consider whether it has any authority deriving from its being given supernaturally by God.

they have discovered the revelation. For in that case they can manifest their commitment to the goals which it offers by pursuing them when it is not certain that those goals are there to be had. If it is on balance probable, but no more than probable, that a human has discovered the way to Heaven, then he will manifest his commitment to the goal of Heaven above all things by pursuing it over a period of time when there is some doubt whether his quest will be successful. Such pursuit will involve a more total commitment to Heaven—indicate more definitely that that is the goal he chooses above all—and so thus also be more worthy of reward; and, since by pursuing some goal steadfastly we often come to desire to pursue it, it will be likely to make the human one who desires Heaven alone above all things. Hence such pursuit will be likely to make the pursuer fitted for Heaven; and since happiness comes from doing and having what you most desire, the more someone desires Heaven, the happier he will be when he gets there.

So there is a priori reason for supposing that the revelation which God provides will be such as requires searching out with the help of others, and such as not to be completely evident even to those who have found it. I am not arguing that it must have such a character; there is a point in not making my salvation too much influenced by what you or I bother to do about it. All I am arguing is that, although it might be good that God reveal himself in other ways, the way which I have described would be good. Butler emphasized the value of investigation in discovering the content of revelation and of uncertainty about it:

If a prince ... desire to exercise or in any sense prove, the understanding or loyalty of a servant, he would not always give his orders in such a plain manner ... Ignorance and doubt afford scope for probation in all senses ... Men's moral probation may also be, whether they will take due care to inform themselves by impartial consideration, and afterwards whether they will act as the case requires upon the evidence which they have, however doubtful.[8]

But he did not bring out the value of mutual help in this respect.[9]

Revelation for Different Cultures

How is the revelation to be made to different centuries and cultures? Of course, God could ensure that, subsequent to his revelation, there

---

[8] J. Butler, *The Analogy of Religion*, pt. II, ch. 6 (pp. 272–3).
[9] For a fuller and more satisfactory development of the point see David Brown, *The Divine Trinity* (Duckworth, 1985), 70–5.

was only one century and culture on Earth. But there would seem to be no reason for him to restrict so narrowly the possibilities for human diversity. Yet, given that he is concerned to reveal himself to different centuries and cultures, he could make a separate revelation to each culture and century. Hinduism and other religions have claimed that he has done just that. However, any division between cultures and centuries is a highly arbitrary one, as any historian will tell us. Humans are too similar to each other, too much in contact with each other, capable of understanding each other's ideas and adopting each other's customs. Men of one culture are capable of transmitting a revelation to men of another culture, and it is good that they should have the opportunity of doing so. Further, if I am right in supposing that man needs not only revelation but atonement and that God might well become incarnate in order to make that atonement, then, if he does so, either there have to be many atonements, or at most one of many revelations can be associated with the one atonement. Atonements are costly, and God would not make many atonements unless one would not suffice for the whole human race. But, if God living on Earth a perfect human life would be an adequate atonement for a few million humans, surely it would avail for the whole human race. It trivializes the notion of a perfect atoning life to suppose otherwise; what atones is the quality of one life, not the number of lives. One perfect atonement must suffice for the whole human race. So any revelation of that atonement must have enough connection with the century and culture in which it took place by being derived from detailed reports of it, made by men of that century and culture, to provide reliable evidence of it. And that means that there cannot be totally separate revelations for different centuries and cultures. Or at least it is an argument for one *final* major revelation, reporting that atonement. Before that atonement and to others who have not heard of it there is perhaps more scope for lesser revelations of the non-historical parts of what subsequently becomes the final revelation, partially inter-communicable between cultures.

But now we come to a serious problem. We need in any one culture a revelation accessible to old and young, male and female, the clever and the stupid, the uneducated and the learned. And this revelation must be transmittable to men of another culture with totally different backgrounds of religion, ethics, theoretical science, philosophy, and technology. What *could* such a revelation be like?

God could provide a revelation of one or other of two simple extreme kinds. The first kind of revelation is a culture-relative revelation, one expressed in terms of the scientific, historical, and even perhaps theological presuppositions (false as well as true) of the culture to which it is addressed, and giving moral instruction applicable to the situation of members of that culture. Thus the doctrine of creation might be expressed on the assumption that the world was as described by the current science, for instance a flat Earth, covered by a dome, above which was Heaven—'God made the Heaven and the Earth.'[10] On the assumption that the world came into existence 4,000 years ago, it would teach that it was then that God caused it to be. It would teach that God had made atonement, using the analogies of sacrifice and law familiar to those in the culture. It would teach the moral truths which those living in that culture needed to know (for example, those concerned with whether men ought to pay taxes to the Roman emperor, or to obey the Jewish food laws); but it would contain no guidance on the morality of artificial insemination by donor, or medical research on embryos. It would offer the hope of Heaven to those who lived the right life; and it would express this hope using such a presupposition of the culture as that Heaven was above the Earth.

Such a revelation would be perfectly adequate for providing its immediate recipients with guidance on how to live their lives on Earth, have the right attitude to God, plead an atonement for the forgiveness of their sins, and aspire to Heaven; it would, that is, provide enough information of the kind earlier described for the people of that culture to live saintly lives. The limitation of its moral instruction to that relevant to that community would hardly matter, and its metaphors and analogies would be comprehensible there. False scientific presuppositions would make no difference to the religious content of the message, that is, to the kind of life and worship which it sought to encourage. A mistaken view of what God had created, or where Heaven was, would not affect the praiseworthiness of God, or the desirability of Heaven. It therefore follows from the argument of Chapter 2 that, so long as context allows a clear distinction between statement and presupposition, false scientific presuppositions would not render the revelation false. That clear distinction could be made if, for example, the revelation was announced as a rival to some other metaphysical message or moral code which nevertheless shared the same scientific world-view. That would show that the world-view was not part of the revelation but rather something taken for granted in the culture with which the revelation was not concerned.

[10] Gen. 1:1.

The problem is however that a revelation of that kind could not be transmitted, as it stood, to those of another culture. Such a revelation would be of little use, as it stood, to the philosophers who met on Mars Hill, Athens, in the first century AD; let alone to literate and numerate Anglo-Americans of today. It would need to be translated into the vocabulary of each new culture. That could only be done by someone who could think away the presuppositions of the two cultures, and make the distinction between the presuppositionless message and presuppositions in terms of which it may be clad. An intellectual can to some extent perform this exercise, but in so far as he can he has a grasp of the message expressible by presuppositionless sentences. Can there be such a person? Yes, but only in so far as there could be a culturally independent revelation. To this issue I now turn.

The second kind of revelation which God could provide would be a culturally independent one. In a way this could be done. God would give us a creed formed of sentences which made no scientific or historical presuppositions. But such a creed would still not necessarily serve the purpose of providing sentences translatable into other languages and usable by other cultures, which provided clear guidance of the kind described above. And this for the reason described in Chapter 2. You can express claims which do not presuppose the scientific and historical presuppositions of the culture; but those presuppositions still function, not as presuppositions, but as boundaries fixing the range within which your sentences make clear claims with clear entailments. The consequences of your sentences become less clear when your scientific and historical world-view changes.

God could give us a statement in human language of the doctrine of creation without using the cultural presupposition of a flat Earth covered by a dome, but any way in which he does this is open to possible misunderstanding, especially when the revelation is translated into other languages and different questions are raised about it by other cultures. We could avoid more and more such misunderstandings by making the statement more and more rigorous, but there is no maximum degree of rigour, and the possibility of misunderstanding will always remain. (By 'misunderstanding' I mean being understood in a way in which God did not intend it to be understood.)

Thus suppose God gives us the doctrine of creation by conveying to us the sentence 'God created everything.' That could be understood as implying that God created God, which is self-contradictory. Perhaps God would do better with the sentence 'God created everything other than God.' But that might seem to have the consequence that God created logical truths, for example God made it the case that 'for all propositions p, not both p and not-p' (the law of non-contradiction). But that apparent consequence does not seem true (surely the law of non-contradiction would hold, even if there was no God); and in any case hardly seems what the doctrine of creation was getting at. Let us try 'God created everything logically contingent other than God.' But since unicorns are things logically contingent other than God, this might seem to have the consequence that God created unicorns. So it had better be phrased, 'God created everything which exists, and whose existence is logically contingent, other than himself.' I could go on improving this sentence for a long time—indeed much of my book *The Coherence of Theism*[11] was an exercise is spelling out coherently and rigorously the claim that there is a God, along the lines which I have begun to pursue in this paragraph for the doctrine that God is creator. I was trying to spell out with considerable philosophical rigour, avoiding the scientific assumptions of my culture, what the claim that there is a God amounted to. But I would have been deluding myself if I had supposed that I had achieved maximum rigour. There is no such thing. At best I have provided a spelling-out which gives a clear answer to the main concerns of our culture about that doctrine. But I did not phrase it and could not have phrased it in such a way that it would be clear what were the consequences of the doctrine with respect to questions which might interest *any* culture.

The reason for this is the philosophical reason set out in Chapter 2. It is the nature of language that we learn and manifest our understanding of the meaning of words and sentence forms by using them in a publicly agreed way in familiar circumstances. We learn and show our understanding of the terms by which 'God' is defined—'person', 'able to do everything', 'knows everything', and so on—and the other terms used in expositions of the doctrine of creation—'create', 'logically contingent'—by seeing them or terms by which they are defined used in mundane situations, and by using them ourselves. That gives us a grasp of their meaning which allows us to use them in many new and different situations, and to use them to discuss many new possibilities; but it does not give us an understanding of their meaning sufficient to guide us as to how to apply them in some utterly different situations, or in discussing hitherto quite unenvisaged possibilities.

[11] Clarendon Press, 1977.

'God created everything' is a satisfactory account of the doctrine of
creation, given that the only possible kinds of 'thing' we envisage are
such things as trees and humans and lakes and plants and angels. The
doctrine has the consequence for each such, that God is its creator. But
once a culture begins to consider other possible cases of 'things', for
example logical truths, it is unclear what 'God created everything' has
to say about these. Is it committed to holding that God created logical
truths? We can improve the formulation to make the answer clear.
Other possible 'things' are then brought to our attention, for example
unicorns; we then legislate that really there are no such 'things'. And so
we go on. New cultures always raise new questions of interpretation,
and the consequences of unreformed old sentences for their concerns
become unclear. The explicit mention of the presuppositions of the
culture may have been eliminated from the sentences of a creed. The
sentences may no longer make explicit reference to 'Heaven and Earth'.
But the presuppositions still operate in a different way: to determine for
which areas of enquiry (i.e. those of which the culture is well aware) the
sentences have clear consequences, and for which areas they do not.
Sentences of a human language only have meaning to the extent to
which its speakers can grasp that meaning, and as (being only human)
they cannot conceive of all the possible concerns of future cultures they
cannot have sentences whose consequences for the concerns of those
cultures are always clear. If God chooses to reveal his message in
human language, he chooses a tool too feeble to convey an unequivocal
message to all nations and generations—unless backed up in some way.

Two further empirical considerations add to this formal logical
difficulty standing in the way of God conveying his revelation by means
of presuppositionless sentences which can be handed on from one
culture to another. The first is that the more presuppositions are removed from revealed sentences, and they are made logically rigorous,
the less accessible they will be to the relatively uneducated majority
of members of that culture, who will then need an élite to translate to
them the message in terms which they can understand. The second
further difficulty is that if the revelation involves a demanding morality,
then those who hear it have all sorts of bad reasons for forcing upon
it an interpretation of their own. If correctly translated, it may demand too much of them in the way of time, energy, and change of
perspective.

So the message of a revelation will inevitably become less clear as it is
passed from one culture to another. There are a number of ways in

which God could make the original such that the process of obscuration was slower. He could provide both a culture-relative and a culturally independent revelation, such that each could provide a check on the interpretations drawn from the other—a New Testament as well as a *Summa*-cum-Denzinger.[12] And he could perhaps even provide simultaneously, together with a revelation in terms of one culture, a translation of it in terms of another culture. If you have, as well as an original literary work, one translation of it into one foreign language, authorized by the author, you will then be able to see far better how to translate it into different foreign languages. For you will be helped to see from the example provided what has to be preserved in translation, and what can be altered. But all of this would still not be enough to counter the processes of obscuration which I have described. The content of the message still would not be guaranteed always to be evident to other cultures with new interests and concerns. Not even God can give unambiguous culturally independent instructions accessible to humans limited not merely by the knowledge, but by the concerns and interests, of their own culture.

An effective revelation cannot consist solely of original documents or other proclamations; *continuing* guidance is required, a mechanism which helps translators of the original revelation to get their translation correct. There need to be documents containing statements of the revelation in one or more cultures. For given that obscurity will infect even a culturally independent revelation, there is everything to be said for an initial revelation which is at any rate accessible to most people in an original culture. Perhaps also there could be a more culture-free statement as to how the revelation is to be translated so as to make it accessible to other cultures. But, as well, there must be such a thing as a Church in which translations have a better chance of success than they would otherwise. There are various ways in which God could effect that result through a Church. There could be an infallible authority in the Church which pronounced from time to time on which interpretations were correct. In his *An Essay on the Development of Christian Doctrine*, Newman argued that:

---

[12] The great medieval philosopher-theologians, such as St Thomas Aquinas, each wrote a *Summa theologiae*, a very lengthy detailed and interconnected exposition and justification of their theological systems. In the nineteenth century H. Denzinger collected together all the proclamations of Councils and popes which he regarded as being authorative expositions of the Christian revelation, in an *Enchiridion symbolorum* (a handbook of definitions); later editions of Denzinger have been produced by others.

In proportion to the probability of true developments of doctrine and practice in the Divine Scheme, so is the probability also of the appointment in that scheme of an external authority to decide upon them, thereby separating them from the mass of mere human speculation, extravagance, corruption and error, in and out of which they grow. This is the doctrine of the infallibility of the Church.[13]

This infallibility could be mediated through an individual or through the majority vote of some Council chosen by a certain procedure. Alternatively, God might ensure that, while no one mechanism guaranteed truth, truth would emerge in the long run by consensus within the Church, distinguished as such by some organizational continuity and continuity of doctrine with the original revelation. The consensus would be obtained by moral, scientific, and philosophical reflection in the light of experience on the original content of revelation, and the way in which it had been developed and expounded in intervening centuries. There would be no one stopping-point to controversy, but a general direction by God of interpretation, compatible with some error by individuals, groups, or even generations. God could have provided either of these methods for guaranteeing the preservation of his revelation for new centuries and cultures. The former method might seem to grant an all-or-nothing status to some written documents—you believe that or nothing; there is little scope for an individual to work out for himself which parts of revelation fit best with other parts and with what his natural reason tells him about God. At least, that is so in so far as it is fairly certain what (if there has been a revelation) is the infallible authority for interpreting it; otherwise, of course, the individual will have plenty of work to do to discover if there is an infallible authority—and part of that work will consist in considering whether the 'interpretations' proclaimed by a given purported authority are plausible interpretations of the original revelation.[14] All the same, it gives much less scope than the consensus method for the individual to sort

---

[13] 1st pub. 1845; 1878 ed., Longmans, Green & Co., 1906: 78. Newman held that the process of doctrinal evolution consisted in developing, by a process more intuitive than deduction, ideas which were implicit in an original formulation. See my fuller discussion in ch. 8.

[14] As Newman urged, asking rhetorically, 'What is inconsistent' in the idea of 'a probable infallibility'? (*Essay*, 81). And he went on to claim: 'We have then, no warrant at all for saying that an accredited revelation will exclude the existence of doubts and difficulties on the part of those whom it addresses, or dispense with anxious diligence on their part.' And after the qualifying clause, 'though it may in its own nature tend to do so', he boldly added, 'Infallibility does not interfere with moral probation; the two notions are absolutely distinct' (ibid. 82–3).

things out for himself, to take individual doctrines seriously and reflect upon them. On the other hand, the consensus method of guaranteeing the preservation of revelation could prove rather weak. A priori considerations do not seem to me to give much greater prior probability to one over the other method of ensuring the preservation of a revelation. But some method there must be if the revelation is not to die out.

So far I have been arguing that if there is a God there is good a priori reason for expecting a propositional revelation, in connection with an atoning incarnation; and for expecting some means to be provided for preserving and rightly interpreting that revelation for new centuries and cultures. I have not yet considered what form the original revelation might take, except to suggest that, at any rate in part, it will be formulated in terms of the presuppositions of the original culture. Again there are various possibilities. At one extreme is a Quran, a book dictated by the original revealer, or prophet, as I shall call him. (Indeed it seems more accurate to say that in Islam the vehicle of the original revelation is a text, the Quran, rather than a prophet or community; the role of Muhammad was simply to receive and transmit the word-by-word inspiration coming from God himself.) Alternatively, the original prophet might talk and various others record some of the things which he said; and the kind of life he led, and the recorders described him as having led, might help us to understand the kind of life which he was commending us to lead. The former method would have the disadvantage that it might encourage excessive literalism of observance, making it difficult for future generations to have the courage to apply an original command, intended only for a particular culture, to a new culture. If the prophet (who was God Incarnate, or at least his very special messenger) wrote that it was wrong to take money on usury, or laid down rules for the right way to treat slaves, and these were his *ipsissima verba*, then future generations would find it difficult to introduce a system of lending money on interest for commercial investment or to abolish slavery—thinking that God himself had forbidden taking interest, and had commended slavery, for all time. A little distancing of the revelation from the prophet, and plenty of versions of it on which new generations can get to work to apply it to new circumstances, has much to be said for it.

So perhaps many books written by many authors, each recording and applying the teaching of the prophet; overlapping, stressing different aspects of revelation, and occasionally contradicting each other. Plenty of scope to ferret out the original teaching, plenty of examples to see how it applies thirty years later. Among the tasks of the later community will be to say which historical documents contain the original revelation; and that too is something on which they might change their view marginally over the years.

The later community will have to make the distinction between the presuppositions of the original documents and their informative content. One help here will be if there are examples in the original revelation of that revelation cast into different philosophical or scientific moulds. Another help is if the intervening centuries have reinterpreted the revelation into the terms of their own culture. Later generations can then look back and, seeing what was taken for granted in one culture, see the revelation as that content which went beyond the presuppositions of the culture, and remained the same when it was put in terms of a new culture. However, to repeat my earlier point, distinguishing the presuppositions of the original revelation from its informative content is not enough. If revelation is to answer questions raised by a new culture, it needs a Church to interpret it, in one of the ways compatible with its original meaning rather than in other ways, so as to give true answers to the questions of the new culture, answers which could not have been provided in sentences available to members of the culture of the original revelation. And it is notable that the need for authorized interpreters was soon recognized even in Islam, the religion *par excellence* of the Book; and who was qualified to interpret became the subject of much continuing dispute.[15]

---

[15] See A. J. Arberry, *Revelation and Reason in Islam* (Allen & Unwin, 1957), 16–17.

6

The Tests of Content and Miracle

So much for the sort of revelation we might expect to find. What will show, among candidate revelations of this or some other kind, that we have got it? A candidate revelation purports to be a message from God, and in order to see whether it is that, we must apply the kind of tests which we apply to a letter to see whether it comes from whom it claims to come. Evidence on such matters is traditionally classified as internal and external. Internal evidence is the evidence of the letter itself, whether it is the kind of thing the purported author is likely to have written at this time and place. External evidence is the evidence of how the letter arrived, others who report it having been sent, and so on. In the case of a purported revelation from God, internal evidence will concern whether it is relevant to our needs, deep, and, as far as we can judge by criteria other than its having been revealed, true (for a good God who knows everything will not lie to us). External evidence will be the circumstance of the revelation's origin. I am concerned, to begin with, with the tests for the genuineness of an original revelation, given by some prophet purporting to come from God. I will come later to the tests of genuine interpretation of such revelation in later tradition.

The Test of Content

The internal evidence concerns the content of the purported revelation—and by the content I mean the message as opposed to the presuppositions in terms of which it is cast. The content must be relevant—it must provide information of a kind necessary for our deepest well-being. In particular, as I argued in the last chapter, it may be expected to provide information by way of general moral truths, by way of the details of what God is like and has done for us needed for applying those moral truths, and by way of details of the afterlife to encourage us in our pursuit of the good, to help us in our process of character formation. I argued in the last chapter for the relevance of information of these kinds. There may be other kinds of information important for our well-being whose relevance is not evident in advance. In that case one would expect the purported revelation to show the relevance, for otherwise its recipients would not know what to do with it, and it would be of no use for the perfecting of character, or achieving any other aspect of well-being.

Secondly the content must, as far as we can judge by independent criteria, be true. The evidence that it is true will be, first, that none of the prophet's teaching is evidently false. His teaching on morality, for example, must not involve his telling men that they ought to do what is evidently morally wrong—the prophet who commends cheating and child torture can be dismissed straight away. Likewise no factual teaching must be provably false. If the prophet teaches that, whatever men do, the world will end in exactly thirty years time, and the world fails to end then, the prophet must be rejected. Note here, however, as again in what I shall write below, that we must keep clear all the time the distinction between the message and its presuppositions. Thus if the prophet were to say, 'Slaves, be obedient to your masters',[1] or 'Soldiers, be content with your wages',[2] and declare that he was transmitting the commands of God, in a society in which slavery and soldiering were parts of normal life, those commands cannot in general be seen as endorsements of slavery and soldiering. The prophet may be presupposing the existence of the institutions and simply telling individuals caught up in them how to behave. What these commands clearly rule out is disobedient slaves and soldiers mutinying for money at the time and in the circumstances of the commandment being issued. Whether they rule out more can only be determined by a more detailed study of the context. This might reveal that the society was debating hotly whether slavery was legitimate, or war was ever justified; in that case these sayings would need to be understood in a wider way. Again, teaching about geography or past or future history needs to be construed carefully, to see whether it is the message of the prophet or whether it is the vehicle, the presupposition, in terms of which the message is cast.

It is important to bear in mind too, when considering the prophet's moral teaching, that he may be announcing either moral truths which

---

[1] Eph. 6: 5; other verses in other of St Paul's and St Peter's Epistles contain similar commands.

[2] Luke 3: 14, a saying attributed to John the Baptist.

hold independently of the will of God or ones which are made such by divine command. If God is our creator, he has the right (within limits) to command us to do things; and doing those things becomes our duty, when it was not a duty (and not wrong) before the command was issued. Such commands might be made known to men through a prophet. Hence it is no objection to the prophet's teaching on morality that he tells us that it is our duty to do some action, when it would not be our duty to do that action but for a divine command—so long as the action is not intrinsically immoral.[3]

Thirdly, positive evidence in favour of the truth of the prophet's teaching will be provided if its claims subsequently prove true. He might make very detailed factual predictions, for example about his own death and resurrection, or about the course of world history in the longer term. Or more vaguely but none the less relevantly, subsequent experience would confirm a prophet's teaching if the sort of teaching about God, his nature, and action in history which the prophet gives makes sense of the investigator's own private and public experience, in the sense of making probable a course of experience which would not otherwise be probable. The course of a person's life, the answering of his prayers, and particular 'religious experiences' within that life might be such as the God proclaimed by the prophet would be expected to bring about. Or again, the prophet's moral teaching might be confirmed if reflection and experience began to show us that a certain life-style, though it seemed initially pointless, was in fact greatly worthwhile.[4] A special case of evidence in favour of the prophet's teaching will be where he tells us that certain very unusual historical events have occurred or will occur, and that they are brought about by divine intervention and have deep moral significance. If it is initially plausible that God might himself intervene to bring about such events, and there is evidence to show that those events occurred and the evidence is

---

[3] On God's right to command, and its limits, see my *The Coherence of Theism* (Clarendon Press, 1977), ch. 11, and *Responsibility and Atonement* (Clarendon Press, 1989), ch. 8.

[4] Although Paley thinks that the conveying of moral instruction was not the main point of Jesus' teaching (which in his view was the affirming of reward in Heaven and punishment in Hell for good and bad conduct respectively), he does make the point that a revelation is confirmed by a prophet's moral teaching being true and deep. See W. Paley, *A View of the Evidences of Christianity* (1st pub. 1794), pt. II, ch. 2, 'Of the Morality of the Gospel'. He argues that the moral teaching of Christianity is 'such as, without allowing some degree of reality to the character and pretension of the religion, it is difficult to account for'. He goes on to argue that Christianity commended virtues ignored by the ancient world and refused to commend ones which appealed to that world.

ambiguous as to whether mere human processes brought the events about; then the occurrence of the events is some evidence that the prophet's teaching about their significance is true.

Generally evidence for and against the truth of the prophet's teaching must be weighed in the same way as evidence for and against the truth of any other body of claims, be it the story told by a witness in a criminal trial, or a scientific or historical theory. But in this case, with the qualifications above, any falsity at all is enough to dismiss the whole: earthly witnesses in a criminal trial can make a few mistakes without their testimony as a whole being regarded as worthless, but a prophet purporting to have a message from God must be assessed by more stringent standards.

What applies to the prophet's own teaching applies also to its elaboration and clarification in a church; although here (if the weaker position of the last chapter is taken) there can be temporary falsity on central matters, and continuing debate on more peripheral matters. Only the general drift and permanent central features of that teaching can be thus assessed. In so far as that can be checked out, it must contain no falsity and much truth; and it will be further evidence in favour of the genuineness of the revelation if some parts of it which do not seem initially true (and especially parts which would not naturally have occurred to humans on their own) turn out to seem true on investigation and reflection. Some version of where the boundaries of the revelation lie may have the consequence that there lies within those boundaries an account of the kind of revelation which has occurred and the test of its genuineness. To be acceptable what the version claims to lie within its boundaries must be self-consistent. For example suppose that the version says 'everything which the Pope proclaims *ex cathedra* about faith and morals is true', and it also lays down an account of which proclamations of the Pope are *ex cathedra* (and what is the test for some individual being Pope), then it cannot have the consequence that two such proclamations are not consistent with each other.

Some, perhaps most, of the content of a purported revelation, although relevant and if true deep, may be expected to be such that we cannot now check it out by experience or reflection. For revelation seeks to tell us deep things that we cannot find out for ourselves—and it would be a fairly thin revelation if its only role was to suggest things that we could immediately check. It would serve no role for us or the rest of the human race, after it had been checked out and found probably true. If our need for revelation is as great as I suggested in Chapter

5, it cannot be so easily dispensed with. It contains predictions of the future (e.g. about the afterlife) which we cannot yet check out, and moral teaching which is puzzling and easy to ignore but for the authority of revelation, and teaching about the detailed nature of God and aspects of what he has done for us and how to worship him in consequence, to which we could have no other access than the word of God himself. Hence we need some evidence that what the prophet says is true when we cannot check independently whether it is or not. The fact that some of what the prophet teaches is seen to be true and deeply relevant is indeed some evidence that the other things which he said are true and deeply relevant. If someone says what is true on one deep matter, that is some evidence for supposing that he is a wise man, and so for supposing that what he says on other deep matters is true. But it is not very strong evidence—many teachers who teach deep truths teach falsities also, and prophets who agree over one range of their teaching disagree over another range.

However, the evidence of content would be substantially very much stronger indeed if the content contained elements which subsequently proved true but which at the time could only have been known to God himself. Deep moral and philosophical truths are eternal and necessary truths, and although humans might not be able enough to find them out, some very wise humans may suddenly glimpse some of them, or some non-human being who was not God might nevertheless see them. There are some very deep such truths perhaps which God alone can see, but in that case they are not ones about which we humans can have independent evidence. There is however one element of purported revelation which God alone can know at the time of the revelation, but which humans can certainly discover afterward. This is statements announcing God's intentions to act in history in ways not predictable from natural laws. God alone can know his intentions before he acts, unless they are intentions of which he has already given some indication (his having kept the laws of nature operative until now is some indication of his intention to continue to do so) or unless he has some moral obligation to fulfil them (e.g. unless he has made a promise to do some act). But that God would perform a miracle, in the sense of violate laws of nature (an expression whose meaning I will clarify further below) in ways which he was in no way obliged to do, is something which God himself alone knows, apart from any to whom he announces that intention. If some prophet predicts such a violation and it occurs, that is substantial evidence that the prophet's message comes from God.

Miracle

So before taking the argument further, I need in this context[5] to spell out this understanding of miracle more fully and to consider what would be evidence for the occurrence of a miracle in this sense. To repeat, I understand by a miracle a violation of the laws of nature, that is, a non-repeatable exception to the operation of these laws, brought about by God. Laws of nature have the form of universal statements 'all *A*s are *B*', and state how bodies behave of physical necessity.[6] Thus Kepler's three laws of planetary motion state how the planets move. The first law states that all planets move in ellipses with the sun at one focus. If this purported law is to be a law of nature, planets must in general move as it states.

What however is to be said about an isolated exception to a purported law of nature? Suppose that one day Mars moves out of its elliptical path for a brief period and then returns to the path. There are two possibilities. This wandering of Mars may occur because of some current condition of the universe (e.g. the proximity of Jupiter drawing Mars out of its elliptical path), such that if the condition were to be repeated the event would happen again. In this case the phenomenon is an entirely regular phenomenon. The trouble is that what might have appeared originally to be a basic law of nature (Kepler's first law) proves now not to be one. It proves to be a consequence of more fundamental laws (namely Newton's laws of motion and gravitational attraction) that the original purported law normally holds, but that under circumstances describable in general terms (e.g. 'when planets are close to each other') there are exceptions to it. Such repeatable exceptions to purported laws merely show that the purported laws are not basic laws of nature. The other possibility is that the exception to the law was not caused by some current condition, in such a way that if the condition were to recur the event would happen again. In this case we have a non-repeatable exception to a law of nature. But how are we to describe

[5] I repeat here what I have written elsewhere on this topic. See my *The Concept of Miracle* (Macmillan, 1970); *The Existence of God* (Clarendon Press, 1979) ch. 12; and R. Swinburne (ed.) *Miracles* (Collier-Macmillan, 1989), introduction and chs. 8 and 13.

[6] This is an over-simplification. Some laws of nature have the form of statements of physical probability. They state that there is such-and-such a probability of an *A* being *B*. A 'violation' of a law of nature will then consist of the occurrence of something vastly improbable given those laws, e.g. something of a kind most unlikely to occur given those laws, in the whole history of the universe. On this see *The Concept of Miracle*, 30–1.

this event further? There are two possible moves. We may say that if there occurs an exception to a purported law of nature, the purported law can be no law. If the purported law says 'all As are B' and there is an A which is not B, then 'all As are B' is no law. The trouble with saying that is that the purported law may be a very good device for giving accurate predictions in our field of study; it may be by far the best general formula for describing what happens in the field which there is. (I understand by a general formula a formula which describes what happens in all circumstances of a certain kind, but does not mention by name particular individuals, times, or places.) To deny that the purported law is a law, when there is no more accurate general formula, just because there is an isolated exception to its operation, is to ignore its enormous ability to predict what happens in the field.

For this reason it seems not unnatural to say that the purported law is no less a law for there being a non-repeatable exception to it; and then to describe the exception as a 'violation' of the law. At any rate this is a coherent way of talking, and I think that it is what those who use such expressions as 'violation' of a law of nature are getting at. In this case we must amend our understanding of what is a law of nature. To say that a generalization 'all As are B' is a universal law of nature is to say that being A physically necessitates being B, and so that any A will be B—apart from violations.

But how do we know that some event such as the wandering of Mars from its elliptical path is a non-repeatable rather than a repeatable exception to a purported law of nature? We have grounds for believing that the exception is non-repeatable in so far as any attempt to amend the purported law of nature, so that it predicted the wandering of Mars as well as all the other observed positions of Mars, would make it so complicated and *ad hoc* that we would have no grounds for trusting its future predictions. It is no good for example amending the law so that it reads: 'all planets move in ellipses with the sun at one focus, except in years when there is a competition for the World Chess Championship between two players both of whose surnames begin with K.' Why not? Because this proposed law mentions properties which have no other place in physics (no other physical law invokes this sort of property) and it mentions them in an *ad hoc* way (that is, the proposed new law has the form 'so-and-so holds except under such-and-such circumstances', when the only reason for adding the exceptive clause is that otherwise the law would be incompatible with observations; the clause does not follow naturally from the theory). What we need if we are to have a more adequate law is a general formula of which it is an entirely natural consequence that the exception to the original law occurs when it does.

In these ways we could have grounds for believing that an exception to a purported law was non-repeatable and so a violation of a natural law. Claims of this sort are of course corrigible—we could be wrong; what seemed inexplicable by natural causes might be explicable after all. But then we could be wrong about most things including claims of the opposite kind. When I drop a piece of chalk and it falls to the ground, every one supposes that here is an event perfectly explicable by natural laws. But we could be wrong. Maybe the laws of nature are much more complicated than we suppose, and Newton's and Einstein's laws are mere approximations to the true laws of mechanics. Maybe the true laws of mechanics predict that almost always, when released from the hand, chalk will fall to the ground, but not today because of a slightly abnormal distribution of distant galaxies. However, although the true laws of nature predict that the chalk will rise, in fact it falls. Here is a stark violation of natural laws, but one which no one detects because of their ignorance of natural laws. 'You could be wrong' is a knife which cuts both ways. What seem to be perfectly explicable events might prove, when we come to know the laws of nature much better, to be violations. But of course this is not very likely. The reasonable man goes by the available evidence here, and also in the converse case. He supposes that what is, on all the evidence, a violation of natural laws really is one. There is good reason to suppose that events such as the following if they occurred would be violations of laws of nature: levitation, that is, a man rising in the air against gravity without the operation of magnetism or any other known physical force; resurrection from the dead of a man whose heart has not been beating for twenty-four hours and who counts as dead by other currently used criteria; water turning into wine without the assistance of chemical apparatus or catalysts; a man growing a new arm from the stump of an old one.

Since the occurrence of a violation of natural laws cannot be explained in the normal way, either it has no explanation or it is to be explained in a different way. The obvious explanation exists if there is a God who is responsible for the whole order of nature, including its conformity to natural laws, and who therefore can on occasion suspend the normal operation of natural laws and bring about or allow someone else to bring about events, not via this normal route. We should suppose that events have explanations if suggested explanations are at all plausible. If there is quite a bit of evidence that there is a God responsible for the natural order[7] then any violations are plausibly attributed to his agency and so plausibly recognized as miracles—at least so long as those violations are not ruled out by such evidence as we may have from other sources about God's character.[8] God's permitting a law of nature to be violated is clearly necessary for this to occur if he is the author of nature; and in the absence of evidence that any other agent had a hand in the miracle, it ought to be attributed to God's sole agency. But if there is evidence, say, that it happens after a command (as opposed to a request to God) for it to happen issued by another agent, then the miracle is to be attributed to a joint agency.

I have not considered here the kind of historical evidence needed to prove the occurrence of an event which if it occurred would be a violation, but clearly it will be of the same kind as the evidence for any other historical event. There is the evidence of one's own senses, the testimony of others (oral and written), and the evidence of traces (effects left by events, such as footprints, fingerprints, cigarette ash, etc.). I see no reason in principle why there should not be evidence of this kind to show the occurrence of a levitation or a resurrection from the dead.[9]

So if the prophet of a purported revelation announces as part of the content of the revelation that such an event will occur in certain circumstances and it does, that is substantial grounds for supposing the revelation to be genuine—given that there is every reason to suppose that the event is a violation of a law of nature, and in so far as there is evidence that there is a God and so that violations can only take place by his agency or consent.

External Evidence

We test the genuineness of a letter, whether its author is the purported author, not only from its content, but from the circumstances of its

---

[7] As I claimed in *The Existence of God*.

[8] I argue in *The Coherence of Theism* that necessarily an omnipotent, omniscient, and perfectly free God must be perfectly good.

[9] Hume however famously thought otherwise. See David Hume, *An Enquiry Concerning Human Understanding*, s. 10. For discussion of his argument and for analysis of these kinds of evidence which we have for the occurrence of historical events and of their force, see my *The Concept of Miracle*, ch. 4, reprinted in *Miracles*, ch. 13.

origin. We look at the messenger who brought the letter to see whether
he is in general trustworthy and whether he brings with him any mark
of authentication in terms of the author's seal or signature.

In the case of a purported revelation, there can be no parallel to
evidence about whether the messenger could have made the journey:
God is everywhere, and can make himself accessible to whomever he
chooses. The character of the messenger is however indeed open to
examination. His general goodness would be evidence that he believed
what he said—that his message came from God. So too would any will-
ingness to be tortured or die rather than deny the divine origin of his
message.

But what mark of authentication of the messenger's belief could there
be? A mark of authentication such as a seal or signature becomes such
in virtue of two considerations. First, no one other than the purported
author could, it is generally believed, have made it. Signatures or seals
are recognized as authenticating, in part because they are things easy
for one individual to produce and almost impossible for any one else to
produce. Secondly, the local conventions are such that a mark of that
kind is generally made only in order to authenticate. Signatures and
seals are recognized by convention as authenticating devices, whereas
fingerprints are not—even though they too are marks very difficult for
others than their author to produce. So what mark of authentication
could God give to a revelation?

A mark would be one which, it would be reasonably believed, God
alone could have made, if it was a clear instance of a miracle. The local
conventions of most cultures would recognize a miracle as designed to
authenticate a revelation, if it occurred in answer to a prayer or prediction that it would serve for that purpose; or if it manifestly forwarded
the promulgation of the revelation, especially if but for the miracle the
revelation could not have been promulgated. Given those conventions,
the miracle would therefore (by the argument of pp. 26–7), if it
occurred, have the meaning of authenticating the revelation.

Such external evidence as I have described for the genuineness of the
original revelation would be reinforced in so far as the subsequent
church which interpreted the original revelation showed similar goodness of character and its promulgation of the message was boosted by
similar miracle. Indeed many such miracles—for example a heavenly
voice daily proclaiming its truth, in ways utterly contrary to physical
laws, loudly in a way audible to all—would give it almost overwhelming
force. Such an authentication of a revelation would however defeat its

purposes, if my account of those purposes in the last chapter is correct. The point of a revelation is to provide humans who search it out diligently with some information, quite likely to be true, about the way to Heaven, on which honest and diligent inquirers who want Heaven above all can rely. Too much evidence of the truth of a revelation would make the attainment of Heaven so easy that it became available to those who had not formed a settled determination to pursue it as their supreme goal. But Heaven is so important a thing that there is reason not to give it to those who do not have a settled will to pursue it above all.[10] And the admission of the latter into the church would dilute its power to sanctify. We should expect some evidence of miracle in favour of a revelation, but not overwhelming evidence of such a kind.

Non-Christian Religions

If the above are the tests for the genuineness of a revelation, I suggest that, before we ever come to look at the details of its message and method of promulgation, there is, among the so-called great religions of the world, only one serious candidate for having a body of doctrine which is to be believed on the grounds that it is revealed, and that is the Christian revelation. I do very much hope that this last sentence will not be misunderstood. I am not saying that there is only one serious candidate for being 'a' true or even 'the' true religion, or even only one serious candidate for having a revelation; only that there is only one serious candidate with a body of doctrine which is to be believed on the grounds that it has been revealed.

Many Eastern religions do not purport to announce a revelation. The grounds for believing Buddhism are not supposed to be that the Buddhist message comes from God; whether or not there is a God is not a central matter for Buddhism, and even if there is, the grounds for believing the Buddhist message (e.g. about the goodness of pursuing the noble eightfold path) are not that it has been revealed by God, but rather its intrinsic plausibility and that it has been found by wise men in some sense to 'work'. The same goes for the messages of Confucianism and Taoism. Certainly Hinduism often claims that God has become incarnate on various occasions, and revealed certain things about the divine nature and the goodness of certain ways of conduct. But

[10] For argument on this, see my *Faith and Reason* (Clarendon Press, 1981), 155–6.

the grounds for believing those things, for instance the message of the *Bhagavad gita*, are not that this is a revelation. Rather the process of inference must go the other way round. The message seems on other grounds to be true, and that is some reason for supposing that it comes from God. My grounds for saying that the process of inference 'must' go the other way round are that Hinduism makes no detailed claim to evidence of revelation other than the content of the message, no appeal to particular historical facts concerning its promulgation which might authenticate the message. And the content of the message concerns not any particular future acts of God but general truths of a kind on which wise human thinkers might stumble.

By contrast, Judaism claims to proclaim a law initially revealed on Mount Sinai to a chosen people. And the survival of that people through more than three millenniums of adverse circumstances is sometimes adduced as support for the revealed nature of that law. But it has seldom made appeal to the details of particular allegedly miraculous events (e.g. the crossing of the Red Sea by the Israelites escaping from Egypt) as the substantiating sign thereof; and if it had done so, I suggest that (whatever the reader's views about the strength of the evidence for the resurrection of Christ) the evidence in favour of the miraculous nature of such events would be significantly less than the evidence in favour of the miraculous resurrection of Christ. Such events as the crossing of the Red Sea happened in times well covered by the mists of history in comparison with the events in first-century AD Palestine; and, even if they happened, are far more readily susceptible of non-miraculous explanation than is Christ's resurrection. And the survival of the Jews, through three millenniums, remarkable though it is, does not seem to violate any obvious statable law of nature. The appeal of Judaism, like the appeal of the other great religions, must turn on the intrinsic plausibility of its doctrine. If that doctrine is in fact revealed, its intrinsic plausibility is the evidence thereof and not vice versa. (Of course, in so far as Christianity incorporates Judaism any miraculous evidence in its favour will count in favour of it with Judaism as a component.)

This point applies even more strongly to Islam. Islam claims very firmly that the Quran is God's revelation to Muhammad and through him to the world. But Muhammad explicitly denied any claim to have wrought a miracle other than the Quran. The Meccans asked, 'if he really was the prophet of God, why did he bring no sign to confirm his statements. Muhammed's answer was that the Quran with its inimitable language was itself the sign he brought.'[11] The claim that the Quran is 'inimitable' has been based on three different grounds: (1) its success, (2) its content, including information which could not by normal processes have become available to Muhammad, an illiterate prophet, (3) its artistic style.[12] The trouble is that we have no plausible cases of natural laws which the success of the Quran, things known to an illiterate, or the production of a new style of writing might seem to violate. We have no reason to suspect that illiterate creative genius cannot guess at truths normally accessible only to the literate, or create a new style or a successful movement. So there is no strong reason to suppose that natural law has been violated. We do not know what are the natural possibilities in this area. With Christ's resurrection it is different; if it happened in anything like the form recorded, it clearly violated natural laws. Islam may well be revealed, but it has slender basis for appealing to us on those grounds; for it the truth and depth of its message are the grounds for believing it to be revealed.

With Christianity it is different. It too appeals to the intrinsic plausibility of its doctrine as evidence that that doctrine is revealed; but it also appeals, significantly and substantially, to authenticating signs that it has a revealed doctrine as evidence of the truth of that doctrine. It has always appealed (except when we come to some very radical forms of Christianity from the eighteenth century onwards, very untypical of mainstream Christianity) to miracles, and above all to the miracle of the Resurrection, as evidence of the revealed truth of its doctrines, as I shall illustrate in due course. It is therefore appropriate to examine in the final part, in more detail, the nature of that claim, and the kind of detailed historical evidence by which it needs to be substantiated.

[11] A. Guillaume, *Islam* (Penguin Books, 2nd ed., 1956), 33.
[12] On these interpretations of the Quran's 'inimitability', see J. Wansbrough, *Quranic Studies: Sources and Methods of Scriptural Interpretation* (Oxford University Press, 1977), 77–8.

PART III

The Christian Revelation

7

The Original Revelation

So I turn to examine the nature of the Christian claim to have a revelation, and the kind of evidence which can be adduced in its favour. I shall not examine that historical evidence in any detail—that is a task for others—but I shall seek to show the relevance of such evidence and the kind of strength it needs to possess in order to be substantial evidence of a revelation. I seek to provide a matrix into which the detailed historical work of the past century, and work yet to be done on the events of the first century in Palestine and the subsequent development of the Christian Church, can be slotted to yield theological conclusions.

The original propositional revelation was the teaching of God to the Israelites of the centuries BC about himself and his dealings with them and other nations, culminating in the teaching of Jesus Christ, including his teaching about the significance of his actions, and the teaching of the first apostles about the significance of those actions. This is the virtually unanimous claim of Christians over two millenniums; and it is that on which the enquirer into Christian claims must pass his judgement. No doubt what Jesus did, such as allowing himself to be crucified, was at least as important as, if not more important than, what he taught. But our concern in this book is only with propositional revelation, and that, according to Christian tradition, includes the teaching of Jesus about the significance of his life and actions, about who he was (e.g. the Christ or Messiah), and that his death was an offering for the sins of the world—if that was what he taught. It also includes certain truths supposedly revealed directly by God, that is, not through the mouth of Jesus, to the first apostles, for instance that the Gospel and the Church were available equally to Gentiles as to Jews.[1] It also includes God's teaching to Israel before Jesus; but Jesus himself taught and the apostles taught that some of that teaching had been misunder-

[1] Acts 10.

stood, and some was of only temporary and limited application[2]—so Christians have always maintained. So the purported revelation on which the enquirer must pass his judgement is to include that part of God's purported teaching to Israel, set down in the Old Testament, which was proclaimed by Christ and his apostles as such. But, the claim is, the core of the Christian revelation was the teaching of Jesus Christ.[3] Protestants and Catholics alike have taught that revelation came to an end with the death of the last apostle.[4]

The Gospels claim (among other things) to contain a record of the teaching of Jesus, and they were given their status as Scripture in the Church on the grounds (whether justified or not) that that record was a true one. St Paul claims in his Epistles for his central message that he received it 'from the Lord', that is, that it was a message handed down to him by those who heard the Lord; and he contrasts what he received 'from the Lord' with other things which he had to say.[5] Christian writers of the next two centuries were concerned to show that the teaching which they had received from the apostles really did come from those who had heard and seen the Lord; and that the teaching of various sects was not so derived. All this, for example, is a constant theme of Irenaeus' *Adversus haereses*.

The reason why I wrote above that the claim of Christians that the original propositional revelation was the teaching of Jesus (as qualified above) was only a 'virtually' unanimous one is that there has been a strain in Protestantism, with its immense reverence for Scripture, to

[2] See Christ's comment on the Mosaic Law on divorce (Matt. 19: 9); and the decision of the apostolic 'Council of Jerusalem' that the requirement of circumcision did not apply to the Gentiles (Acts 15: 1 and 28–9).

[3] The Council of Trent declared that 'our Lord Jesus Christ first promulgated the Gospel with his own mouth, which was promised beforehand through the Prophets in the Holy Scriptures', but it goes on to amplify this by writing that this 'truth and discipline', i.e. theoretical and moral truth, consisted of 'things received from the mouth of Christ himself by the apostles or received from the apostles themselves under the dictation of the Holy Spirit' (Denzinger 1501). In writing that the original revelation was the 'teaching' of Jesus Christ, I mean that it was what he proclaimed as his message, not anything he said, let alone presupposed, about other matters—e.g. history or geography.

[4] For the Catholic tradition, see the listing as a Modernist error, in the 1907 decree of the Holy Office *Lamentabili*, the view that revelation was not brought to completion 'with the apostles' (Denzinger 3421).

[5] Contrast (e.g.) 1 Cor. 7: 10 and 11: 23 with 1 Cor. 7: 25. 1 Cor. 11: 23 in which Paul claims that he received the details of the Last Supper 'from the Lord' shows that this phrase is to be interpreted as referring not to private inspiration, but to public tradition. Paul would hardly be claiming to have learnt by private inspiration historical details which were otherwise publicly accessible, unless he provided a lot more by way of explanation and justification of how that could be provided.

write of Holy Scripture itself as the original revelation; what was given by God was the Bible. But that surely fits very badly with other things that those same Protestants wish to say: for example that there were Christians in the first four centuries AD. For the books of the New Testament were not written down until from twenty to seventy years after Christ taught on Earth, and were only put together and recognized as a New Testament in final form in the fourth century AD. If the books themselves were the revelation, how could there be Christians when there were no books?[6] Holy Scripture must be regarded by Protestants as it is by Catholics, as no more than a true record of a revelation which existed before it.

And how are we to know what Jesus Christ did teach? The primary process for finding that out must be historical investigation of just the same kind as that which would be pursued by historians investigating the teaching of any other teacher. This is the kind of work which New Testament scholars have been doing so very well with rich energy and ingenuity for the past hundred or so years.[7] I do not propose to do more such work here or even to summarize existing work; but for those unfamiliar with this work, it is worthwhile my drawing attention to the sources for that teaching and to the difficulties in interpreting them.

The main sources for that teaching are the four Gospels, other New Testament writings, Christian literature of the second century AD, and a few reports of the teaching in non-Christian literature. Scholars have drawn our attention to three major factors at work which have the consequence that the Gospels cannot be taken without caution as straightforward accounts of the teaching or actions of Jesus. First, the Gospels are composite works and their authors relied on various sources for their information. The approach to Bible criticism known as 'source criticism' drew attention to the diversity of sources whose information transmitted through various channels reached its final form in the four Gospels. The normal historical tests for accidental error and doctrinal

---

[6] 'How should it be if the apostles themselves had not left us writings? Would it not be necessary then, to follow the course of the tradition which they handed down to those to whom they did commit the churches?' (Irenaeus, *Adversus haereses*, 3. 4. 1). And Papias, in the early 2nd century AD, as quoted by Eusebius, records how he was ever enquiring diligently of those who heard the apostles teach exactly what they said, adding, 'for I do not think that I derived so much benefit from books as from the living voice of those that are still surviving' (Eusebius, *Ecclesiastical History*, 3: 39).

[7] For a history of this work and the kind of theories to which it has given rise, see S. Neill and T. Wright, *The Interpretation of the New Testament* (Oxford University Press, 1988).

bias must be applied. Then there is the fact that the various Gospel incidents and stories have often had a use, as part of liturgy or to illustrate a point of teaching relevant to a later decade, and have been put together and tailored for that purpose, before subsequently being used as part of a Gospel. 'Form criticism' drew attention to that source of distortion. But even in so far as this was done (and it was probably not the route of transmission for all Gospel incidents), it worked by knocking previous matter into a shape suitable for theological use or other later Church use; and the critic may be able to discern the original material underlying its transformed version. And finally the Gospel writers themselves were writing 'Gospels', summaries of the Christian good news. They were not 'biographies' of Jesus. The genre of Gospel dictates how the passages within it are to be read—literally or metaphorically. In general it seems plausible to suppose that the Gospel writers were intending to recount a series of historical incidents—things actually done and taught by Jesus—which they believed to have world-shattering significance. But it is by no means always clear when they are telling a simple story, by using words literally; and when they are describing the deep significance of some incident or aspect of Jesus' life, by writing a prose poem about it, using words metaphorically. Our hesitation on this point arises most acutely with respect to St John's Gospel.

Consider for example the story of the healing of the paralytic in the pool of Bethesda (John 5: 2–9). The story assumes that any sick person who gets first into the water of the pool after the water is 'troubled' will be healed. (Verses 3–4, which may be a later insertion into the text, put this assumption into words.) Jesus found there a man who had been paralysed for thirty-eight years, who complained, 'Sir, I have no man when the water is troubled to put me in the pool: but while I am coming, another steppeth down before me.' Whereupon Jesus commanded him, 'Take up thy bed and walk', and so he did. Now this story is open to an obvious allegorical interpretation, suggested by the figure thirty-eight. It was, according to the Book of Deuteronomy,[8] after thirty-eight years of wandering in the wilderness, waiting for God's action, that God commanded his people Israel to go forward to Canaan to claim their promised land. The paralytic represents Israel waiting for God to bring him to the spiritual promised land; the command of Jesus allows Israel to go forward. The five porches of the

---

[8] Deut. 2: 14.

pool (5: 2) perhaps represent the five books of the Law, under whose shadow the paralytic has spent the thirty-eight years. The water is perhaps the water of baptism which is the means of healing. On this interpretation St John is not purporting to tell us a story about a literal healing of paralysis, but telling us in allegorical language what Jesus accomplished for Israel by his intervention in history.

A third possible interpretation beside the literal one that John recorded the exact details of a healing miracle with no symbolic significance, and the allegorical interpretation sketched above, is that John is saying both that the literal story is true and that it symbolized the redemption of Israel, sketched in the allegorical interpretation above. The coincidence of literal story and story rich in symbolic significance came about either because John selected from among the healing miracles of Jesus one with such symbolic significance and thus his narrative had a double meaning, or because Jesus himself performed the act as a symbolic act, intending thereby to convey the claim that he was redeeming Israel.

To see which of these interpretations of what St John is saying is correct is very difficult, but not in principle impossible. For example, we might be able to discover (via other ancient documents) whether such a miracle was generally (either among the Christian community or more widely) believed to have occurred. If it was not, then John was probably making only an allegorical claim. If it was, then probably John was making at least the literal claim and maybe the allegorical claim as well. Such evidence, if it could be had, and much further evidence—for instance about first-century genre conventions—could help to make clear the meaning of the text.

So, as with any historical enterprise, the historian tries to discover 'what really happened' by considering possible sources of distortion underlying the reports of what happened. If the New Testament critic had only one book (e.g. one Gospel) on which to work in order to discover what really happened, his task would indeed be difficult. But he has four Gospels, many letters written by St Paul within twenty to thirty years of the incidents in the life of Christ of which they make mention, and many later documents (within and outside the New Testament) influenced in various ways by incidents in the life of Christ. The task of discovering some vague outlines of what Jesus said and did and what happened to him is not, I suggest, an impossible one. It would be odd if with so many documents contained in the New Testament, as well as extra-Testamental documents, some reasonable, if vague, conclusions about the teaching and actions which gave rise to those documents could not be reached. However it must be acknowledged that such enquiry cannot yield certainty, only a significant balance of probability; and only a somewhat vague conclusion as to the general tenor of Christ's message, not his exact words; and when a miracle is alleged, any background evidence of its intrinsic improbability must be crucially qualified to the extent to which there is evidence that there is a God likely to intervene in history. What happened at the pool of Bethesda, and what St John himself was trying to say in his story about it, are perhaps things ever beyond the ability of human historians to discover. (However, as a later chapter will suggest, to say that is not at all to say that we cannot discover 'the' meaning of the story in St John's Gospel.)

However, there are various crucial qualifications to be put on the general conclusion of the last paragraph. The first is that 'acts speak louder than words'. A single statement uttered by Jesus might well be misreported; even if it was repeated many times and reported by different witnesses, there is still *some* risk of misreporting under the pressure of doctrinal bias. But deeds are better remembered, and even if the historian is biased, his bias is more likely to give rise to a biased commentary on what was done rather than a total misreporting of what the agent did.[9] The Gospel writers all agree that Jesus did a number of significant deeds and that certain significant things happened to him; they report these differently, but by and large they all report them. These acts were done among the Jews whose understanding of their significance was formed by the Old Testament, and especially the 'Law' and the 'Prophets' within it, and by contemporary thought about it, and thus constituted a non-verbal communication of the kind discussed at the end of Chapter 1. Some acts leave long enduring marks, and anyone who wished to leave a permanent message in an age before television and tape recorders were invented would have been well advised to use acts as part of his way of doing so.[10]

[9] This point is well brought out with respect to the Gospels by the fact that the first three Gospel writers feel obliged to record (and John seems to allude to) an incident which they must have found embarrassing: the baptism of Jesus. The incident must have been embarrassing: for if Christ needed baptism, did it not follow that he was corrupted by sin; and if he was baptized by John, did it not follow that he was inferior to John? Hence St Matthew added, in the mouth of Jesus, an explanatory commentary (Matt. 3: 13–15). (To say this is not to deny that Jesus may in fact have said the words there reported.)

[10] The view that the life and message of Jesus can best be reconstructed by starting with the acts rather than the words of Jesus is the view of E. P. Sanders in his balanced

I comment on the significance of three groups of acts of Jesus, as I see them, which seem to me to have enormous importance for the understanding of revelation.[11] The first group of acts are those which constitute the founding of a Church. Jesus appointed twelve apostles; that there were twelve chief followers is known to many New Testament writings, though those which have lists have slightly differing lists of who the twelve were. The old Israel deriving from Abraham had (in the common belief of first-century Jews) twelve tribes deriving from twelve tribe-founding individuals. A Jewish prophet who founded a community based on twelve leaders could only be read as claiming to found a new reformed Israel. Further, the Gospels report or acknowledge[12] the institution by Jesus of a ceremony in which he and the original twelve were the first participants, the eucharist. Early Christian communities were all characterized by the celebration of the eucharist. These two acts[13] constitute performative actions, more evident and enduring than words, of founding a new reformed Israel deriving from the twelve and characterized by a special ceremony.[14] Such a new Israel I shall call a Church; without intending thereby to beg any questions about whether Jesus supposed that it would absorb the old Israel or come to exist separately from it.[15]

and widely influential book *Jesus and Judaism* (SCM Press, 1985) which seeks to do just that. He writes (11–12) that 'There are several facts about Jesus' career and its aftermath which can be known beyond doubt.' By contrast he regards the 'sayings material' as (15–16) 'having been subject to change in ways that cannot be precisely assessed'. Sanders however is concerned only to show what can be established without bringing in the Church's authority; and on that basis his conclusions are understandably fairly sparse. I shall be arguing that his limitation is an unreasonable one, and once we (justifiably) bring in the Church's authority, as well as considerations about whether and how God is likely to give a revelation, we can learn a lot more.

[11] I choose these three groups of acts as crucial for authenticating the Church's subsequent teaching, without wishing to deny the importance of other acts—e.g. Jesus eating with outcasts.

[12] St John's Gospel does not report this institution. But it is implausible to read that Gospel without seeing a vast eucharistic-size gap in John's report of the supper of the day before the crucifixion. Talk of the 'body' or 'flesh' and 'blood' of Jesus which his disciples must consume in order to have eternal life is a prominent theme of the Gospel—see John 6 throughout. St John takes for granted the institution of the eucharist and reports instead an incident of Jesus washing his disciples' feet which must be read as his interpretation of the significance of the eucharist.

[13] Sanders (*Jesus and Judaism*, 11) lists among his 'almost indisputable facts' that 'Jesus called disciples and spoke of there being twelve', and regards (307) the Last Supper as being 'almost equally certain' with one of those facts.

[14] See Additional Note 6.

[15] In making this claim I am of course supposing that adequate arguments can be given against the view deriving from Schweizer that Jesus expected the end of the world

The second group of acts are those centred on the 'Passion', the story of Jesus' betrayal, arrest, trial, and crucifixion which all the Gospels record in considerable and very similar detail. In a way these seem things which happened to Jesus rather than things which he did, but the Gospels are all keen to emphasize that he voluntarily allowed himself to be taken prisoner under circumstances where crucifixion was a likely outcome. Now of course the Gospel writers might have said this in order to magnify the power of Jesus over events. But there are a number of acts (rather than mere words) in his ministry which seem to me to constitute a challenge to the authorities, and especially the act (on the occurrence of which almost all historians agree) of overthrowing the 'tables' in the Temple after riding into Jerusalem surrounded by cheering crowds—a challenge deriving from the interpretation which contemporaries would naturally put on these acts to a claim by Jesus of a very high God-granted status; Jesus must have realized that such a challenge involved a serious risk to his life.[16] And there is another crucial indication in an act (or the words which were inseparably joined to the repeated performance of an act) that foresaw the Passion as the outcome of his ministry. Central to the eucharistic ceremony which Jesus instituted was the interpretation of the bread as his 'body', the wine as his 'blood', implying that the eucharist was constituted to commemorate a sacrificial death, which of course occurred only after that institution whose benefits became available to the members of the new Church.[17]

The Passion then is to be regarded as something which Jesus allowed to happen to him.[18] The Gospel writers record the various incidents of the Passion in great detail, and that can only be because they regard

immediately at or after the time of the Passion. It seems to me that the institution of the eucharist must count decisively against that view. For more detailed exposition of and objections to Schweizer's work see Neill and Wright, *Interpretation*, 205–15.

[16] Sanders interprets the 'overthrowing' of the tables as a prophecy of the destruction of the Temple, and sees its challenging nature as arising from that; rather than it symbolizing the need for cleansing the worship of the Temple from corruption (*Jesus and Judaism*, chs. 1 and 2). Sanders (332) endorses the view of C. F. D. Moule (*The Origin of Christology* (Cambridge University Press, 1977), 109) that Jesus 'did not seek death; he did not go up to Jerusalem in order to die; but he did pursue, with inflexible devotion, a way of truth that inevitably led him to death, and he did not seek to escape'.

[17] See Additional Note 7.

[18] That Jesus allowed himself to be crucified, 'his life and death being openly intended by him as an offering to God to make expiation in some way for the sins of men'—which I now suggest is shown by my second group of acts—was a crucial premiss in the argument of *Responsibility and Atonement* (see p. 122 of that book) for which at that stage I did not outline an argument.

those details as of great significance. The details all echo Old Testament acts (and so plausibly 'fulfil' them in a wide sense to be considered later), and the central such one is the Exodus of the Jews from Egypt, commemorated annually in the Jewish Passover. Jesus died on the Cross either on the day of the Passover, or the day after it, in which latter case it was the eucharist which was instituted on Passover Day. The Exodus involved an escape from slavery to freedom through the shedding of blood; and the Gospel writers are all telling us that the crucifixion involved an escape from slavery (not to a literal foreign power, but to sinfulness, guilt, and death) to a freedom in the service of God here and hereafter, made possible by the shedding of blood, the voluntary giving of a life by Jesus. Every detail has much significance in this regard. My only point here is that if Jesus allowed himself to be crucified at Passover time subsequently to instituting the eucharist, he inevitably proclaimed in the contemporary culture an understanding of it of this kind.

So the spoken teaching of Jesus was, I suggest, clarified and re-inforced by two central groups of acts, proclaiming that in some sense his death was an atonement, and that the teaching would be continued in the Church deriving from his initial group. The broadest outlines of some other of his teaching is also not too difficult to discern from the written records—the importance of forgiving enemies, praying for them, and being generous to them and all human beings, for example—and the occurrence of a life after death, in which the good will be rewarded and the bad punished. But I doubt if normal historical enquiry will allow us to establish much more about the content of Jesus' teaching with any very great degree of confidence. The Gospels (and even the Epistles) are too susceptible of divergent interpretation and open to accusation (however false) of having poor sources or being biased.

Almost anything that anybody writes about the New Testament has been disputed by some scholar, but there would, I suggest, be a considerable consensus about the occurrence and significance of the acts which I have described, and the vague account of Jesus' teaching—very much greater consensus than would be found with respect to the details of Jesus' teaching. I have not argued for my interpretation; that is a matter for historians.

The point to be made here however is that unless there is some sort of evidence of the kind indicated that Christ founded a Church to whom he entrusted the propagation of his message, and unless there is evidence (of a kind to which we will come shortly) that the Church's interpretation of that message is likely to be correct, we would have to rely on the fairly slender amount of evidence for which there is good historical support in the New Testament as to what that message was; and unless Christ made provision for the continued propagation of that message, he cannot reasonably be supposed to have intended it for future generations. Given such evidence of his founding a Church, the plausibility of its interpretation is only open to independent check, if to some extent we have access to the original revelation, as I have suggested that we do. Of course the amount of historical evidence of the two kinds which we need will depend on the amount of background evidence we have that there is a God and that he is likely to have operated in this way. But, although we do have substantial such evidence, it is not overwhelming; and we cannot, I suggest, rely exclusively upon it.

But, given evidence as to what Jesus did and said, we need evidence that, through Jesus, God was speaking. I urged in the last chapter that we need for this kind of claim both some independent evidence that it is true and also historical evidence of a miracle brought about by God to authenticate the message. There is a third group of public events, one of whose roles is to do just that—although their agent is not, according to the New Testament, unequivocally Jesus, but God the Father himself.

The tradition records that Jesus rose bodily from the dead and manifested his risen self to his disciples on several occasions. Despite some New Testament critics claiming that the writers of Gospels and Epistles did not intend that tradition to be taken literally, it seems to me quite clear that they did. They report that such events described in a very down-to-earth way were used by Christians as evidence that he was risen and thus (at least) Messiah.

If the events of the first Easter occurred in anything like the form recorded in the Gospels, there is a clear case of a violation of a natural law. As a violation of natural law, it would (for reasons already stated) be plausibly explained by the action of God intervening in human history. The terminology of 'natural law' and so of a violation thereof belongs, of course, to the last five centuries; but the basic idea was readily available to earlier centuries. The ancients and medievals thought of objects as having powers to bring about effects; and objects of the same kind as having in the natural course of things the same powers. Animate objects could choose whether or not to exercise their powers. Inanimate objects had unavoidable liabilities to exercise their powers under various circumstances. Humans had limited powers to run and climb which they could choose whether or not to exercise. Water had the power to quench thirst or clean skin which when drunk or rubbed on the skin it was liable to exercise—all of course within specifiable limits. What later centuries called laws of nature are simply the regularities of objects of a given kind having certain powers which they are liable or able to exercise under certain circumstances. Hence a violation of a law of nature is, in the ancient terminology, an object exercising powers which did not belong to it as a member of its natural kind—for instance a human walking on water—or an inanimate object exercising a power when it had no natural liability to do so (or not exercising it when it did have such a liability)—for instance wood spontaneously catching fire, without being lit by other fire, heated, or rubbed. A human dead for thirty-six hours rising again was clearly exercising powers beyond the human on a grand scale. Our 'violation' is the ancient's 'object acting supernaturally', and so requires a supernatural explanation. Given a God of the sort that the Jews acknowledged, objects had their powers because he conserved them, and hence if an object acted super naturally, that could only be because God caused it or permitted some lesser agent to cause it to do so.[19]

It follows that, like other theists, the Jews must reasonably construe the events of the first Easter (if they occurred in anything like the stated form) as God intervening in human history. But, given Jewish tradition, the Jews for whom these events were in the first instance performed were in a position to put a more detailed interpretation upon the events. For bringing to life a prophet crucified for saying certain things is *par excellence* vindicating that message, declaring it to be true.[20] For it is God himself declaring that the life had been given so

[19] Jewish recognition of the need for supernatural explanation of the lesser acts of Jesus which went beyond normal human powers is seen by the suggestion (which the Church can hardly have invented) that he did these acts because he was in league with the Devil (Matt. 12: 24). Jesus reasonably urged that that was not a plausible explanation of acts of love, and that he acted by the 'Spirit of God' was a more plausible explanation (Matt. 12: 28). If the Resurrection was due to the act of any lesser agent, it could only be one permitted by God so to act, with the consequence that the community would reasonably construe it in the way stated in the text. The goodness of Jesus manifested in his life and teaching, as well as the implausibility of supposing that God would allow some devil to intervene in history with the typical divine signs described in the text so as to deceive humans on so massive a scale, is further evidence that any lesser agent of the Resurrection is not a devil permitted by God to act contrary to his wishes.

[20] The Resurrection as well as being interpreted as the divine vindication of Christ's teaching must also, I have claimed in *Responsibility and Atonement*, be interpreted as the acceptance of his sacrifice on the Cross.

Revolution in the
original revelation —
the others are illuminations
112   *The Christian Revelation*

generously in such a worthy cause that Jesus was worthy of life in the
Kingdom of God. In the Old Testament stories God took away only
the most worthy of men (Enoch, Elijah), and even so he took them
secretly so as not to be seen. But to take a man in such a way that his
tomb was empty and his living body seen by disciples was a semi-public
taking; and a taking which would inevitably lead to the propagation of
that message. If the Resurrection occurred as reported in these respects,
it was God's own act and must be interpreted by the conventions of
those to whom it was addressed. (Of course the Church has always
regarded the Resurrection as something vastly more mysterious and of
vastly greater significance than 'the resuscitation of a corpse'—to use a
phrase coined by those who reject the normal view of the Resurrection,
to characterize that view—but it has also normally regarded that Resurrection as involving 'resuscitation' as a minimal mundane historical
element. And by speaking of the Resurrection occurring 'as reported'
it is to the mundane elements of the empty tomb and the bodily appearances of the risen Christ that I am referring.)

    The issue then is did the Resurrection happen in roughly the way the
Gospels record? I argued in Chapter 6 that evidence for a miracle will
be of two kinds—background evidence, from the existence of God, as
to how likely it is that God would bring about a miracle of this kind;
and historical evidence from reports of witnesses that it happened. As
regards the background evidence, I argued in Chapter 5 that it might
be expected that God would give a revelation and in Chapter 6 that a
miracle would be needed to authenticate one. If the content of the
Christian revelation has some prior probability, then the background
evidence gives some reasonable support to the view that the Resurrection took place. The historical evidence is the records of the Gospels
and Epistles, with their various different writers, of the death of Jesus,
of the empty tomb, of the appearances of Jesus to the disciples after
that, the evident failure of the Roman or Jewish authorities to produce
the corpse of him whom the disciples claimed to be risen; the conviction of the disciples as to these things and what they signified being
shown by the effect on their lives, their missionary activity, and willing-
ness to die for their faith. Again, I do not propose to assess the historical evidence in detail—that is not my expertise; my point here is that if
the background evidence is fairly strong, as I have suggested that it is,
we do not need too much in the way of historical evidence to make it on
balance probable that the Resurrection took place.

MAIN
POINT   If the Resurrection did take place, then it constitutes God's authenti-

cation of the teaching of Jesus, including his teaching (by deed) that the twelve apostles constituted the foundations of a Church to carry on his work and be the vehicle for the promulgation of his teaching. I noted in the last chapter that if an original revelation was to be of any use to subsequent generations, there must be some reason to believe that the Church's interpretation of it was basically correct. If God authenticated Jesus' teaching that the Church would be the vehicle of that teaching, he thereby guaranteed that its interpretation would be basically correct. It would follow that we know a lot more about what Jesus taught than normal historical enquiry reveals. For it would follow that he taught what the Church said he taught; and since in due course it came to say that the New Testament gave a basically reliable account of this, it would follow that it did (subject to any qualifications which the Church put on how it is to be interpreted—on this, see Chapter 10).

Historical evidence for the Resurrection, although for reasons given above it need not be too strong, must exist and constitute an essential plank of Christian apologetic. It certainly seems to have played that role in the first century AD. The early speeches of the apostles, recorded in the Acts of the Apostles, emphasize that they witnessed this event and that was the central justification of their faith.[21] The rest of the New Testament echoes that,[22] and stresses the observational basis of the evidence for the Resurrection. And the subapostolic age does the same.[23]

There are however two strains of apologetic justification for the truth of the Gospel message which have secured undue influence at later periods. The first is the argument from prophecy, in the narrow sense of a claim that many detailed predictions of the Old Testament about the life of the Messiah proved true of Jesus, and so he was the Messiah and is for that reason to be believed.[24] Now which verses of the Old

---

[21] See Peter's Pentecost speech, esp. Acts 2: 32. Also Acts 3: 15, 4: 33, etc.

[22] e.g. 1 Cor. 15: 1–11; 'A critical sifting of the New Testament materials makes it indubitable that the Resurrection of Jesus held a place of unique importance in the earliest Christian apologetic' (A. Dulles, *A History of Apologetics* (Hutchinson, 1971), 19).

[23] See 1 Clement 42 and Ignatius, *Epistle to the Smyrnaeans*, 3.

[24] Ignatius comments unfavourably on those who rely too much on 'fulfilment of prophecy' for their evidence for the Christian revelation: 'Certain people declared in my hearing, "Unless I can find a thing in our ancient records, I refuse to believe it in the Gospel"; and when I assured them that it is indeed in the ancient scriptures, they retorted, "That has got to be proved." But for my part, my records are Jesus Christ; for me, the sacrosanct records are His cross and death and resurrection, and the faith that comes through Him. And it is by these, and by the help of your prayers, that I am hoping to be justified.' (*Epistle to the Philadelphians*, 8.)

Testament are to be interpreted as prophecies of a Messiah is not a matter of how the original author of the strand of the Old Testament book intended them to be taken. It is a matter of what their meaning is as part of the Scriptures of the old Israel, and that is a matter of how Israel in the centuries immediately before and after Christ understood them. I shall emphasize in Chapter 10, following up the general points made in Chapter 4, how meaning is a function of context. If Christ set out to 'fulfil' Old Testament prophecies, he presumably wished to be understood by his contemporaries as doing so, and so he would have endeavoured to fulfil them in the way in which they understood them (except in so far as he deliberately sought to transform their understanding of them). Hence, if we are to consider whether he did fulfil prophecy or not, it is prophecy so understood which is at stake.

Now no doubt there are some Old Testament verses which are to be understood as prophecies of a Messiah, given the context described above. And in so far as we have enough knowledge of contemporary conventions to read them aright, we can see that some of them are fulfilled in Jesus. One example might be Jesus riding into Jerusalem on the 'first Palm Sunday' with cheering crowds, declaring his lordship over the Temple by overthrowing the tables of the money-changers, but riding not on a war horse but on a colt, in fulfilment of Zechariah's saying: 'Rejoice greatly, O daughter of Zion; shout, O daughter of Jerusalem: behold thy king cometh unto thee: he is just and having salvation; lowly, and riding upon an ass, even upon a colt the foal of an ass.'[25] And in so far as we have ground for supposing the Old Testament itself to record a lesser revelation, then that sort of fulfilment of prophecy can provide some evidence of the truth of the teaching of Jesus. But this route of proof is a long and arduous one, and the total support which it provides for the truth of Christ's revelation—at any rate for us who are fairly ignorant of the conventions of Old Testament interpretation prevalent in the first century AD—is small. The theologians of the first and second centuries were in a better position to assess this evidence.

However our limited knowledge of the contemporary conventions of Old Testament interpretation may well suggest that while some New Testament claims that Jesus fulfilled prophecy are initially plausible, others are not. One well-known example of the latter is St Paul's claim

---

[25] Zech. 9: 9, referred to explicitly by both Matthew and John in their accounts of the entry into Jerusalem (Matt. 21: 5 and John 12: 15).

in his Epistle to the Galatians[26] that the promises recorded in the Book of Genesis as having been made by God to Abraham and his 'seed' were to be construed as having been made to a single individual, and so plausibly to Christ, rather than to many 'seeds'. It is very doubtful whether Genesis was so interpreted in contemporary Judaism. In such a case we cannot have an argument from prophecy, understood as such by independent criteria, to Christ as its fulfilment; and Paul could not either. But in such cases St Paul may not be giving an argument from prophecy whose meaning is given by entirely independent criteria; but rather saying that, given that the Old Testament was addressed by God to Israel of the first century AD as well as Israel of earlier centuries and therefore to be understood in the light of what happened in that century, the heir of the promise to Abraham and his 'seed' is most plausibly seen as one individual, namely Christ, and so the singular 'seed' is of crucial importance for understanding the text—not the text as understood by its human author many centuries BC, but the text as promulgated through him by God for the century who witnessed Christ. That texts change their meaning in crucial ways when their author and audience changes is a point which I made in Chapter 4 and shall hammer home with regard to the way the Bible is to be understood in Chapter 10. My purpose in anticipating that discussion here is to make the point that while Jesus may well be regarded as the fulfilment of Old Testament prophecies in all the detailed ways which the New Testament claims, we cannot have an argument to his Messiahship from all of those prophecies interpreted as such by independent criteria. Often, but not always, the way prophecy is to be read is shown by what happened to Jesus, the Messiah, rather than Jesus being the Messiah being shown by his fulfilment of prophecy. One possible example is the suffering servant passages of Isaiah about one (perhaps one person, perhaps Israel) whose suffering will bring salvation to Israel and the world,[27] but which may not have been understood as Messianic prophecies by contemporary Judaism. What may have happened here is that there is a strand of thought in the Old Testament which is given a concrete and fuller realization by the deliberate acts of Jesus. Even the appeals to Jesus as fulfilment of prophecies, least plausible given an independent understanding of the prophecies, can be so construed—given that the way the 'prophecies' are to be understood is determined by what happens later. I shall give a

---

[26] Gal. 3: 16.   [27] Isa. 42: 1–4; 49: 1–7; 50: 4–11; and 52: 13–53: 12.

pattern of argument in Chapter 10, which has the consequence that
such understanding is often reasonable.

In some of the apologists of the second century AD, unlike in the
New Testament, the appeal to Christ as the fulfilment of prophecy
becomes the dominant argument for the truth of the Christian
revelation—but that argument will not bear the weight put upon it.
The main burden of argument must be the other way round.[28] As the
Clementine Recognitions put it, 'Jesus is not to be believed because the
prophets foretold him, but rather the prophets are to be believed to be
true prophets because Christ bore witness to them.'[29]

However, in a more general sense of 'fulfil' there is plenty of independent reason for saying that Jesus fulfilled the Old Testament—he
provided what so many writers of the Old Testament inchoately longed
for: deep prophecy, true revelation from God, true incarnation of God,
true sacrifice for sin. By some of his actions Jesus showed that he
regarded himself as the 'new' and greater Moses and Elijah;[30] that is, he
played their role in a larger way. Old Testament people and their
actions are historical 'types' of Jesus and his actions; and since it is by
his deliberate action that Jesus makes himself thus, his so doing is
another way in which he conveys meaning by symbolic action, a process
familiar to the contemporary culture, as I noted in Chapter 4. And it is
the major theme of the Epistle to the Hebrews that Jesus made available that expiation from sin which it was the purpose of the sacrifices
laid down in the Old Testament law to provide, but which the Old
Testament prophets emphasized that they were unable to do. The
author draws strikingly to our attention the many similarities between
the details of Christ's Passion and the detailed sacrificial requirements
of the Old Testament. To any who are at all convinced independently
that the deep insights of ancient Israel recorded in parts of the Old

---

[28] In Justin's *Dialogue with Trypho*, the dispute between the Christian apologist and
the Jew turns on which prophecies are Messianic. Justin considered Isaiah 7 to be a
Messianic prophecy, whereas Trypho thought that it was prophesying only the birth of
Hezekiah. For this and other illustrations of the point that Christianity determines in
large part which prophecies and types are to be taken as Messianic, see J. Barton,
'Judaism and Christianity: Prophecy and Fulfilment', *Theology*, 79 (1976), 260–6. For
the method of exegesis of the Old Testament practised by Christians in the early Church
being unique to them, see also J. N. D. Kelly, *Early Christian Doctrines* (5th ed., A. & C.
Black, 1977), 32 and ch. 3.

[29] Clementine Recognitions, 1. 59. Quoted in J. Barton, *People of the Book?* (SCM
Press, 1988), 22.

[30] See the feeding of the 5,000 (e.g. Mark 6: 35–44) as a magnified repetition of
Elijah's feeding of the 100 (2 Kgs. 4: 42–4).

Testament about God and human needs constitute a lesser revelation, the ability of Christ to meet those needs may play a significant role in a cumulative case for the Christian revelation. The deep moral teaching, explicit in the prophets and wisdom literature and implicit in much of the Law, gives us some grounds for that conviction; but, as I commented in the last chapter, the evidence of miracle to authenticate it as especially divine is not strong in comparison with evidence for the Resurrection. And hence for us with respect to this wider kind of fulfilment, as for first-century Jews with respect to the narrower more literal kind of fulfilment, the argument must go the other way round. The insights of the old revelation are indeed a revelation, because they are announced as true insights deepened by the words and acts of Jesus in the Christian revelation.

The other strain of apologetic justification for the Gospel message, if one can call it that, which has secured undue influence at later stages of Christian history is the claim of many Protestants that Scripture wears its truth on its face. Calvin wrote that 'Scripture exhibits fully as clear evidence of its own truth as white and black things do of their colour, or sweet and bitter things do of their taste.'[31] And he would attribute our seeing that evident truth, to the work of God the Holy Spirit—as did the Westminster Confession when it taught that 'our full persuasion and assurance of the infallible truth and divine authority [of Holy Scripture] is from the inward work of the Holy Spirit, bearing witness, by and with the Word, in our hearts.'[32] Now if some one really does see something as overwhelmingly obvious, then indeed he ought to believe and live by what he 'sees'. But, as I shall emphasize in Chapter 10, it is very far from obvious how certain parts of the Bible are to be understood—we need a context to make the meaning of the sentences clear—and different readers to whom the truth of Scripture has seemed evident have understood it to mean very different things. Very few parts of the Bible seem to claim either 'self-evident' authority or indeed even to be the immediate 'word of the Lord';[33] much more do they claim to provide grounds for belief about the acts and words of God, which are the true vehicles of revelation. And thirdly of course much of

---

[31] J. Calvin, *Institutes of the Christian Religion*, (trans. F. L. Battles (Westminster Press, 1960), I. 7. 2.

[32] In H. Bettenson, *Documents of the Christian Church*, (Oxford University Press, 1943), 344.

[33] See Barton, *People of the Book?*, 45 f.

Scripture has not seemed self-evident to so many of its readers; argument is needed to show how it is to be understood, and why it is to be believed. Those to whom Scripture seems 'self-evident' are well advised to reflect on these facts before reaffirming their conviction that its truth needs no argument.

So the original revelation is the words of Jesus, and the acts of Jesus and the teaching of the Old Testament as interpreted by Jesus and his apostles. We can have, at the initial stage of historical enquiry, only the most general idea of what the teaching was, but it included the foundation of a Church to continue that teaching. The Resurrection subsequent to the events of the Passion would provide a guarantee of the truth of the original teaching and so of the basic reliability of the Church's subsequent declaration as to what that teaching was and how it was to be interpreted. In so far as there is historical evidence for the Resurrection of modest strength, there are good grounds for supposing that what it guaranteed is true. And so I turn next to the interpretation of revelation in the Church.

[Handwritten annotations in margins:]

Question
Did Jesus intend to found a Church

+ different audience
* Context changes the meaning
Dynamic view of interpretation

Original revelation – Jesus
Community is responsible
for the
Continuous interpretation

before in Decrees
Loaves of 7 God's Work
Canonical –
divisely

Callous for dynamic view

Catholic – meaning above the original meaning

Can have
Historical criticism

new minds
Must agree that different things mean at canonical

8

Church

Question
Was the original revelation final? Did it close with the death of the apostles?

The Church, traditionally, has many roles—to convert, to baptize the converted and bring them into the scheme of salvation, to comfort and strengthen the faithful in their pursuit of the Christian way, to manifest God's love in charitable action, and above all to worship God especially by celebrating the eucharist and thereby incorporating the faithful regularly into the benefits of Christ's death. But it is to be expected that among its roles, if my argument in Chapter 5 is correct, and necessary for pursuit of some of the other roles, would be to interpret the original revelation to later generations with their presuppositions and their interests. If the argument of Chapter 5 is correct and God gives a revelation for later generations to interpret, he must provide a Church in *allows for tradition* which such interpretations have some chance of being correct. If Jesus Christ did indeed found a Church to carry on his work, as I suggested in Chapter 7, and his work and teaching was given its divine authentication by the Resurrection, then the Church itself received divine authentication as the interpreter of that revelation. *Whole argument*

The word is 'interpreter'. If the Church had become the vehicle of new revelation, then there would no longer be an 'original revelation' whose meaning and consequences Church members could tease out by argument and experience and interpret for the benefit of other cultures, and many of the advantages alleged for a revelation in Chapter 5 would not be available. Catholic, Orthodox, and Protestant alike have always maintained that the most that a Church can do is to interpret the original revelation. *Church interprets*

How is the later Church to be recognized? Over the past two millenniums mainstream Christianity has split like an amoeba so often; and new sects have arisen within it claiming to be the whole or part of the true Church. One test which might be applied for which is the true Church is the test of doctrine, that that Church is the true Church which correctly interprets the original revelation. But if that test were the only test for a true Church, then the need for a Church as an interpreter of doctrine would not have been satisfied. For the whole point of a Church in this connection was to provide some independent test for the correctness of interpretation. The arguments of Chapter 5 suggested that interpretation of an original revelation would be very difficult without a Church in which some chance of success was guaranteed. That would be so even if the original revelation was in the form of a document authenticated by a divine miracle. When we have only the fairly slender and vague picture of it left as a result of historical work on what Jesus Christ said and did, quite obviously enough knowledge of what that revelation was to guide conduct in later centuries would be totally unobtainable without an independent guarantee of the reliability of interpretation. Even if you think that the Bible provides a totally true and perspicuous account of what Christ did and said, you need (as I pointed out in Chapter 7) some grounds for supposing that that is so, and the only remotely plausible such grounds are that it was authenticated by the Church which Christ founded. But for those grounds for operate, there must be a test for which society is the Church other than the fidelity of the teaching of that society to the original revelation—otherwise the argument moves in a vicious circle into which we can never break.

Identity of Societies

For all societies of humans, states or clubs, businesses or sports teams, a later society being the same society as an earlier society is a matter of its continuity with it in two respects: aim and organization. To be the same football team as an 'earlier one, you have to continue to play football; and to be the Oxford college founded in the fourteenth century, you have to do the same job—teaching and research—as it did. And there has to be continuity over the interval in the pursuit of the aim. But continuity of aim is not enough. If the college became bankrupt and sold its buildings to an American university who set up an Oxford campus, the latter would not be the college founded in the fourteenth century—it would simply be a different society doing the same job at the same place. For sameness we need also continuity of organization. What that will amount to will depend on the way the original society was organized. Let us consider a chess club which has a constitution adopted at a general meeting when it was formed. The constitution lays down how the committee and officers are to be elected, new members admitted, and present members excluded; and also makes provision for how the constitution itself can be changed (e.g. how the club can agree to have different officers, elected by different procedures). Then a later club is the same as an earlier club, by this criterion, if its committee and officers are elected by the same procedures as those of the original club, or by new procedures adopted after following duly the procedures for constitutional change laid down in the original constitution; and the club consists of members who fulfil the requirements of the original constitution or a properly amended constitution for being members. Of course not all societies have written constitutions, at any rate to begin with (constitution writing often occurs at a later stage of their history). In that case there may be an 'unwritten constitution' in the sense that those who were evidently much involved in the organization could tell an enquirer what the procedures were. But organizations exist even before that stage is reached. And then one may say that there is continuity of organization if changes in officers, committee, and membership are recognized as such by almost all members (either formally acclaimed or implicitly accepted); all previous members that is, or at any rate all of them who wish to continue to be members. That is a very rough description of what continuity of organization amounts to in the absence of a constitution, but then such continuity will be a rough matter: there will be clear cases of continuity, clear cases of discontinuity, and a wide border area when there will be no true answer as to whether continuity has been preserved.

Even with a written constitution, there can be much unclarity as to whether a later society is the same as an earlier one. There can be unclarity as to whether the aim is the same. If the rules of chess are changed is it still the same club? Yes, if they are changed gradually and the later game is recognizably similar to the earlier game. No, if the members suddenly agree to play a form of 'chess' on a football field which resembles football more than it resembles chess. And as for continuity of organization—no written constitution can foresee every eventuality, and circumstances may arise for which it contains no clear provision. Maybe the constitution says that all elections of the committee must be held at a general meeting convened by a committee member, and then all committee members are killed simultaneously in a road accident. If a non-committee member then convenes the general meeting which elects a new committee, is it the same chess club? Our intuitions are, I think, to say yes, even though constitutional procedures have not been followed. There are ways of continuing contrary to a constitution which nevertheless constitute continuity of organization.

What is however evident is that if there is a clear 'best candidate'[1] for continuity with the original society, then no other society can be the original society. Suppose that a society S_2 exists today with continuity of organization and aim with those of an original society S_1 100 years ago (although with marginally different aims, and a somewhat different constitution, though one reached after due constitutional process). Now a few members of the public greatly admiring the original society form a society S_3 with exactly the same aims and constitution as S_1. Which society—S_2 or S_3—is the same society as S_1? Clearly S_2 is. The most difficult issues as to which subsequent society is the original society arise when the original society splits. If the split results in one society which does and one society which does not preserve the organization and aims of the original, then it is clear what to say: the former *is* the old society, the latter is not. But splits often result from a difference of interpretation of the rules (written or unwritten) and different understanding of the aims. Here there may be a clear answer as to which has preserved continuity which outsiders can detect, but there may not. One resultant society may be following the constitution much more obviously, the other more obviously conforming to the aims. Here the only thing to say is that the original society has split into two societies, neither of which is *the* original society; only together do they constitute that, and they are not functioning properly as that society.

Twin Criteria for the Church

If Christ founded anything like an earthly society, then he must have understood something along these lines as necessary for its sameness over time. The continuity of the old Israel was a matter of continuity of organization, as well as continuity of aim including teaching doctrine (proclaiming the same God); and in founding a society on twelve apostles, Christ was clearly intending to found a society with public continuity. And, I suggest (though here again we pass beyond my limits into the realm of historical enquiry), the New Testament beyond the Gospels clearly thinks of the Church in the same way. St Paul's talk of

---

[1] In Nozick's terminology, such a candidate is the original because it is the 'closest continuer' of the original. Nozick's analysis of identity over time in terms of closest continuers seems to me highly plausible for societies, artefacts, and plants, which he mentions; but not for the case to which he wishes mainly to apply it—persons. See R. Nozick, *Philosophical Explanations* (Clarendon Press, 1981), ch. 1.

the body of Christ of which individual Christians are made members by their baptism,[2] and St John the Divine's talk of the names of the twelve apostles as written on the twelve foundations of the wall of the heavenly Jerusalem, when the names of the twelve tribes of Israel are written on the gates of the city,[3] both thereby emphasize the public organized nature of the Church.

The vast majority of Christian denominations have an ancestry deriving from the Church of the twelve apostles. Relatively seldom have groups of non-church members come together to form a church; all the major Christian denominations have arisen as the result of a split in an existing denomination. Eastern Orthodox and Roman Catholic separated in the tenth century, Catholic and many of the Protestant denominations separated in the sixteenth; and innumerable greater and lesser splits have occurred in Christian history (as have also a few amalgamations). Across the split there has been a continuity of aim, including teaching doctrine, between successor bodies and the original body, a continuity often more evident to independent witnesses of later centuries than to those most immediately involved. The similarities between major Christian denominations must strike an outsider as far more evident than any differences. Also, there has always been *some* continuity of organization across the split: for instance there have been ministers of religion, worship on Sundays, baptisms and eucharists, and the Bible, in both successor communities as in the previous Church, before and after the Catholic/Protestant split; and the same goes for all other major divisions in Christian history.

But, all that said, the teaching of different Christian churches does differ; and how shall an enquirer discover the correct interpretation of the original revelation whose outlines history has blurred, that is, how shall he discover which ecclesiastical body provides the best interpretation of that revelation? If my analogy with earthly societies is justified, it will be that ecclesiastical body which is the same church as the apostolic Church, for it is to that body that God entrusted his revelation and in which he provides some guarantee of its availability. That body will be the one, if there is one, which best satisfies the criteria of continuity of aim and organization with the apostolic Church. Continuity of aim is dictated by continuity of doctrine. For the other aims of the Church are largely controlled by that aim: the Church must convert, but what conversion consists in depends on what Gospel it is

---

[2] e.g. 1 Cor. 12: 12–31.   [3] Rev. 21: 12–14.

teaching, and so on continuity of doctrine. But continuity of aim in the application of teaching to evangelism, worship, and charity is also required. A body which had forgotten to worship, to convert, or to inspire acts of charity for two centuries could hardly claim to be the Church, whatever it 'taught'. However, the differences between denominations turn little on whether doctrine is applied (most have applied central elements of their doctrine, albeit with much half-heartedness); the differences turn rather on the details of what that doctrine is.

So, for a later body to be the Church or part of it, it must be propagating the original revelation, or something not too distant from it, and there must be a continuity in its doing so back to the apostolic Church. However, just as a chess club might still remain a chess club even if temporarily it agreed to play only draughts during the summer, so a body might remain the Church even if it temporarily ceases to teach one or two essential parts of a much richer original revelation, but only temporarily and marginally so. The trouble is that since the original revelation is difficult to discern except in its barest outlines, the test of propagating that revelation is not easy to apply directly. However, continuity over many centuries provides a much stronger test for eliminating possible candidates for being the Church or part of it. The teaching of a body wildly out of line with the teaching of all earlier Christian bodies with which it can claim any continuity of organization cannot be the Church. For if the Church is the vehicle of revelation, it is the vehicle of revelation for the third and fourth and fourteenth centuries as well as the twentieth century. And a twentieth-century 'Gospel' which bore no relation to a fourth- or fourteenth-century Gospel could not claim for it the authority of a first-century revelation mediated through the Church. True, given that part of the purpose of a revelation must be to give believers something to sort out for themselves, the removal of minor inconsistencies within previous doctrine would be compatible with that. But the overthrow of a major part of past doctrine could only be achieved by denying that the fact of its being taught by the Church was substantial evidence of its truth, and to deny that is to deny that we have any more access to the original revelation than historical enquiry can provide.

Continuity of doctrine, as far as can be discovered, back to the apostles, in its central elements, has always been the claim of mainstream Christian denominations until the present century. Origen began *De principiis* with a list of such central doctrines 'which are believed in plain terms through the apostolic teaching'.[4] He acknowledged that 'many of those who profess to believe in Christ hold conflicting opinions not only on small and literal questions but also on some that are great and important'. On some of those which he lists he comments that the true view 'is not *yet* clearly known', but he foresees the true view being worked out within the Church's tradition (i.e. from Holy Scripture, as interpreted within the Church).

After the doctrine test has been applied, the organization test must be applied. Church organization is a matter of admission procedures (e.g. baptism), kinds of worship (e.g. the eucharist), who conducts the worship (e.g. episcopally ordained priests), how officers are appointed (e.g. elected by the congregation, or appointed by the Pope) and how they are installed (e.g. whether bishops are consecrated by bishops, or by congregations), and how interpretations of doctrine are worked out and proclaimed. A setting up of an independent body by unconstitutional procedures, where there is no question of the parent body having changed its aims, must constitute a 'schism', in which the independent body has broken away from the Church. The trouble is that this test, like the doctrine test, is not very easy to apply in practice to the cases which give rise to dispute. Splits often arise because the breakaway body claims that the original body has been changing its teaching gradually from the original teaching, so much that if this process continues, the Church will cease to exist. To save doctrine, unconstitutional procedures must be used. And, as we saw with the chess club, the use of unconstitutional procedures does not necessarily bring about the non-existence of the society. And anyway the Church did not in the beginning have a written constitution, and even when in many ways the machinery of all its successor bodies became subject to very precise written rules (e.g. with respect to the ceremonies of ordination and consecration of bishops), the extent of power which could be exercised by different organs—for instance by the Pope as opposed to a General Council—was subject to acute dispute within as well as between all Christian denominations, for almost all the Christian centuries. There is however no substitute for looking at the record of history to see which of either body produced by a split can reasonably claim to be the one true successor of the previous body; or at least, within the limit of time, energy, and capacity available to the enquirer,

[4] *De principiis*, bk. 1, preface.

to reach a view with respect to those major splits which have left plausible rival candidates for being the true Church, or part of it.

The twin appeal to continuity of doctrine and organization is in fact
common to Roman Catholic, Orthodox, and quite a bit of Anglican[5]
and Protestant teaching. It might be thought that for Roman
Catholicism, the test of organization sufficed; we do not need to check
for continuity of doctrine, since whatever the Pope pronounces *de fide*
or *de moribus ex cathedra* is the Catholic faith: 'such definitions of the
Roman Pontiff by themselves, not as a result of any consent of the
Church, are irreformable', said the First Vatican Council, declaring
papal infallibility.[6] However, there remains the issue of who is the Pope
(and for a hundred years of the Middle Ages there were rival claimants
for this office), and which of his pronouncements are *de fide* or *de
moribus ex cathedra*. In case of doubt, any such pronouncements have to
satisfy a further test. The Second Vatican Council voted against an
amendment which Pope Paul VI wished to add to the Council's decree
Lumen gentium, saying that the Pope owed account to God alone; its
theological commission added a note of explanation of the rejection:
'The Roman Pontiff is bound to abide by Revelation itself, the basic
structure of the church, the sacraments, the definitions of the first
councils etc. It is impossible to list them all.' In effect there are tests *ab
extra* of what constitutes a true papal definition.[7] It must however be
granted that this point is hardly emphasized in Roman Catholic teaching. It has been a little more to the fore in the teaching of the Eastern
Orthodox Church. The Eastern Orthodox Church has had very high
respect for the ecumenical Councils of the Church, as the vehicles for
the interpretation of revelation. Such Councils had to be validly
convoked, but a further test that a Council was an ecumenical Council
was its fidelity to tradition, and especially to the decisions of previous

---

[5] For the 17th-century exponent of Anglicanism Richard Hooker, the Church was 'the
visible Church', i.e. constituted by outward organization as well as conformity to true
doctrine. See his *Laws of Ecclesiastical Polity*, III. i. 14.

[6] Denzinger 3074.

[7] On this, see J. M. R. Tillard, *The Bishop of Rome*, trans. J. De Satge (SPCK, 1983),
41. See too Rahner, that most influential of modern Roman Catholic theologians: 'Any
fresh dogmas which might possibly be conceived of would still in any case continue to
relate to the former ones as remaining in force. A pope who altogether failed to recognise
this fact in his new definition, and ran counter in it to earlier definitions, would show
himself to be a heretic who had lost his doctrinal authority' (K. Rahner, *Theological
Investigations*, xiv, (trans. D. Bourke, (Darton, Longman, & Todd, 1976), 81).

Councils.[8] And of course Anglicanism and Protestantism have insisted that all ecclesiastical pronouncements depend for their authority on their provability from Scripture.[9]

The test of continuity of doctrine has of course been to the fore in Protestantism in the form of this appeal to Scripture. The Church is the Church, on a Protestant view, in virtue of its conformity to Scripture; much else crept into its teaching in the Middle Ages and corrupted it, which led to the need for reformation.[10] But, Protestantism can point out, the Catholic Church has always stressed that the interpretation of revelation was the interpretation of Scripture (as well as sometimes also, what on the Protestant view should not have crept in, unwritten tradition). Yet even supposing that it was clear what can and cannot be proved from Scripture, why is Scripture the fount of authority, why are certain books and not others the touchstone of doctrine? Only in the fourth century AD was the canon (the definite list) of books of the New Testament finally recognized as such.[11] The rabbis came to agree on which books constituted the Old Testament around AD 100, but why should the Church take their list? The Latin Church from the fourth century onward did not.[12] It included as canonical the books of the Old Testament Apocrypha, which the Reformers relegated to a secondary place as suitable for 'example of life and instruction of manners' but not 'to establish any doctrine'.[13] Yet Roman Catholicism makes no difference in canonical status between the Apocrypha and the rest of the Old Testament, and so in this respect it is still a matter of

---

[8] 'Fundamentally, then, a doctrine did not become orthodox because a council said it was, but a council was orthodox—and therefore binding—because the doctrine it confessed was orthodox' (J. Pelikan, *The Christian Tradition*, ii: *The Spirit of Eastern Christendom* (University of Chicago Press, 1974), 24.

[9] See (e.g.) arts. 20 and 21 of the Thirty-Nine Articles of the Church of England.

[10] Thus Luther: 'Where God's word is purely taught, there is the upright and true church; for the true church is supported by the Holy Ghost, not by succession of inheritance' (*Table Talk*, § 370, trans. W. Hazlitt (H. G. Bohn, 1857)). Despite the medieval Church teaching things contrary to Scripture, God had miraculously preserved it in a distorted form, Luther held, through its period of 'Babylonian Captivity' to false doctrine. But he seems to have taught that the Church may teach things beyond what is contained in Scripture, so long as it does not actually contradict Scripture—see P. Althaus, *The Theology of Martin Luther*, trans. R. C. Schultz (Fortress Press, 1966), 335.

[11] For the story of the formation of the canon of the New Testament, see e.g. B. M. Metzger, *The Canon of the New Testament* (Clarendon Press, 1987).

[12] For an account of how the Christian canon of the Old Testament came to include the Apocrypha, see P. R. Ackroyd and C. F. Evans (eds.), *The Cambridge History of the Bible*, i (Cambridge University Press, 1970), 532–5.

[13] Art. 6 of the Thirty-Nine Articles.

dispute what is the canon, that is, which books form the Bible.[14] As for the Church in the East—according to one tabulation, even in the tenth century AD there were no fewer than six different lists of Scriptures of the Old and New Testaments with authority.[15]

There is a Protestant position to which I referred in the last chapter—that the authority of Scripture is its self-evidence. For the reasons given there that is hardly a plausible position. The only plausible Protestant position must be that the Church early recognized the New Testament as expressing the Gospel, and the Old Testament as qualified by the New, and thereafter submitted its doctrinal authority to Scripture. But 'early' can at best be construed as 'by the fourth century'. For in the first four centuries some Christians had very different views as to the limits of Scripture from those which eventually prevailed. For Marcion in the middle of the second century AD, Scripture consisted only of expurgated versions of St Luke's Gospel and ten Pauline Epistles, and no other books of New or Old Testaments.[16] Why one list rather than another? The answer must be because in the second and third centuries less formally and in the fourth century more formally the Church approved one list rather than another.[17] (Of course given a largely agreed corpus one might include one book or set of books—for instance the Apocrypha—rather than another on grounds of consistency with the rest, but that cannot be the solution when very

---

[14] As it is also a matter of dispute whether certain passages of books—e.g. John 7: 53–8: 11 or 2 Esd. 7: 36–105—belong to the Bible. Those who dispute about these matters seem to me not always clear as to what criteria they are using. John 7: 53–8: 11 is omitted from some modern versions of the Bible on the grounds that it is 'not to be found in most ancient manuscripts' of St John's Gospel. Maybe, but many books of the Bible are compilations of passages which previously existed separately. Why omit this passage alone on the grounds of it having a separate origin? It would be more relevant to omit it on the grounds that when St John's Gospel was recognized as canonical by the Church in the 3rd and 4th centuries, it did not include that passage.

[15] B. F. Westcott, *The Bible in the Church* (1st pub. 1864; Eerdmans, 1980), 227. Quoted in Metzger, *Canon of the New Testament*, 217. St John Damascene (*De fide orthodoxa*, 4. 17) does not accept the Old Testament Apocrypha as canonical. He describes Ecclesiasticus and the Wisdom of Solomon as 'virtuous and noble', but states that 'they are not counted nor were they placed in the ark'.

[16] See J. N. D. Kelly, *Early Christian Doctrines* (A. & C. Black, 5th edn., 1977), 57. See Metzger, *Canon of the New Testament*, esp. 251–4 for the three criteria used in the early Church for determining whether a book should be included in the New Testament: its fidelity to basic Christian tradition, its deriving from the teaching of an apostle, and its widespread and continuing acceptance by the Church.

[17] Augustine has something approaching a calculus for computing, in his day before a final list of canonical books had been established, whether a book was sufficiently well recognized in the Church to be deemed canonical. See his *De doctrina Christiana*, 2. 8. 12.

different lists are proposed.) What is to count as the Church for the purpose of authenticating Scripture must be established by other criteria—for example continuity of doctrine in non-scriptural respects, and continuity of organization. If one supposed that normal historical criteria showed, as on the whole many Reformers supposed, that the books of the New Testament were all, every word of them, apart from St Paul's Epistles, written by apostles or other disciples who had listened in detail to Christ or to a major apostle, that all reports of his teaching were committed to memory and written down therefrom more or less verbatim, then much of the New Testament could be used as a very precise test for the nature of the original revelation and the rest would be authenticated by its conformity with that part. But, alas, the application of normal historical criteria since the nineteenth century has shown (what would not have been very surprising to the earlier Fathers who cross-checked what they read in Scripture by any other sources they could get[18]) that all those books reveal is a rather vague picture of that original revelation, certainly not enough to provide a test of doctrine which does not assume already the truth of Scripture. We must therefore bring in the criterion of continuity of organization to show which body could justifiably claim the authority to authenticate Scripture—even if thereafter we see no need for such a criterion.

However, it seems highly implausible to me to confine the role of the Church in the interpretation of revelation to that of validating the canon of Scripture. Anyone knowing nothing about the history of Christianity reading the Bible could hardly get anywhere constructing anything like the creeds of the Church, which Christians have regarded for most of the Church's history as summaries of their faith. It labours the obvious to point out how many and diverse have been the interpretations of Scripture since the Reformation on central matters of faith, even by those aware of the history of the Church. The diversity of interpretations which would be produced by those unaware of that history defies imagination. Suppose that Christianity had been eliminated in the persecutions of the early centuries AD, and that the last Christian martyr had buried the last copy of the Bible in the sands of Egypt; but that copy had been found again in the twentieth century, and various persons impressed by its teaching had tried to construct Christian doctrine therefrom, how could they even have begun? If the arguments of Chapter 5 for the need of an interpreting Church have

---

[18] See the saying of Papias quoted in ch. 7 n. 6.

any worth, that need could hardly have been superseded by the promulgation of the canon of Scripture.

The Nature of Interpretation

Continuity of doctrine must involve in large part continuity with
respect to the content of doctrine; but since it has been a normal part of
that content that the promulgation of doctrine involves 'interpretation'
of an original revelation, continuity will also involve continuity with
respect to the method of that interpretation.

Eastern Orthodoxy and Roman Catholicism, indeed the vast majority
of those who called themselves Christians until the Reformation and the
majority of such thereafter,[19] always recognized the need for continuing
interpretation. There are differences however in respect of what the
interpretation was of, what were the rules for interpreting, and in what
form with what status the interpretation was promulgated. The
interpretation was, all would agree, of the original revelation, but they
disagreed as to what more immediate documents or traditions
describing the original revelation, often called 'the deposit of faith', the
interpreting Church went to work on. Holy Scripture was certainly the
core such datum, once it had been set down and canonized, but before
then traditions were unwritten or at any rate uncanonized (i.e. not
immediately recognized as Scripture). Protestants have always insisted
that once there was a canon of Scripture, that was the only datum; and
I believe that most Orthodox theologians would also hold that view.[20]
Roman Catholicism of the last five centuries has insisted that the
Church possessed 'unwritten traditions' as well which were equally data
for interpretation.[21] Some of the early Fathers said the same.[22] But the
medieval Catholic Church held that Scripture was the only datum for

---

[19] See Additional Note 8.

[20] See A. Nichols, *From Newman to Congar* (T. & T. Clark, 1990), appendix, 'The
Idea of Doctrinal Development in Eastern Orthodox Theology'.

[21] The Council of Trent stated that the revelation was contained both 'in written
books and in traditions unwritten'. (Denzinger 1501). The Second Vatican Council
reaffirmed the double source of revelation: 'it is not from Sacred Scripture alone that the
Church draws certainty about everything which has been revealed. Therefore both sacred
tradition and sacred Scripture are to be accepted and venerated with the same sense of
devotion and reverence' (*Dei Verbum*, 9).

[22] St Basil of Caesarea writes that 'a whole day would be needed for me to discuss the
mysteries of the Church which are not written down' in Scripture (*On the Holy Spirit*, 27.
67). He makes this assertion in the course of arguing that if the divinity of the Holy Spirit
were not explicitly stated in Scripture, that would not suffice to dismiss it as an essential

the derivation of doctrine.[23] The Church of pre-Reformation centuries interestingly gave a particular primacy of interpretation to the Fathers, that is Christian theologians of the first five centuries AD. In any theological argument, wrote the seventh-century Byzantine theologian Maximus the Confessor, it was necessary to produce 'the voices of the fathers as evidence for the faith of the Church'; the faith is 'what the fathers have taught us'.[24] The Council of Trent also declared that no one should interpret Scripture 'contrary to the unanimous consensus of the Fathers'.[25] Their primacy presumably arose from their having written down the 'unwritten' (i.e. unwritten in Scripture) traditions, and having shown how to interpret Scripture.

Once an interpretation was promulgated, it then—on Roman Catholic and Orthodox views—passed into the category of a datum, describing the original revelation, with whatever status (e.g. infallible, or somewhat less) that interpretation had, for yet subsequent interpretation to get to work on. And even on the view of the classical Reformers, the way in which Scripture has been interpreted in the past has some degree of authority for how it should be interpreted in future.[26]

There are also differences among those who believe that doctrine should be 'derived' from the original datum, about what derivability involved. Aquinas held that the content of later doctrinal statements is contained 'implicitly' in what has gone before,[27] but the issue is just what 'implicitly' involves. At one extreme is the view of Bossuet and other French Roman Catholics of the seventeenth century that new statements of doctrine could only be restatements of the datum—in their case Scripture and the Fathers, perhaps in different words but with the same meaning. 'The Christian religion came from its Lord complete and perfect',[28] in the form of unwritten traditions which the

part of the Catholic faith. The divinity of the Spirit, he argues, is clearly implicit in the Church's liturgical tradition.

[23] See A. E. McGrath, *Intellectual Origins of the European Reformation* (Basil Blackwell, 1987), ch. 5. Duns Scotus, among others, taught the sufficiency of Holy Scripture for the genesis of Christian doctrine—see *Ordinatio*, Prologus, pt. 2, q. 1.

[24] PG 91: 465.

[25] Denzinger 1507.

[26] See McGrath, *Intellectual Origins*, 149. Luther seems to have taught that the Church set the limits to possible interpretations of Scripture. Scripture could not be interpreted out of line with a unanimous past tradition of interpretation. See also my n. 10 above.

[27] St Thomas Aquinas, *Summa theologiae*, 2a. 2ae. 1. 7.

[28] Owen Chadwick, *From Bossuet to Newman* (Cambridge University Press, 2nd edn., 1987), 5.

biblical authors and Fathers gradually committed to writing. The
Church never made up her mind, never discovered anything, merely
put it in new and clear words. Jansen apparently remarked that
'theology was an affair of the memory, not of the reasoning faculty'.[29]
This view does seem very implausible as an account of what has
happened to Christian doctrine over two millenniums. It does look as if
Christian bodies in the sixteenth century were doing rather more than
rephrase the teachings of the Bible, or even of the Bible and the
Fathers.

A more common view is the view that deriving is deducing. (An
inference from premises to conclusion is a valid deductive inference,
i.e. follows a logical entailment, if someone asserting the premises but
denying the conclusion would be contradicting himself. It just draws
out the consequences of what is already there. Much inference in
science, history, and ordinary life is not deductive, but ampliative—in
going beyond the premises—to a merely probable conclusion or at any
rate one whose probability is increased by the premises. The latter
type of inference is inductive inference.) Duns Scotus seems to have
advocated that deriving is deducing, when he wrote that 'Many essential truths are not expounded in sacred Scripture, although they are
contained there implicitly (*virtualiter*), just as conclusions are contained
in premises (*principia*).'[30] This is a more plausible view than that of
Bossuet, for, as all philosophers know well, deductions of any length
and complexity can often yield new and surprising conclusions—as
when a surprising mathematical theorem is deduced from familiar
premises—and thus it is better able to account for the apparent development of Christian doctrine over two millenniums.

The Jesuits of the Spanish Counter-Reformation tried to spell out in
detail what the 'deduction' view amounted to and different of them
gave different accounts of the matter.[31] Their accounts all assume that
deductive reasoning is always syllogistic reasoning, that is, that
premises and conclusion are in the form of universal ('all *A*s are *B*') or
particular ('some *A*s are *B*' or 'a [name] is *B*') statements; and that all
reasoning can be analysed as reasoning from two premises to a
conclusion. Suarez's account is as follows. There is revelation of two

---

[29] Ibid. 7.   [30] *Ordinatio*, Prologus 123.
[31] For a general account of their controversies, see Chadwick, *From Bossuet to
Newman*, ch. 2.

kinds: formal and virtual. A statement is formally revealed if (1) it is contained in Scripture, or (2) it is officially promulgated by the Church, or (3) it can be deduced from such statements alone, or (4) it can be deduced from a universal revealed statement (of one of the former kinds) and a particular statement known by 'natural reason'. Under (1) it is allowable that the statement be expressed in words other than those found in Scripture. Thus, Suarez writes that 'God being infinite or incorporeal are sufficiently [*satis*] immediately revealed in Scripture, if not in the same words, at any rate in equivalent ones.'[32] Under (3) it could be deduced from two revealed premisses, (*a*) 'God was in Christ', (*b*) 'Christ was human', as the Council of Chalcedon affirmed, that 'in Christ were two natures, human and divine'.[33] 'Known by natural reason' was so understood as to include everything known without recourse to revelation. Thus from the revealed universal premiss 'every human correctly baptized when there is no impediment is justified' (i.e. is regarded by God as guiltless) and the particular premiss given by 'natural reason' 'This infant has been correctly baptized' we can derive (since the only possible impediment of disbelief would not arise for an infant) 'this infant is justified'.[34] However, if the premiss of natural reason is a universal one, for instance 'every human can smile' when conjoined to the particular revealed premiss 'Christ is human' to yield 'Christ can smile', the conclusion is not formally revealed; the revelation is merely virtual.[35] Why this difference arising from whether the premiss of natural reason is universal or particular? Suarez's answer is that in a universal statement 'all its particular consequences are contained in a formal way, although confusedly';[36] for example, 'every human correctly baptized without impediment is justified' is really about every human, such as this infant, correctly baptized without impediment, saying that every such is justified. All the same, it only follows given a premiss of natural reason that it is about this infant. Suarez goes on from here to claim that what is formally revealed is *de fide*, whether or not the Church has yet declared it to be so; whereas what is virtually revealed is not *de fide*, until the Church declares it to be so.[37] So the only way in which the Church's derivation added to the

---

[32] F. Suarez, *De fide*, disp. 3. 11. 12.

[33] The example is taken from Chadwick, *From Bossuet to Newman*, 26–7. The revealed premisses were themselves, the claim would be, rephrasings of such biblical statements as those to be quoted on 135–9 below.

[34] *De fide*, disp. 3. 11. 5.   [35] Ibid. 3. 11. 5.   [36] Ibid. 3. 11. 6.
[37] Ibid. 3. 11. 11.

sum of doctrine to be believed was by deduction from a universal premiss given by natural reason and a particular premiss given by faith.
Only if the Church were to promulgate it as a doctrine would 'Christ
can smile' become a doctrine imposed on believers. But doctrines
formally revealed are already doctrines requiring assent, before the
Church declares them to be such. The way Suarez applied his
distinctions would naturally yield the result that while Christ having
two natures, human and divine (the definition of the Council of
Chalcedon), was formally revealed, that Christ had two wills, one
human and one divine, was only virtually revealed and so not *de fide*
until declared to be so by the Third Council of Constantinople.[38]

Other Jesuits in Counter-Reformation Spain diverged from Suarez in
different directions. Vásquez held that any inference from one revealed
premiss and one premiss given by natural reason was *de fide*, even if the
revealed premiss was not universal. Molina contended that those
conclusions which Suarez called 'virtually revealed' were not revealed at
all, but did become morally certain when the Church declared them.

Clearly if any of these accounts of revelation are even to begin to
have some appeal they have to be phrased so as to allow that not all
deduction has the form of a syllogism, and in that case an account will
have to be given in more general terms of which premisses of natural
reason can play a role in the deduction. We can, I think, not unfairly
suppose that what Suarez was getting at, in allowing particular but
disallowing universal statements known by natural reason to play a role
in establishing a statement as formally revealed, was that statements
that have the certainty of the deliverances of immediate sense can play
such a role (and he supposed these to be the particular statements
known by natural reason), but those that merely have the certainty of
some philosophical or scientific theory cannot play such a role (and he
supposed these to be the universal statements known by natural reason).
We could replace the three Jesuit theories by theories phrased in terms
of deducibility (whether syllogistic or not) from revealed premisses and
premisses of natural reason, the latter being distinguished no longer by
their universal or particular form, but instead by the kind of certainty
they have. But the whole enterprise seems a misguided one. The view
that the later doctrines of creeds and Church declarations are contained
explicitly in Scripture or can be deduced therefrom (even with the aid

---

[38] See Chadwick, *From Bossuet to Newman*, 32.

of some premisses given by 'natural reason') seems to me implausible—for the following reasons: scriptural sentences need interpretation, as we shall see in Chapter 10; and they sometimes appear to contradict each other. If we interpret the sentences of Scripture in the most natural ways suggested by the texts in isolation, they contradict each other; and from a self-contradictory datum you can prove anything you like. Only in the light of an already partly developed doctrine can those sentences be given interpretations which do not contradict each other, and allow the development of a consistent system of doctrine. Further, the biblical writers, like many of the Fathers, did not express their views in terms whose consequences for statements expressed in the philosophical categories of Plato or Aristotle are in any way clear.

I do not find the 'deduction' view in Aquinas. Aquinas held indeed that the content of later doctrinal statements was contained 'implicitly' in what had gone before, but he does not say that mere deduction (let alone deduction in the pattern of a syllogism) could draw out what was implicit, and his examples of things 'implicit' in other things are very far from suggesting that. Aquinas thought of the Church as beginning with Abraham, not with Christ, and that 'all the articles of faith are contained implicitly in certain primary things to be believed, namely that God exists and has providence over man's salvation'; and he cannot have thought that mere deduction would give us the Nicene Creed from those primary things. Indeed, in another paragraph[39] he compares God's revelation in the Old Testament and then in the New Testament to that of a teacher who does not teach a discipline all at once to a pupil who could not absorb it, but teaches it little by little; and he makes no distinction between the New Testament drawing out what was implicit in the Old, and the creeds drawing out what is implicit in Scripture as a whole. So Aquinas clearly holds that what is 'implicit' is made explicit by a process much more subtle and less rigorous than deduction. And hence his view seems to me very similar to that expounded by Newman in the nineteenth century. For Newman the derivation of a new formula was the perception of its 'congruity' with Scripture and the 'intuitive sense' of the Church. Looking back, the Church perceived a rational 'development', a 'logical sequence'. But 'the "logical sequence" of Newman is not the "logical implication" of the scholastics, though the latter might be a part or aspect of the former. It means rather a

---

[39] *Summa theologiae*, 2a. 2ae. 1. 7 ad. 2.

harmony or congruity or "naturalness" in the way which ideas have developed.'[40]

Because Newman was not a rigorous thinker, he did not put his account of derivation in a rigorous way, but I believe that it is not too dissimilar from the following account which is, I suggest, the correct account of how early Church proclamations of doctrine were 'derived' from Scripture. Clearly at the early stage unwritten tradition was also operative, in saying for example—in ways which I shall develop more fully in Chapter 10—which parts of Scripture were crucial for interpreting others (e.g. that the Old Testament should be interpreted in the light of the New), and thus in saying what are the core elements of the Christian faith. Derivation then consists in finding overall clear and precise statements, expressed by sentences which as far as possible use words in literal or at any rate analogical senses, which do best justice to the general tendency of the datum. This involves taking most of its sentences in the senses most naturally suggested by the text, and interpreting other sentences in ways consistent with the former; and developing the simplest metaphysical account which systematizes those data. I argue at length in Chapter 10 that sorting out the meaning of scriptural teaching (and of any other datum) involves comparing passages with each other and with our knowledge of the core elements of Christian doctrine and our knowledge of other matters: namely science and history, psychology and morals. This process clearly gives great scope for spiritual reflection (facing up to things honestly and pursuing them thoroughly) and intellectual systematization. The practice of all this, I claimed in Chapter 5, was part of the point of revelation. It is made possible by the existence in the New Testament of very different traditions of thought in terms of which the core message of the Gospel is expressed—the Palestinian Jewish (e.g. of the opening chapters of St Matthew's Gospel), Pauline, and Johannine traditions. The hard work of Christian derivation involves getting them into one focus.

Let me illustrate this process of 'deriving' by the derivation in the Church of the doctrine of the Trinity. There are a few passages in the New Testament which state and many more which presuppose or entail that Jesus Christ is God. The opening passage of St John's Gospel, for example, speaking of Jesus Christ, the Son of God, claims that (1: 1)

---

[40] J. H. Newman, *The Idea of the Development of Christian Doctrine*; expounded in Chadwick, *From Bossuet to Newman*, ch. 7. See p. 157.

'The Word was God' and (1: 14) 'The Word became flesh and dwelt among us.' St John distinguishes elsewhere in the Gospel between Jesus Christ and God the Father who sent him. There are other passages in the New Testament which distinguish the Holy Spirit from the Father and the Son and seem to presuppose that he is on the divine side of the divine/creature divide. There are a few 'Trinitarian formulae' in the New Testament which put the three persons of the Holy Trinity on a level; notably the command at the end of St Matthew's Gospel (28: 19) to baptize 'in the name of the Father, and of the Son, and of the Holy Spirit'. Liturgical practice in the early Church contained other non-scriptural Trinitarian formulae. The early Church believed that the practice and doctrine which it inherited were divinely revealed; and it saw the books which it therefore came to recognize as canonical Scripture as incorporating that revelation; and the New Testament, and especially the Gospels, to be the core of that revelation, by which other scriptural books were to be interpreted. It felt itself aware of God in its worship and prayer, and there was scriptural authority that what it would be then aware of was the Holy Spirit. Some theologians came to teach that a unique God who was Love would need a God or Gods to whom to express that love.[41]

So in the course of the third and fourth centuries AD the Church tried to devise a formula to systematize these Trinitarian intuitions. There were various formulae, around which doctrinal battles raged. The view that the Son was 'of like substance' with the Father nearly won the day; but it was eventually defeated because it suggested that the Son was less divine than the Father. The preferred formula adopted by the Council of Nicaea in AD 325 was that the Son was 'of the same substance' with the Father. The three entities came to be called three hypostases, or persons; and all to be 'of the same substance'—distinct yet equally divine. Such was the teaching of the Council of Constantinople in AD 381. But what 'of the same substance' meant was unclear. Did it mean that all three persons belonged to the same genus, the divine, in no stronger a sense than three humans all belong to the *genus humanum*? or did it mean that all three were in some sense the same individual thing? Later theologians and Councils tried to sort that out.

---

[41] For justification of some of the early stages of the 'derivation' of the doctrines of the Trinity and the Incarnation, see David Brown, *The Divine Trinity* (Duckworth, 1985), chs. 3 and 4. For doubt on the legitimacy of the development see J. Hick (ed.), *The Myth of God Incarnate* (SCM Press, 1977), pt. I.

The 'derivation' from Scripture can hardly be deduction. There are scriptural passages which taken with their normal meanings imply doctrines contrary to later orthodoxy: for example Christ's statement in St John's Gospel (14: 28) that 'the Father is greater than I'. There are other scriptural passages which are ambiguous, but which perhaps more naturally seem to imply doctrines contrary to later orthodoxy, for instance the reference to Christ in the Epistle to the Colossians (1: 15) as 'the first born of all creation'. What rather has happened is that one party in the Church proposed, and eventually a Church proclaimed as official doctrine, one interpretation which they claim is the most plausible interpretation of the message of Scripture and Church tradition as a whole. This forces them to claim that certain past ways of worship were misleading, and certain statements of past theologians false, and that certain passages of Scripture have to be interpreted with other than their normal meanings (i.e. their meanings if taken in isolation). But the claim is that any rival theory forces us to regard more worship and past theology as mistaken and forces more passages to be taken with other than their normal meanings. There is a right and wrong derivation from Scripture. I shall seek to show in Chapter 10 in detail how Church tradition (i.e. the majority tradition of worship and theology) and other passages of Scripture force interpretations on some passages of Scripture which they would not bear on their own.

This process led theologians guided by the fourth-century Councils to interpret Christ being 'the first born of all creation' in the sense that Christ was 'begotten of the Father before all worlds'; he was not 'created' out of nothing, let alone out of pre-existing non-divine matter, but out of the stuff of the Father—which is why theology came to prefer a word 'begotten' chosen to make clear that neither of the latter views were implied; Christ was 'begotten' of the Father himself 'eternally'. Again the 'Father is greater than I' was to be understood in some sense other than that naturally suggested—for instance Christ, in so far as he was human, was less than the Father.

A similar process was at work in 'deriving' the other great patristic doctrine: that Jesus Christ who walked on Earth was fully God and at the same time fully man. Again there are the New Testament passages already referred to which imply his divinity. But there are also plenty of New Testament passages which imply his humanity. St Paul's Epistle to the Romans (1: 3) speaks of Christ as 'born of the seed of David according to the flesh'. 1 John 4: 2 speaks of Christ as having 'come in the flesh'. The Epistle to the Hebrews (4: 15) stresses that Christ 'hath been in all points tempted like as we are, yet without sin'.

All of these passages could however be read in a 'docetist' way, that is, as implying that Jesus Christ was God and not man; temporarily clothed with flesh, and temporarily suffering, but not truly human. However, the early Church wanted to read them with the interpretation which it held to be best consonant with the rest of Scripture, for it believed that the humanity of Christ was important if he was to be the means of our salvation. So it developed the doctrine which finally received its canonical expression in the declaration of the Council of Chalcedon that 'one Lord Jesus Christ', 'truly God and truly man', was 'of one substance with the Father as regarding his Godhead, and at the same time of one substance with us as regards his manhood'.[42]

I suggest this as a much more plausible account of 'derivation' than that given by Suarez and others in sixteenth-century Spain.

It follows from my account that when we have a canonical Scripture, the datum from which doctrine is derived cannot be just Scripture, but rather Scripture with a certain tradition and balance of interpretation. Whether or not there are other 'unwritten traditions' from which doctrine can be derived, there needs to be at least this unwritten tradition. Yet this tradition, because unwritten and because a matter of a balance implicit in most worship, practice, and theology, is too vague to form an additional premiss in a deductive argument.

While serious consideration of the nature of the derivation from the original revelation involved in the formation of doctrine began in sixteenth-century Spain, it was Newman's *Essay* which made this issue a central one in Catholic theology, and many Catholic writers of the twentieth century have given accounts of derivation very much in the spirit of Newman. The theologian who responded most explicitly to Suarez was F. Marin-Sola.[43] All later doctrine, he held, must cohere rationally with the original revelation, but logical deducibility was not necessary. Hence, contrary to Suarez, all new definitions were indeed derived from the original revelation. Some modern Catholic writers have however given accounts of the derivation involved which have the effect that anything defined was really derived. For example, 'derivation' is allowed to include formalizing the presuppositions of any

---

[42] Denzinger 301.
[43] For an account of his views, see Nichols, *From Newman to Congar*, 178–83. See also Chadwick, *From Bossuet to Newman*, 204–7.

Doesn't allow for a new revelation [handwritten margin note]

patterns of devotion which have developed in the Church. And that, as their critics have pointed out, has the effect that 'derivation' is no longer merely an interpretation of an original deposit but can be in effect new revelation.[44] Such an account is wildly disconsonant with tradition. Of course, various events in the history of thought and practice within and outside the Church, including the development of practices of devotion, can cause Christians to believe that certain doctrines are involved in the original revelation. But what is at stake is, whatever the cause of such a belief, whether there are public rational procedures of argument to show that what some believed to be involved in the original revelation really was—whether these procedures are deductive or of a looser kind. If not, the emergence of the new belief would constitute a new revelation; and all Christian tradition has claimed that there cannot be such.[45]

Finally, there are of course different views about the form and the status in which interpretations are promulgated. The Church's teaching is proclaimed in the teaching of its official teachers, and among them especially those recognized informally as having eminence; in prayers officially sanctioned for liturgical use; and more formally in the declarations of Church Councils and officers. For Eastern Orthodoxy Councils of all properly consecrated and elected bishops of the Church have supreme, though perhaps not infallible, status. For Roman Catholicism of course that status belongs to the teaching of the Pope and of Councils whose declarations are at any rate tacitly approved by him. Later Roman Catholicism developed a distinction between the ordinary and the extraordinary (*ex cathedra*) teaching of the Pope

---

[44] Nichols's book is an account of different theories of doctrinal development, i.e. derivation in my terms, in the Catholic tradition in the period subsequent to Newman. A number of the writers whom he discusses are open to the charge of giving such a vague and general account of 'derivation' that any subsequently promulgated doctrine counts as 'derived'. The declaration of Vatican II (*Dei Verbum*, 8) is also susceptible of an 'anything goes' interpretation: 'There is a growth in the understanding of the realities and the words which have been handed down. This happens through the contemplation and study made by believers who treasure these things in their hearts (cf Luke 2: 19, 51), through the intimate understanding of spiritual things they experience, and through the preaching of those who have received through episcopal successions the sure gift of truth.' For one Anglican exposition of the view that derivation of divine truth from Scripture involves a method more subtle than deduction, a recognition of images, see Austin Farrer, *The Glass of Vision* (Dacre Press, 1948), esp. ch. 3.

[45] For the different ways in which Protestants of the past century have 'derived' doctrines from Scripture, see D. H. Kelsey, *The Uses of Scripture in Recent Theology* (SCM Press, 1975).

(which included his approval of the declarations of Councils), and ascribed infallibility to the latter:

The Roman Pontiff, when he speaks *ex cathedra* (that is when fulfilling the office of Pastor and teacher of all Christians in virtue of his supreme Apostolical authority he defines a doctrine concerning faith or morals to be held by the Universal Church) ... is endowed with that infallibility, with which the Divine Redeemer had willed that His Church—in defining doctrine concerning faith or morals—should be equipped. And therefore such definitions of the Roman Pontiff of themselves—and not by virtue of the consent of the church—are irreformable.[46]

We have already noted the need for external tests in resolving disputes about which Councils were true Councils, or which papal declarations were *ex cathedra*. And we have already noted that to allow a class of fundamental irrevisable doctrinal proclamations is to narrow the scope for individual and collaborative enquiry in the light of personal spiritual experience in working out the meaning of revelation.

I have now described the different views on the nature of the interpretation of the original revelation which the Church has to pursue. There are differences on which are the data in which the original revelation is contained, what processes of logic are involved in the interpretation, and in what form and with what status the interpretation is promulgated. Even where theologians agree on some formula for any of these matters, they may well disagree as to how the formula is to be interpreted. Theologians might agree as to what the datum describing the original revelation was, and that the process involved 'finding overall rigorous philosophical statements which did best justice to the general tendency of the datum', and yet disagree as to which philosophical statements did this. Although there are certainly internal criteria for determining which interpretations of a datum best draw out what is involved in it, the argument of Chapter 2 indicates that there are bound to be border areas where one interpretation is as well justified as another, and even if one interpretation is better justified than another, that will not always be obvious. Hence we need an external criterion for a true development, that is, that it is developed in a Church which is the 'closest continuer' of the Church of the apostles.

There is a framework within which Christians can begin to sort out for themselves the interpretation for their own culture of the

---

[46] Denzinger 3074.

deliverances of the original revelation. It is the framework of Church
organization continuous with the apostles. Christians must belong, in
the case of a split, to that body which preserves the maximum continuity of organization with what has gone before: except in so far as
there is a break in doctrine; except in so far as on important matters
they can show a greater similarity of doctrine to that of an earlier stage
of the Christian body. Among the elements of doctrine on which there
needs to be continuity is the doctrine of how doctrine is to be derived
from the original revelation, and the Church body needs to have
conformed well to its own criteria in this matter. At this point I pass
my baton to the historian to show which present-day body preserves
best in its doctrine and organization continuity with the Church of the
apostles.

One result of such investigation might be to establish as 'the best
continuer' with the Church of the apostles one ecclesiastical body with
clear contours of organization and essential doctrine—for example the
Roman Catholic Church. In that case, if there is a revelation, that
would be where it is to be found today. Were historical investigation to
show that, it would of course make easier the task of determining the
truth about the matters with which creeds have been concerned: but
not that much easier; for, as I argued in Chapter 5, arguments about
whether there was a revelation would then turn crucially on the truth
and interpretation of those doctrines which, if there was a revelation, it
then evidently licensed—evidence that they were false would be
evidence that there was no revelation. And in so far as it did make the
task of sorting out the truth on these matters *too* much easier, that
would begin to defeat the purpose of revelation.

It is possible however that the final result of historical investigation
into all these matters might be a draw: there may be no 'closest
continuer' of the Church of the apostles. It might be that two later
bodies have equal continuity of organization, one showing more continuity in one respect, another in another; or one later body might
preserve continuity of organization better, while only marginally
possessing continuity of doctrine, which was better satisfied by the
other body. What then is to be said? The same as we would say with
respect to an ordinary earthly society of which the same was true: that
the society was split, and in consequence was not functioning properly.
If this was so of the Church, it could only provide interpretation of
revelation in so far as it had announced the interpretation before the
split, or two successor bodies give the same interpretation independ-

ently. Here finally would be applicable the famous canon of Vincent of Lerins that the Catholic faith is 'that which has been believed everywhere, always and by all'.[47] Clearly it will not apply until we know who counts as 'all';[48] but when the tests of continuity of organization and doctrine have done their best, it can take over.[49]

The claim that God has guided the Church to interpret the original revelation correctly is subject to the objection that political forces have often influenced Councils and Popes in proclaiming this doctrine rather than that. That such forces have often had a significant influence cannot be doubted. Irrational forces have so often influenced human decisions on other matters also, including their decisions to proclaim conclusions on matters of secular history and science. But the claim of divine influence over the Church's interpretation of doctrine need be only minimally the claim that where such irrational forces would have forced the Church to adopt false interpretations of doctrine on very fundamental matters God has enabled enough Church leaders to see that theological considerations favour a different interpretation, so as to prevent the Church being saddled permanently with false interpretations. That is quite compatible with God allowing political influences to be decisive on occasions where they inclined the Church to reach interpretations which were true. Those who hold that all official Church interpretations are revisable (e.g. the Eastern Orthodox, if they claim that among the tests that a Council is an ecumenical Council is its fidelity to tradition, so that any interpretation proclaimed by a Council can be shown subsequently not to be faithful to tradition, and so not to have been proclaimed by a proper Council) are not committed to the view that divine

---

[47] *Commonitorium*, 1. 2.

[48] Augustine in one place had a weighted formula for determining what should be believed. Scripture should always be believed—although we need the Church to explain what it means. Councils are to be preferred to post-apostolic bishops, General Councils to local councils, and 'among general councils, earlier ones are often improved (*emendari*) by later ones'. See his *Treatise on Baptism*, 2. 3. 4.

[49] In his *The Identity of Christianity* (SPCK, 1984), Stephen Sykes sees the identity of Christianity as constituted by an ongoing tradition of external form (a 'series of propositions' expressed in 'story, myth, and doctrine'—260) interacting with 'inwardness', 'an internal experience of new life' (i.e. Christians' inward response to this external tradition in a tradition of worship). If we develop Sykes's stress on a tradition of worship into a clear and full-scale public criterion for the identity of Christianity, then it, together with his doctrine test, will give us an account of that identity similar to that of this chapter, public tests which can be used by enquirers into the nature of Christian revelation. As Sykes recognizes, 'inwardness', in effect the guidance of the Holy Spirit, cannot be used as a public criterion without being given more public content.

influence guided Councils or popes on any one particular occasion—or would have guided them otherwise, had they been inclined to promulgate false doctrine—but only that it guided the general drift of theological interpretation over the centuries. And who, looking at the history of theology, could deny that argument, reflection, and prayer, as well as irrational political forces, have played a significant role in the formation of Christian doctrine? The argument to show that God has determined the influence of such argument, reflection, and prayer, whether through natural processes or by intervention in them, sufficiently to prevent the embodiment of false doctrine on fundamental matters must, in view of the impossibility of determining directly just how much different influences influenced different Church leaders at moments of history long ago, proceed by a different route. It must proceed via evidence that there is a God able and willing to intervene in history, evidence of the Resurrection that he would preserve doctrine in a Church, and the prior probability of the doctrines which that Church proclaimed (e.g. of the doctrine of the Trinity), as well as any more direct historical evidence from the teaching of Jesus.

Other Suggested Tests

Besides my twin tests for the true Church of continuity of doctrine and organization, there have been in the history of Christianity two other tests suggested. The first is purity of life. If Christ founded a Church to be his 'body' in the world, one would expect it to evince his holy life; a body which failed to do so, the suggestion goes, could hardly be the Church. This issue was raised in an acute form by Donatism in the fourth century AD.[50] The Donatists claimed that a 'church' which tolerated unworthy bishops and other officers ceased to be part of the true Church; and that they themselves had that purity which made them the true Church. Since that time many other sects have arisen, claiming on grounds of sanctity of life that the main body had unchurched itself through impurity and that they alone had the purity to make them the true Church. Now certainly if a 'church' ceased to teach seriously holiness of life, it would indeed fail to be the true Church—this follows from the test of continuity of doctrine. For obvi-

[50] For Donatism and other 'puritan' movements of the early Church, see S. L. Greenslade, *Schism in the Early Church* (SCM Press, 1953), ch. 6.

ously a crucial part of doctrine concerns the worthwhileness of living a holy life. And if a society taught that seriously, it would tend to make its members more prone to pursue such a life than they would otherwise be. So 'puritans' are right to demand that to be a true Church, a body must be a sanctifying body. But to demand that the members of the Church be fully sanctified before they become members would be to deny the role of the Church as a sanctifying agent: you can only make holy what is not already holy. And to demand that the Church be a society of saints is to refuse to allow it one of its all-important roles, of moulding sinners who choose to be moulded into saints.[51] (To demand sanctity with respect to officers alone would be to refuse to recognize that they too are members on the way to sanctification, and so to make a division between officers and other members far sharper than the history of Christian doctrine could possibly warrant.)

The other suggested test for the true Church is the test of miracles: that the Church's authority be established by many continuing miracles, in a way that its original authority was, it claims, established by the miracle of the Resurrection. There is a New Testament passage that claims that such miracles will be the signs of the Church;[52] and passages which claim that the Church was characterized by such miracles in its very early years.[53] Clearly such evidence would reinforce a 'church's' claim to authority, and from time to time most branches of Christianity have claimed some miraculous backing for their work. But clearly later miracles are not as vital for authenticating revelation (though no doubt desirable for other reasons) as the original miracle of the Resurrection. For a Church recognized as such through the original miracle, its later manifestations can be recognized as such by the tests of continuity of doctrine and organization with the earlier Church. And too much evident miracle would lead people into Christianity for the wrong reasons, as I argued in Chapter 6. That said, some none too evident miracles are perhaps to be expected in connection with the Church, and certainly the occurrence of miracles will reinforce a body's claim to be the Church.

---

[51] On this role see *Responsibility and Atonement* (Clarendon Press, 1989), 163–73.
[52] Mark 16: 17–18, part of the 'longer ending' added on to the last chapter of St Mark's Gospel.
[53] (e.g.) Acts 5: 15–16.

Creeds are the lens to
interpret Scripture -
rather than Scripture
interpreting
Creeds

Creeds are
preface to
Cannot
divine
authorise

Calvin would stipulate matter originated

9

Creeds

So then later bodies teach how the original revelation is to be interpreted; and one criterion, but not the only criterion, of those bodies being parts of the Church just is the plausibility of the interpretation and its fidelity to the tradition of interpretation within the earlier Church. The teaching will appear in documents having varying degrees of official status, varying from prayers officially sanctioned by a local body for local use, to creeds approved by Church Councils; and needs to be weighted accordingly in judging fidelity to the tradition. If any teaching can be identified as infallible, then of course any later interpretations of revelation must be consonant therewith.

The original revelation and any later documents purporting to interpret it will be subject to the complexities and difficulties of interpretation inevitably involved in human language itself which I laid out in Part I. In this chapter I draw out the consequences of those complexities and difficulties for those expositions of Christian doctrine (i.e. interpretations of the original revelation) which seek to lay it out as precisely and clearly as possible. The creeds[1] and declarations of Church Councils have this character, and it is they which have been used as the tests of orthodoxy (possibly, along with certain papal pronouncements). So too do some expositions of doctrine by theologians, which are not also used as tests of orthodoxy. The genre of such documents is thus clear; in them the whole is true if and only if each sentence is true.

Scientific and Historical Presuppositions

The documents will often be subject to presuppositions, scientific and historical. They may presuppose that the sun, stars, and planets spin

---

[1] Creeds typically begin with the words 'I' (or we) 'believe in' certain things; and to believe *in* certain things is not the same as to believe that these things are so. To believe *in* God is not the same as to believe that there is a God. On this, see my *Faith and Reason* (Clarendon Press, 1981), esp. ch. 4. Nevertheless, those who put the creeds forward for

daily from east to west round the Earth and that sun and planets travel among the 'fixed stars' with more complex motions over longer periods; that there are no planets, let alone planets inhabited by rational creatures, beyond the solar system; that men did not evolve from lower animals, but were created directly by God either *ex nihilo* or by 'breathing life into the dust of the ground' (as Genesis 2: 7 states); that the Earth was only a few thousand years old; and other doctrines of ancient and medieval science. Although such presuppositions are there in the writings of theologians, they relatively seldom get into creeds and official declarations. Perhaps this is because the latter need to be precise, and to include only things essential for belief, and unnecessary assumptions therefore get weeded out. One exception to this, and not one usually noticed by those who say the words, is the claim of the Apostles' Creed that God the Father Almighty is the creator 'of Heaven and Earth'.[2] By 'heaven' (οὐρανός, *caelum*) was meant 'the sky', that is, that region in which moon, sun, and planets moved against the background of the fixed stars. 'Heaven' did not mean for the writers of early centuries what it means for us, namely the abode of the blessed after death. Most writers did however hold that the abode of the blessed was in or (more often) beyond the sky.[3] Those who recite the creed today tend, I suspect, to think they are affirming God as creator of this world (the physical universe we live in now, the Earth and, by implication, all that surrounds it) and another world (Heaven, where, by God's mercy, we hope to be). But although the ancients had very many different views about the nature of Heaven, they virtually all thought of it as a realm surrounding or overarching the Earth, where things behaved differently from how they behaved on Earth. The physical universe consisted of two parts: Heaven and Earth. In our way of thinking it does not: it consists of innumerable stars and planets, of which the Earth is one small one.

recitation at baptism and in worship were announcing as the official doctrine of the Church that what the believer is to put his belief in is in fact so.

[2] The final form of the Apostles' Creed, now used very frequently in the Church's worship and often a test for the admission of candidates to baptism, may be as late as the 8th century. It is a variant of the 'old Roman creed', to be dated to the 2nd century. The phrase 'creator of Heaven and Earth' is not in the old Roman creed but is in a number of early creeds. See J. N. D. Kelly, *Early Christian Creeds* (Longmans, 1950), 372–4.

[3] Heaven was however generally regarded as a complicated place with many 'layers' to it, as it were. See (e.g.) St John Damascene, *De fide orthodoxa*, 2. 6. Tatian places Paradise, the abode of the blessed, 'above' Heaven. But not all thinkers placed Paradise in or above Heaven. One who did not was Theophilus of Antioch who placed it on Earth, in a favoured region in the East. On the last two writers see J. Danielou, *Gospel Message and Hellenistic Culture* (Darton, Longman, & Todd, 1973), 393.

Yet in putting the phrase 'Heaven and Earth' in the creed, the authors were not making a point about the constitution of the physical universe. One can see this by the fact that there was available no rival account of it to the very general ancient view of it sketched above. It was just their way of putting a point which could have been put, less committedly, by describing God as the creator of the physical universe; in view of their belief about the nature of that, they naturally described it as 'Heaven and Earth'.

Although their presuppositions can, as we saw in Chapter 2, be removed from creeds and other statements without too much difficulty, creeds, like all other statements, are inevitably addressed to those questions which concerned men of the time and will say which of their answers to those questions was correct, without necessarily enabling us to say which of our answers to their questions was correct. Thus the Nicene Creed has an expanded version of the phrase which I have just been discussing, and expresses its belief in God the Father Almighty 'maker of Heaven and Earth, and of all things visible and invisible'. The expanded phrase makes the point that God created not merely the physical universe, but as well anything non-physical which may exist—for instance angels and the souls of the departed. What it claims is clear in so far as it is clear what counts as a 'thing'. But, as we saw in Chapter 5, that is not at all clear. Certainly if there are angels, and souls of the departed, angels and souls of the departed count as things, and so one who believes the creed believes that God created them; they do not exist under their own powers. So much is uncontroversial. But are space and time, or numbers or logical relations, things? The authors of the creed had probably not given much, if any, attention to such issues. Such 'things' were not what they were talking about; and so even if we do think of time or the number twenty-three as things we must not read the creed as affirming that God created them. Creeds are to be read only as choosing between answers currently available—for example that God did not create the Devil, or that he did create the Devil as well as all other spirits.

Inevitably each new formulation of doctrine raises further questions not raised by the discussions which gave rise to the original formula. If Christ has two natures, as the Council of Chalcedon declared, does it follow that he has two separate wills? The centuries following the Council of Chalcedon tried to answer that question. More generally the meaning of all technical terms will need clarification in terms of the interests and concerns of each new generation. So what does the

Chalcedonian doctrine of the Incarnation commit us to, if we try to avoid stating it in terms of the Greek words ὑπόστασις and φύσις? The arguments of Chapter 2 suggest that the process of clarification is an unending one.

Sometimes however theologians have wanted to say that such matters as the age and size of the universe were part of the content, as opposed to the temporary framework, of revelation. The sixteenth and seventeenth centuries and the nineteenth century saw two well-known controversies, in which scientific discoveries undermined the presuppositions of biblical writers about such matters: the controversy of the sixteenth and seventeenth centuries concerned whether the Earth was stationary and sun, moon, planets, and stars went round it; and the controversy of the nineteenth century concerned the age of the Earth and whether men evolved by a gradual process from lower animals over a long time. The reason why some supposed that Christian revelation contained a view of these matters was because the Bible presupposed and sometimes explicitly affirmed views thereof, and they supposed that the Bible's presuppositions were part of the content of the Christian revelation. But presupposition must be distinguished from content, and just how the Bible is to be read in respect of its 'affirmations' is a matter of some controversy which will be discussed in the next chapter. As we shall see there, earlier centuries were far less 'literalistic' in their reading of the Bible, and so less inclined to regard scientific matters as part of its content. It is for this reason that the only controversies between science and the Bible which produced theological controversy, and had a wide impact on the community, were those of recent centuries. But the clashes between the view of the Bible and the Greek science believed by most of the Christian Fathers would have given rise to controversies just as acute as those of later centuries if early centuries had read the Bible as literally as later ones did. The Old Testament certainly assumes that the Earth is flat and rests on 'foundations' —Greek science knew that it was spherical and floated in empty space. Greek science believed that all water was to be found in the sublunary region, and certainly under the 'firmament' of Heaven formed by the background of the 'fixed stars'. Genesis 1: 7 says that on the second day of creation 'God made the firmament, and divided the waters which were under the firmament, from the waters which were above the firmament.' And so on.

As we shall see, the Fathers had their ways of interpreting the Bible so as not to read it as contradicting the supposedly true Greek science.

But until the sixteenth century such conflicts did not have wide impact, because Church authorities were prepared in general not to insist that history and science formed part of the content of revelation, and allowed that it was permissible to interpret the Bible accordingly. I write 'in general' because clearly the kind of thing announced in early creeds, and which for reasons given in Chapter 5 was the sort of thing with which revelation was concerned, did have some particular implications for history and science. Atonement was made available by the death of Christ on the Cross—hence it ruled out the historical claim of Docetism made in the second century that he did not die there.[4]

The declaration of the Holy Office in 1616 that 'the double motion of the Earth about its axis and about the sun is false, and entirely contrary to Holy Scripture'[5] was the Catholic Church's only official proclamation declaring a theological orthodoxy on matters concerning the age, size, or detailed mode of operation of the universe. It was of course a most unfortunate declaration, and quietly abandoned at the beginning of the nineteenth century. The Darwinian theory of evolution was formally opposed by smaller Church denominations, but in general the larger ones made no formal condemnations. Despite the event of 1616, Protestantism is more at risk from such scientific discoveries—for, just because creeds in general avoid scientific and historical presuppositions, the discoveries cause most problems in respect of their clashes with the Bible. Protestantism has often claimed that the Bible is to be read without using the tradition of the Church as to how it is to be interpreted; and so the latter cannot be invoked to remove apparent conflict.

Univocity in Creeds

Once we have siphoned off their presuppositions from creeds and other theological statements and noted that they cannot be read directly as taking a position with respect to views not even heard of, we must bear in mind that creeds contain much metaphor and analogy. Some credal sentences are, however, given my understanding of the terms as defined in Chapter 3, to be understood quite literally. The occurrence of metaphor and analogy is to be expected in view of the fact that theology makes claims about transcendent matters, but must perforce use ordin-

    [4] See (e.g.) J. N. D. Kelly, *Early Christian Doctrines* (A. & C. Black, 5th edn., 1977), 141–2.
    [5] See (e.g.) A. D. White, *A History of the Warfare of Science with Theology*, i (Dover Publications, 1960), 137–8.

ary human words given their meaning originally by their applicability to very ordinary mundane goings-on. However, it is possible for ordinary words to be applied in quite new circumstances without being used analogically or metaphorically. When a ball is said to have a diameter of 1 metre, a galaxy to have a diameter of 300,000 light years, and an atomic nucleus to have a diameter of 10^{-14} metres, 'diameter' is being used in exactly the same sense throughout. So too is 'cause', when an explosion causes the disintegration of a supernova, or the way someone talks causes his hearers to be annoyed. It just that the diameters are very different, not that the meaning of 'diameter' is in any way different. The same goes for 'cause'. All this follows from the results of Chapter 3. It does however require some careful analysis to see when words in theology are being used univocally, when they are being used analogically, and when they are being used metaphorically. By considering what else those who devised, expounded, and assented to the creeds (or prayers, or other official documents) said on other occasions, we can normally form a reasonable understanding of how literally they intended particular phrases to be understood. I will illustrate univocal, analogical, and metaphorical uses in creeds and other official documents. My discussion of each example will however be fairly brief and contestable; I do not marshal a whole battery of other uses of words by many different theologians or church officials, as I would need to do to justify adequately an interpretation of any one particular phrase. However I hope that I will have said enough to make clear that all three kinds of use are to be found, and to make clear the procedures for sorting out which is the use in a given case.

The ancient creeds all talk of God or the Father as *omnipotens* or παντοκράτωρ, normally translated as 'all-powerful', 'omnipotent', or 'almighty'; and however exactly this is to be spelled out so as to avoid certain logical paradoxes, it clearly involved God as being very 'powerful'. Less frequently, he is referred to as 'perfect' or 'good'; said to be 'wise' and 'to know all things'.[6] By my criteria, 'good', 'wise', and

---

[6] Thus the creed of the Council of Nicaea affirms belief in the 'Father almighty', (παντοκράτωρ) (Denzinger 125) and the 'Roman baptismal order' affirms belief in the 'Father omnipotent' (*omnipotens*) (Denzinger 30). The First Vatican Council spoke of God as *intellectu ac voluntate omnique perfectione infinitum*, 'infinite in intellect and will and all perfection'. The 'Tome of Damasus' (AD 382) spoke of it being a heresy to deny that the Son, like the Father, *omnia posse omnia nosse*, 'is able to do everything, and knows everything' (Denzinger 164). The Third Council of Toledo (AD 589) spoke of the 'goodness' (*bonitas*) of the Trinity (Denzinger 470). And, to take a very recent example, an encyclical of Pope Pius XII spoke of God as 'most wise' (*sapientissimus*) (Denzinger 3781).

'powerful' come out as univocal in their use of men and of God. 'Wise' is used in the same sense in 'God is wise' as in 'Socrates is wise'. There are the same synonyms—'knows many things', 'understands many things'—same antonyms—'foolish'—same determinates and determinables. Of course there are differences in what wisdom amounts to in God from what it amounts to in men. God's wisdom is essential to him, and it is not the result of learning. But if 'God is wise' entails 'God is essentially wise', whereas 'Socrates is wise' does not entail 'Socrates is essentially wise', the difference does not arise because 'wise' has different meanings when applied to God and when applied to Socrates. Rather, the entailment arises because of the meaning of the word 'God'. 'God' is a word used to denote a kind of being who cannot but be wise. (The entailment arises either because '*x* is God' by itself entails '*x* is essentially wise', or because it entails 'if *x* is wise, then he is essentially wise', which, conjoined to '*x* is wise', yields '*x* is essentially wise'.) A similar point applies if 'God's wisdom is not the result of learning' is entailed by 'God is wise'. These entailments do not arise from 'wise' being used of God in a special sense; the contributions of 'wise' to the meaning of 'God is wise' and 'Socrates is wise' are just the same.

Duns Scotus affirmed, as I do, that such terms as 'good', 'wise', and 'powerful' are used univocally of God and man. He defines a word as univocal if it has sufficient unity in itself to serve as the middle term of a valid syllogism (e.g. 'ϕ' is univocal in '*a* is ϕ' and '*b* is ϕ' if from the former and 'All ϕs are ψ' you can deduce '*a* is ψ', and from the latter together with 'All ϕs are ψ' you can deduce '*b* is ψ') and if it cannot be affirmed and denied of the same thing without contradiction.[7] By these tests 'wise' comes out as univocal with its normal use in its application to God. From 'God is wise', and 'Anyone who is wise knows that man is mortal' it follows that 'God knows that man is mortal'; and the same goes if you substitute 'Socrates' for 'God'. And likewise for 'good' and 'powerful'. 'Although it seems to me that Scotus' tests for univocity are not strong enough,[8] they are of the same logical type as mine. Scotus was clearly attempting to elucidate the same kind of understanding of univocity as I am.

Not so Aquinas. Aquinas claimed that predicates such as 'good', 'wise', and 'powerful' were being used analogically of God in compari-

[7] Scotus, *Ordinatio*, 1 dist. 3, q. 1; and *Opus Oxoniense*, 1. 3. 2. 5–6, translated in A. Wolter, *Duns Scotus: Philosophical Writings* (London, 1962), 20.

[8] See Janice Thomas, 'Univocity and Understanding God's Nature', in G. J. Hughes (ed.), *The Philosophical Assessment of Theology* (Search Press, 1987), 90–2.

son with their use of men.[9] Aquinas's reasons for denying univocity
arise from various metaphysical and epistemological doctrines which are
highly dubious if seen as doctrines about analogy of a kind such as I
have been concerned with. Among the metaphysical doctrines are the
doctrine that words are only univocal if they denote properties in beings
which belong to the same genus, or at any rate have the same mode of
existence. Among the epistemological doctrines is the doctrine that
concepts are abstracted from 'phantasmata' derived from sensible
things, and so our language is tied in meaning by its applicability to
sensible things.[10] Such claims of Aquinas seem quite inadequately
justified if Aquinas's sense of 'analogy' is anything like mine. Words
which denote properties in beings of different genera may be univocal
in my sense, and how we derive our understanding of the meaning of a
word is only indirectly relevant to what that meaning is. However, by
these doctrines Aquinas may be elucidating a rather different understanding from mine of 'univocal' and 'analogical'.

Two recent papers have defended the view that the divine
predicates—'good', 'wise', and so on—are used analogically of God
with respect to their use of humans on grounds other than the meta-
physico-epistemological doctrines used by Aquinas. G. J. Hughes
claims that, while argument leads us to use such predicates as 'good' of
God and thus to affirm a resemblance between a divine property and
human goodness, 'we are unable to state in what this resemblance
consists. It "transcends our mode of expression" because God
transcends our way of existing', 'we do not have a grasp of the truth
conditions'[11] for applying such description to God. Now there are
senses of 'state in what this resemblance consists', and 'grasp the truth
conditions' in which what Hughes says is false. God being 'wise', like
Socrates being 'wise' involves knowing and understanding many things,
and the truth-conditions of his being 'wise' are that he does know and
understand many things. But there are of course also senses of the

---

[9] 'It is impossible to predicate anything univocally of God and creatures' (St Thomas
Aquinas, *Summa theologiae*, 1a. 13. 5). The divine predicates 'good', 'wise', etc. are used,
he held, analogically and more specifically in his terminology, by analogy of proper
proportionality. James Ross also holds that both 'wise' and 'powerful' are used of God
only analogically (*Portraying Analogy* (Cambridge University Press, 1981), 170–1), but he
does not give any detailed argument for this. He allows that other words used in religious
discourse are often either univocal or equivocal with normal senses.

[10] For elaboration and criticism of Aquinas's reasons for denying univocity, see Patrick
Sherry, 'Analogy Today', *Philosophy*, 51 (1976), 431–46. See 438–46.

[11] G. J. Hughes, 'Aquinas and the Limits of Agnosticism', in Hughes (ed.), *The
Philosophical Assessment of Theology*. See 48 and 51.

expressions in which what Hughes says is true. We do not know what it is like to be God, how God knows things, from which other essential properties of God his wisdom derives. But then we do not know what it is like to be a bat, how a bat 'perceives objects, and from which essential properties of being a bat its sensory abilities emerge. But we can still truly say, 'bats perceive', and in doing so use the word perceive' univocally with its use in 'humans perceive'. It is the possession of the surface property, not its underlying causes, which constitutes the truth-conditions for the ascription of 'perceive' or 'wise'.

Janice Thomas suggests that the divine predicates applied to God 'may have real senses none of us know';[12] there may be an analogous sense of the word 'wise' which applies to God, and is known only to God. The senses of scientific terms are matters for experts. If we use them, we use them with whatever sense an expert would use them, even if we do not know what that sense is. God is the supreme expert on his own nature. If we say that he is 'wise', we must mean to use the word in his sense and that *may* be at best analogous with our normal sense. Now God may indeed have a property such that, if he decides to call it the property of being 'wise', he would be using the word 'wise' in a sense analogous to the normal sense. But when creeds claim that God is 'wise', are they using a word like 'entropy' of which many of us do not really know the meaning but on which we rely on an expert's authority? Or are they claiming that God is 'wise' in a sense in which we understand the term? I suggest that they are doing the latter. For they are taking over such words from their use in debates between theists and atheists about whether there is a God, in explicating what the disagreement between them amounts to. The theist, if his belief that there is a God is to have any content, if he is to argue with and convert others, must have a grasp of and be able to explain what that belief amounts to, and so must those whom he seeks to convince of the truth thereof. And so the theist explains that to say that there is a God is to say that there is an all-wise, all-powerful, perfectly good, and free creator and sustainer of the world—or something similar thereto. But this exposition would not amount to anything, and so the claim that there is a God would not have any substance, unless the words in terms of which it is expounded are understood by the theist by a route which does not already assume the existence of such a being. For only so would theist and atheist know about what they disagreed.

[12] Thomas, 'Univocity', 94.

Analogy in Creeds

While the divine predicates—'good', 'wise', 'powerful'—are used of God in their literal senses, there seem to me plenty of words which are used (in my sense) analogically of God. First, there are words which imply passion. God is said to be or to be likely to be angry', to 'feel pity', and to 'love'.[13] All of these verbs of emotion seem to involve (as part of their meaning) not just belief (e.g. with anger, that someone has done wrong) and a tendency to action (i.e. acting unless there is reason not to act—e.g. with anger, acting to hurt the wrongdoer unless there is reason not to do so), but also desire (inclination to action despite contrary reason), and even bodily sensation. No one is really angry or feels pity or love unless they feel these things in their stomach or breasts or bowels or behind the eyes; and have an urge, hard to control, to vent their anger or show their pity and love. But traditional Christian theology has affirmed vigorously and constantly that God has no body, and has no inclination to act contrary to reason; and hence the use of such words in official Christian pronouncements must be so interpreted that they do not carry these latter elements of meaning. 'Angry' in both 'God is angry' and 'John is angry' has as synonyms both 'enraged' and 'furious' (though in the former sentence these words are of course also only used by analogy with their literal use), but only 'angry' in 'God is angry' has as a synonym 'believes wrong has been done and seeks to right it unless there is reason not to do so', and only 'angry' in 'John is angry' has as a synonym 'believes wrong has been done and feels an urge to right it'. Other words used analogically of God are words which imply the use of bodily organs to acquire knowledge or perform actions. God is said to 'see' the weakness of men, or to 'put away from' them dangerous things.[14] By using these verbs of God, we discount any implication that sensations or bodily organs are involved. 'Sees' of God is synonymous with 'is aware of'; and of course it is used sometimes of humans also in just this sense, as when someone is said to 'see' the connection between the premises and conclusion of an argument; but it

[13] I take examples this time from prayers of the Book of Common Prayer. God is addressed as 'merciful' in the collect for St John the Evangelist's Day. The Palm Sunday collect speaks of God's 'tender love' towards mankind. The general confession in the Communion service speaks of 'provoking most justly thy [i.e. God's] wrath and indignation against us', and the Litany prays to God: 'be not angry with us forever.'

[14] The BCP collect for the Second Sunday in Lent addressed God who 'sees that we have no power of ourselves to help ourselves'; and the collect for the Eighth Sunday after Trinity asks God to 'put away from us all hurtful things'.

is not used of humans in this sense with respect to things readily detectable by bodily eyes. More usually of humans, 'see' is synonymous with 'is aware of by means of visual sensations (acquired through use of eyes)'. When God is said to 'put away' from humans dangerous things 'put away' is synonymous with 'remove', but not with remove by means of 'bodily movement'.

Clearly theology, in talking of God as 'good' and 'wise', and acting in the world, is using a whole system of person predicates. It is using the model of a person for its thought about God, in the way that science uses the model of a wave for its thought about light (as I analysed it, in Chapter 4). God is often said to be 'personal' and Father, Son, and Holy Spirit are described as the three 'persons' of the Trinity. But theology normally makes a very sharp difference between God the Holy Trinity (and/or each 'person' of the Trinity—I take this extra clause as read in the remaining passages below where its insertion would be appropriate) on the one hand and human persons on the other which leads me to say not merely that it is claiming that God is a very different sort of person from us, but that he is only a 'person' in an analogical sense. This difference is that it seems to me to be part of the meaning of 'person' in the literal sense that the identity of a person is independent of gain or loss of beliefs or powers. I do not cease to be the same person simply in virtue of losing some beliefs or some powers; personal identity persists through (at any rate minor) alterations even of personality; it is what underlies these accidental features. But on the traditional view of God, his omniscience (knowing all true propositions) and omnipotence (being able to do anything logically possible) are properties essential to his identity. He would cease to be the same 'person' if he ceased to be omniscient or omnipotent. And not merely that but, if a being ceased to be omnipotent or omniscient, that being would never at any time have been God. A letter of Pope Leo makes this point by asserting that 'whatever in any way is worthily ascribed to God is not an attribute of him, but his essence'.[15] And that means that, despite the fact that clearly theology supposes him to be a person in much the same sense of 'person' as humans are persons, he cannot be a 'person' in quite the same sense. 'Person' must be being used analogi-

---

[15] Denzinger 285. This kind of claim, which is standard in medieval philosophy, can be read not in the way in which I have read it—so as to affirm that possession of certain properties is essential to the identity of the individual who is God—but so as to affirm that God is the *same thing as* each of his properties (e.g. omniscience) and so that they are the same thing as each other. This I find very difficult to make any sense of.

cally with respect to God.[16] So we need to talk about God not merely
with the model of a person but with some other model, for instance of a
law of nature or a supreme form which could not ever lose the powers
or ways of behaving it has. If the law of gravity that all bodies attract
each other with forces proportional to mm'/r^2 was really a *fundamental*
law of nature (and not a regularity which only holds under certain
conditions, or one which holds only because God allows it to hold),
then it must hold for eternity. Any regularity in nature which ceased to
hold or changed its mode of operation would never have been a fundamental principle governing nature. We need a model of God as a law of
nature or supreme form to qualify the model of God as a person, in the
way in which, as we saw in Chapter 4, the particle model qualifies the
wave model of light, to give us our limited understanding of what God
is like.

Metaphor in Creeds

Senses of words analogical with the literal sense are often there in the
language, ready to be used, listed in dictionaries. Even when a word is
used in a certain analogical sense only with reference to God, it may
have been used frequently in that sense in the past, and so the sense
may be available for use in new theological discourse. Metaphorical
senses (in my sense) are not however already there in dictionaries; they
are created by a context. Like literature and science, theology is full of
metaphors: sentences and parts thereof which in a particular context of
a creed uttered or a book written at a certain time against a certain
philosophical, scientific, and theological background have a meaning
other than a normal meaning, and so constituent words which have a
sense other than an established sense. Metaphor flourishes even in
creeds, and although some new uses of words in creeds tend to utilize a
recently established sense or to create a new sense with which the words
are then used in other sentences, this does not always happen. Creeds
still contain living metaphors, such as the Nicene Creed's statement
about Christ that he is 'light from light' (φῶς ἐκ φωτός).[17] In the literal
sense Jesus Christ, the second person of the Holy Trinity, is clearly not
light. He does not consist of photons of zero mass, such as stream out of

---

[16] I argue this point about the analogical use of 'person' with respect to God in my *The
Coherence of Theism* (Clarendon Press, 1977), ch. 14.
[17] Denzinger 150.

the light bulb when you turn on the light. Nor is he being said to be something similar thereto. 'Light' does have an analogical meaning: as when we talk of some discovery 'throwing light' on something else, we mean that it helps us to understand the something else, in the way that light helps us to see things. But when Christ is said to be Light, something much more is meant than that he helps us to 'see' deep things as they really are—although that is certainly involved. It is rather that he is everywhere at once; just as light seems to travel from one place to another with infinite velocity. As the original light seems to spread itself without ceasing to illuminate somewhere else, and so there seems not to be just a finite quantity of it; so too there is no limit to the power and wisdom of Christ. As Christ is 'light from light' so he derives his illuminating power, as one candle is lit by another without the latter losing any of its illuminating power, from God the Father who also is Light. All of that is involved; but to understand it, we need to do more than look up φῶς in a Greek dictionary. We need to know the background of Christian thought about light in biblical passages (especially Christ's claim in St John's Gospel to be 'the light of the world'[18]), the role of the sun in some pagan religions, the use of 'light' in Gnostic thought, and the beliefs of ancient science about light. Knowing all that, we see the point of the metaphor.

Talk in all creeds of the first person of the Holy Trinity as 'the Father' and of the second person as 'the Son', who was 'begotten' by 'the Father', 'not made', may also be classified as metaphorical; although this use of 'Father' was perhaps sufficiently well established and clear in Jewish thought to be regarded as analogical.

In a literal sense obviously the first person of the Trinity is not supposed to be a 'Father' of anyone—he does not beget anyone through sexual generation, for he has no body. There is no literal 'begetting', and 'the Son' is not literally begotten. The first person is the Father because he is the source of being of all things, especially of his loved and chosen people Israel, and of his 'Son'; he loves and cares for these, and educates and trains Israel. In all these respects he is like a human father in his relation to a human son, and hence the appropriateness of the analogy. The 'Son', however, unlike all other things whom God the Father keeps in being is 'begotten, not made'. A comparison is being made of the relation of the first to the second person of the Trinity, with 'begetting' to be contrasted with 'making'. But what comparison?

---

[18] John 8: 12. See too crucially the claims made about light in the Easter Eve Liturgy.

Hardly the comparison that someone else, a 'Mother', is co-responsible for second person. But to know which comparison, what is the point of the metaphor, we need to be aware of the general Greek belief that, in human generation, the mother contributed no 'matter' (the existence of the human 'egg' was unknown) to the early embryo, but only 'form'; she provided a womb in which the sperm grew into the foetus and the foetus into the body. Hence the child was formed entirely out of the matter of the father. The universe is not formed from the 'stuff' of God the Father, nor is Israel; but God the Son is, claims the Nicene Creed—and it makes this claim by saying that he is 'begotten, not made'. Hence he is more appropriately called a 'Son' than is any human or other creature loved and sustained by God.[19]

Metaphors are illuminating, but metaphors are also vague; their boundaries are unclear. Both the 'Catholics', who held that the Son was eternally begotten by the Father (i.e. was begotten out of time, or in some way always being begotten), and the Arians, who held that the Son was begotten at a moment of time, held that the Son was begotten. The more literal rendering of the metaphor of 'begetting' would seem to favour the Arian position, that there was a time at which the Son 'was not' and so that he was a being inferior to God the Father, as the use of 'Son' would also suggest.[20] So further credal statements were needed to make clear the boundaries of the metaphor, if talk of 'Son' and 'begetting' were to be given a Catholic sense; and such further statements were forthcoming in abundance.

Other examples of metaphor in the 'Nicene Creed', I suggest, are its expression of belief in Christ who 'came down' (κατελθόντα) 'from the heavens' (ἐκ των οὐρανων), 'ascended into the heavens', and 'sitteth on the right hand' of the Father. Taken literally all these claims entail spatial location and movement for the heavenly Christ. Yet Christ is

---

[19] Just these kinds of point about the value and limits of talk of 'Father', 'Son', and 'begetting' are made by, among other authors, St Hilary, *De Trinitate*, 6. 9 and 7. 28. Thus: 'Comparisons drawn from human experience are not of perfect application to the mysteries of divine power. When One is born from One, God born from God, the circumstances of human birth enable us to apprehend the fact; but a birth which presupposes intercourse and conception and time and travail can give us no clue to the divine method' (6. 9).

[20] For the point that the orthodox had to interpret Scripture, which was the source of the words 'Father', 'Son', and 'beget' used in the formulation of the doctrine of the Trinity, in a less literal sense than did the Arians, and that the champion of the orthodox, St Athanasius, gradually became aware of this and stressed it, see P. R. Ackroyd and C. F. Evans (eds.), *The Cambridge History of the Bible*, i (Cambridge University Press, 1970), 447–8.

said to be 'true God' in the very same creed. That God has no spatial location is common currency among the Fathers and these claims have to be read in the light of that currency.[21] A more explicit account of the relation of God the Son to space is given in the declaration of the Lateran Council of AD 649 that Christ was *circumscriptum corpore, incircumscriptum deitate*[22]—that is, there was a spatial boundary to his human body, but none to his deity. So before taking a human nature and so a body he cannot literally have been in one place rather than another; and so 'came down' cannot be read literally. Yet there is no obvious available analogical sense, and so we must construe it metaphorically. 'Descending' is going lower, and by the customs of the ancient world as well as ours a low position indicates smallness of status and power. Christ's 'descent' was his taking on human limitations, including a human body with the limitations on what could be done and known through it. So too, therefore, 'from the heavens' must be read metaphorically as 'from being God alone'. Analogously also, therefore, belief in Christ who 'ascended' (ἀνελθόντα) 'into the heavens' must be regarded as belief that he divested himself of those limitations; if Christ still has his human body after the Ascension it does not limit his knowledge and mode of operation in the way (whatever way that was) it did so previously. However, if he does still have that body, as the Catholic tradition affirmed, clearly it must have a spatial place; but the parallel with the earlier phrase ('came down from the heavens') suggests that the 'ascended into the heavens' is not to be read as making a claim about the post-Ascension destination of Christ's human body, since the earlier phrase is not making a claim about spatial movement at all. All of this is of course compatible with a belief that Jesus symbolized his 'ascending to the heavens' by rising into the sky (the literal οὐρανός),[23] being covered by a cloud[24] at the end of his earthly ministry, as is claimed by St Luke's Gospel and the Acts of the Apostles. But the later occurrences of οὐρανός in the creed cannot be taken in the same way as its earlier occurrence—at least not if the creed is to be read consistently with the other things that those theologians who affirmed that creed also affirmed.

This interpretation is reinforced by the claim that the ascended Christ is 'seated at the right hand of the Father' (καθεζόμενον ἐν δεξιᾷ τον Πατρός). As the Father has no spatial location, he has no

---

[21] Origen denies that 'the Son of God is contained in any place' (*De principiis*, 4. 1).
[22] Denzinger 504.　　[23] Luke 24: 51.　　[24] Acts 1: 9.

right hand in a literal sense. But there is a clear metaphorical sense, suggested by the customs of the ancient world that the place at the right of the president of a banquet is the place for an honoured guest of equal status or slightly lower status, that Christ returned to exercise his glory and reign. This phrase and the previous phrase are taken over without being the subject of any credal disputes from 1 Peter 3: 22 which speaks of Christ 'who is on the right hand of God, having gone into heaven', the way of expression being ultimately derived from Psalm 110: 1, 'The Lord said unto my Lord: sit thou at my right hand, until I make thine enemies my footstool.' These expressions might have had a more literal meaning in earlier contexts. But the metaphorical understanding of Christ's session at the right hand in the century of credal formation was clearly expounded by Augustine.[25]

Which uses of words in which credal documents are literal, which analogical, and which metaphorical is a matter for detailed analysis in each case. The analysis will be an analysis of which meanings can be plausibly ascribed to creeds given the other beliefs of those who wrote and subsequently affirmed the creeds. Some of my brief analyses above might be open to challenge, but I give them as plausible illustrations of the prevalence of the usages in creeds which we may pick out with modern understandings of 'analogy' and 'metaphor'.

The Fathers of the first few Christian centuries were well aware that the Bible was sometimes to be interpreted in ways other than the literal (as I shall discuss in the next chapter), but they hardly discussed the issue of how far credal and other official Church declarations were subject to difficulties of interpretation arising from the inadequacies of human language. There are occasional references in the New Testament to the inadequacy of our understanding of God;[26] and the Fathers do of course sometimes echo these sentiments. But they have no general well articulated doctrine of the inadequacy of human language. There developed however from the sixth century onward a movement which coloured much Christian theology for the next five centuries, the *via negativa*. This, very loosely, claimed that all that could be said about God was what he is *not*, and what were the effects of his actions in the world. We could know nothing about what God was like in himself; and

---

[25] *Treatise on Faith and the Creed*, 7. In the previous chapter, 6, Augustine acknowledges that Christ's human body was taken into Heaven'. He is agnostic about how this is to be read. But he would deny that Christ himself was located spatially only where his human body was located.

[26] (e.g.) 1 Cor. 13: 12.

so all credal claims and prayers were to be read with this restriction. A claim that God is powerful was to be read as a claim that he is not weak; a claim that God is good was to be read as a claim that he is not evil, and so on.

The thinker who began this way of thought in Christian theology (probably deriving it from the fifth-century Neoplatonist Proclus) was Pseudo-Dionysius, the unknown writer who wrote under the name of Dionysius, St Paul's Athenian convert, and whose writings were generally believed for the next few centuries to be those of Dionysius. Although he allowed a place for the positive way, that is, some positive content to God being 'good', 'wise', and so on, he thought it slender in comparison with the negative content.[27] Dionysius' way of thought inspired the ninth-century Irish philosopher John Scotus Eriugena, the lone significant Western philosopher between the sixth-century Boethius and the eleventh-century Anselm; and the theologians of the Eastern Church St Maximus the Confessor[28] and St John Damascene. This powerful current left Christianity with a deep awareness of the inadequacy of human language to express the divine; even when the thirteenth-century philosophers of the West, and especially St Thomas Aquinas, reasserted the availability to man of significant knowledge of the divine, through natural reason and revelation, available in human language. While disagreeing with Aquinas's detailed account of analogy, my sympathies are with his overall approach—that sentences of human language can tell us quite a bit about God; but that they are very inadequate tools for the job. I have given in this chapter an account of how language works to make this possible.[29] If sentences of human language cannot tell us quite a bit about God, there can be no significant propositional revelation. The central Christian claim that there is such revelation must therefore be read in the light of my account.

[27] 'αἱ μὲν ἀποφάσεις ἐπὶ τῶν θείων ἀληθεῖς, αἱ δὲ καταφάσεις ἀνάρμοστοι', 'Negative statements about divine matters are true, while positive statements are incongruous' (Dionysius, *De coelesti hierarchia*, 2. 3 (PG 3: 141)).

[28] Thus Maximus writes that we must think of God as nothing since he is none of the things that are, and as 'everywhere and nowhere' at the same time (*Scholia on De divinis nominibus* (PG 4: 204)).

[29] See Additional Note 9.

10

Bible

The Church which declared that creeds expressed the essence of revelation also declared at least from the second century onwards that Holy Scripture was the paramount vehicle of revelation. I alluded briefly in Chapter 8 to the process by which the Old and New Testaments gradually came to attain a more or less final form by the end of the fourth century AD.

The New Testament had a fairly high view of the divinely inspired status of the Old Testament; thus 2 Timothy 3: 15–16 asserts that 'all Scripture [i.e. the Old Testament] is inspired by God and profitable for teaching, for reproof, for correction and for training in righteousness'. Yet the apparent contrast between some of the teaching of Jesus and that of certain parts of the Old Testament produced some hostility in the Church of the first two centuries towards the Old Testament, culminating in the second-century Marcion's denial that the Old Testament was a Christian book at all. The orthodox reassertion of the Old Testament was led by St Irenaeus, but he stressed the temporary and symbolic nature of certain parts of it. And so, while a very high doctrine of the authority of Scripture emerged—God the Holy Spirit inspired the writing of each bit of it, and all its sentences were true—it went with a view that Scripture was unclear and difficult to understand, and not always to be taken literally. Scripture was 'tricky'. Certainly the creeds came to enshrine the doctrine that God the Holy Spirit 'spoke through the prophets', but the Old Testament could not be understood without the New, and pre-Christian Israel had a limited understanding of the scriptural message. Nor could the whole Bible be understood without the Church's tradition of interpretation. It was the Church's function to declare which books constituted Scripture, and to provide guidance on how it was to be interpreted.

Bearing these points in mind, let us apply to the smallest units of the Bible, then the whole books of the Bible, and then the whole Bible the rules for interpretation of texts generated in Part I, bearing in mind above all how the genre of a work, and who is its author and intended audience, determines how its sentences are to be understood, and in particular how a statement is to be distinguished from its presuppositions, and literal senses are to be distinguished from metaphorical senses.

The Smallest Units of the Bible

The Bible is a big book, composed of many smaller books, most of them woven together out of yet smaller strands of writings, each with a different social and cultural context and a different literary context (embedded in a different religious work) at each stage of its production and subsequent use. The meaning of any sentence within it will therefore depend on which larger unit it is thought of as belonging to; and also on who is the author of that unit. I shall throughout this section make a crucial assumption that the 'author' of each unit is the human author who would be picked out as such by ordinary historical investigation. I shall then consider later what difference it would make to the meaning of what is said if we drop that assumption and suppose that God is the author, speaking through human authors.

So let us begin by going back to the smallest units, the bits of poetry and story and oracle from various sources from which the books of the Bible were put together, the units which do not contain any smaller units which had any life of their own in speech or writing. It was modern 'form criticism' which drew our attention to these smallest units. The Bible scholar, inspired by this movement, seeks to isolate each smallest unit and ask of it what did it mean when it was originally used, orally or, as the case may be, in writing? To answer this the scholar must locate the original social context and the original cultural context (discover the common beliefs of the society). He must identify the unit as belonging to a genre and show what are the conventions for understanding units of that genre. Discovering social and cultural context is not easy, and some of the results of biblical scholars in this area are somewhat speculative. But their problem is a soluble one and, in so far as they can solve it, they can tell us the meaning of the unit as originally used.

The social context will reveal the reference of the terms. If Psalm 21 was originally used as a hymn in a New Year festival for the enthronement of the king in the first Temple, then we know to whom 'the king' refers—the king currently being enthroned. The cultural context enables us to recognize and interpret any metaphorical use of words. Consider Revelation 1: 8, 'I am the Alpha and the Omega, saith the Lord God.' Taken literally, God is making a claim to be identical with each of two different Greek letters. The obvious falsity of what is said directs us to find a metaphorical interpretation.[1] For this we look to beliefs common in the society: that alpha is the first letter of the alphabet and omega the last. This firstness of alpha and the lastness of omega suggest that what is being said by the human author of this part of the Book of Revelation is that God claims to be the first thing on which other things depend and after which they follow; and that the final purpose of things depends on their relation to God, who will determine what ultimately happens to them.

Knowledge of the cultural context will enable us to recognize instances of different literary genres and thus to see to what extent the truth-value of the whole is a function of the truth-value of its constituent sentences. However, the literary genres to which biblical units belong are ones unfamiliar to modern men. To detect the literary genre we must compare the unit in question with similar units of Middle Eastern literature, and see how these functioned in the society. Much more hard work by biblical scholars is necessary before we can be reasonably sure which genres have truth-value and what are the criteria for their truth, and maybe we can never make more than a reasonable guess at this. Thus, to use the example discussed in Chapter 4, biblical scholars dispute whether a parable has an allegorical interpretation: that is, whether each referring term, predicate, and so forth of each parable has an interpretation peculiar to that text (e.g. that in the parable of the sower (Mark 4: 3–9) Jesus is the sower, the 'seed' is the Gospel message, and so on). If so, individual sentences of a parable will have a truth-value. Alternatively, the parable as a whole may have a truth-value, though individual sentences do not. Or, finally, the parable may not have a truth-value at all, merely be 'inspiring' or 'deep'.

Even when and if we are clear about the truth criteria of different biblical genres, it is often far from clear to which genre a particular unit belongs; and again, much scholarly work is required to answer such questions. Isaiah 5: 1–7 is an obvious parable, but what of Daniel 6 (the story of Daniel and his friends in the burning fiery furnace)? Is this

---

[1] For a full discussion of some of the tests which can be used to detect when words of some biblical fragment are being used metaphorically, see G. B. Caird, *The Language and Imagery of the Bible* (Duckworth, 1980), ch. 11.

supposed to be a true historical record, or is it a parable? If the latter, does it have an obvious message which can be assessed as true, or is even this inappropriate? Locating a sentence as part of a hymn means that it is only to be assessed as true or false in so far as it contributes to the theological message of the hymn; the latter alone is true or false. If the hymn 'There is green hill far away' is to have a truth-value, it is not one which would be affected by discovering that the Hill of Calvary is normally brown or that the hymn was originally written in Israel. And so likewise with Psalm 105, an obvious hymn. Verse 18 reports of the captured Joseph: 'His feet they hurt with fetters; he was laid in chains of iron.' Genesis does not give explicitly these details of Joseph's imprisonment. But it is obviously irrelevant to the truth of the psalm whether he was bound with chains of iron, or some other metal, or rope. Yet whether he was imprisoned at all is, I suggest, relevant to the truth. Crucial issues, however, concern which biblical units are hymns in this respect. My view is that Genesis 1 is a hymn; in that case dates and order are no more relevant to its truth than they are for 'All things bright and beautiful'.

Another important kind of unit of which the Bible, and especially the Old Testament, is built is the prophecy; and which modern genre is closest to the genre of biblical prophecy is not at all clear. The crucial issue is, was a 'prophecy' intended to be unconditional (this is what will happen, whatever you do) or conditional (this is what will happen unless you do something to stop it)? Twentieth-century prophecies of political disaster sometimes have an unexpressed clause ('unless you do something about it') and there is plenty of evidence internal to the Old Testament that biblical prophecies were normally (but not always) so understood.[2] Again, how we are to understand Jeremiah's prophecy to Zedekiah (on behalf of the Lord) (Jer. 33: 17–18), 'David shall never want a man to sit on the throne of the house of Israel; neither shall the priests, the Levites, want a man before me to offer burnt offerings, and to burn oblations and to do sacrifice', depends on whether we are to regard it as false if and only if there is no king of Israel or the priests do not continue to do sacrifice, or as false if and only if these things do not happen even though Israel behaves well.

Cultural context is also crucial for distinguishing what is said from the presuppositions in terms of which is cast. The sentences of the

---

[2] See Ezek. 33: 14–15 for explicit affirmation that prophecies of doom were to be so interpreted. See also the whole story of Jonah.

Bible often have false scientific or historical presuppositions. They often, for example, presuppose that the Earth is flat, square, and stationary, covered with a dome across which the sun, moon, and stars travel by day and night. But the cultural context reveals these as common presuppositions of the society, and the social context typically reveals the main message as not to communicate these but something else by means of them. The falsity of the presuppositions does not, therefore (by the argument of Chapter 2), affect the truth-value of the sentence which uses them. Psalm 104 praises God for many marvels of nature including that 'he laid the foundations of the Earth, that it should not be moved forever' (104: 5). Now the earth has no 'foundations' in some other body, as the Psalmist supposed. But what he was getting at was the Earth is not wobbly, you can build on it, it is firm; and he expressed the claim that God is responsible for this, using the presuppositions of his culture. If God is indeed responsible for this stability, the sentence is true. Genesis 8: 2 tells us that at the end of the flood 'the windows of heaven were stopped'. Heaven has no windows out of which the rain comes, but the quoted sentence is just the author's way of saying, within the presuppositions of his culture, that the rain ceased. If it did, the sentence is true. More generally, the cultural context of the cosmological beliefs common in the Middle East in the first millennium BC, as shown by the similar creation stories in circulation there, helps us to recognize as the messages of the opening chapters of Genesis those aspects of them which diverge significantly from those common presuppositions. Thus other creation stories always pictured the act of divine making of the Earth as shaping a pre-existent matter; Genesis 1: 1 seems to affirm that there was no matter before God acted.[3]

Individual Books of the Bible

So much for the criteria of truth of the smallest units of the Bible as originally uttered or written. But often compilers put the units together into larger units with the addition of connecting verses until we have whole strands, such as the J, E, D, and P sources in the Pentateuch,

[3] 'It is correct to say that the verb bara, "create", contains the idea both of complete effortlessness and *creatio ex nihilo*, since it is never connected with any statement of the material' (G. Von Rad, *Genesis*, trans. J. H. Marks (SCM Press, 3rd rev ed., 1972), 49.

having continuity and unity. These were put together into the individual books of the Old and New Testaments as we know them (although there are clearly a few books which were written straight off by one author). I assume, as in the last section, that the author or compiler is the human author or compiler.

We saw in Chapter 4 how units change their meaning when inserted into larger wholes. This is because the insertion into a larger whole gives the sentences of the unit a different literary context, a different social context (the author is now the author of the larger whole, and the work is addressed to a different audience), and a different cultural context (the culture is now that of the new author and his audience). Although there can be few examples in modern literature of a whole formed by sewing together units of some antiquity written by different authors and groups, the examples of Chapter 4 illustrate what happens to the meaning of the units under these circumstances.

We noted there first the process of quotation. In the Bible the prophetic books contain 'oracles', namely separate speeches, which are in the edited book said to have been spoken by (for example) Jeremiah at a certain place (Jer. 7: 1–2). In the case of the Bible, however, the process of quotation seldom makes any difference to what is asserted, since almost the only speakers for whom a full oracle which existed previously as a separate unit is quoted are those supposed to be inspired to speak the truth, and so ones whose speeches are endorsed by the compiler. There are, however, crucial biblical examples where the addition of a preface or appendix changes the whole tone of the book. The whole tone of the Book of Ecclesiastes is changed by the addition of certain verses, especially at the end (12: 13–14), which purport to summarize its message but really give it a radically new look. A sceptical book becomes a God-centred book. But, as with the Osiander preface, if we take the whole book including that preface, that is the way the book is to be read—that is the meaning it has when that preface is seen as an integral part of it. Another very similar example is 2 Esdras. 2 Esdras 3–14 seems to be a Jewish non-Christian work; but chapters 1–2 and 15–16 are Christian works. Adding Chapters 1–2 and 15–16 to chapters 3–14 changes the tone of the latter. Its pessimistic outlook about the fate of humanity is transformed by the good news of Christ and the Church, and encouragement to Christians to resist bravely in time of persecution.

Footnotes are not a device known to ancient writers. Their substitute for a correcting or amplifying footnote is a verse correcting the previous verse, or a connecting verse saying that the next paragraph fills out the previous one. Daniel 12: 12 seems to be a verse correcting the previous verse in respect to the number of days until the 'end'. An interesting example of a connecting verse is Genesis 2: 4*a*. This has the function, according to B. S. Childs,[4] of explaining that the narrative of Genesis 2, which in various ways contradicts that of Genesis 1 (one example is that plants seem to be created before man in Genesis 1, but after man in Genesis 2—see Gen. 2: 5, 7, and 9), is to be read as a detailed filling out in some respects of Genesis 1.

Correction of verses so as to make the whole consistent or to have a different message is not a process which is obvious unless we have the original, and it is most in evidence in the corrections to St Mark (or his source) made in the Gospels of St Matthew and St Luke (e.g. the insertion of the clause 'except for fornication' in Matt. 19: 9; Matt. 19: 3–11 seems to derive from Mark 10: 2–12). Sometimes the correction seems to derive from a misunderstanding of the original, for example by taking literally what was not meant to be taken too literally (e.g. Matthew taking literally Mark's report that at the Crucifixion 'the veil of the temple was rent in twain from the top to the bottom'[5]).

Changing the context of the units and sewing them together into a literary work has different effects in different places. One interesting example concerns the psalms. Many of them originally had a social context (in the rituals of the first Temple) which was lost when they came to form a collection of hymns for private or synagogic use. The compiler of the Book of Psalms must have supposed many of the psalms to have meanings (e.g. as expressions of personal devotion) other than their original meaning.

Just as the genre of the individual unit is hard for the modern reader to recognize, so is the genre of the biblical book. In my view the Books of Ruth and Jonah are parables; and these parables do not have a truth which consists in the correspondence of each of their sentences to historical facts.[6] But they are easy cases, and the conventions of other books of the Old and New Testaments are much more difficult to

---

[4] See B. S. Childs, *Introduction to the Old Testament as Scripture* (SCM Press, 2nd ed., 1983), 150. See also J. Barton, *Reading the Old Testament*, (Darton, Longman, & Todd, 1984), 50–1.

[5] See the discussion of this and other examples in Caird, *Language and Imagery*, 184–6 and 213–15.

[6] Perhaps the most openly fictional work is the Book of Judith. See the discussion in Caird, *Language and Imagery*, 206.

detect. The Book of Job is obviously concerned with the problem of evil, but is it a treatise which seeks to provide a theodicy, or a work which seeks to stimulate the philosophical imagination, or a work which records the story and perplexity of a particular individual? In the first and third cases its truth-value is a function of the truth-value of (some of) the constituent sentences, in the second case not.

Apocalyptic—Daniel and Revelation—raises in an acute form the problem of just how literally biblical writing was intended to be taken. My own view, for what it is worth, is that dates were intended to be taken literally but talk of beasts and lightning is poetic. Daniel is concerned to predict an end which will happen an exact specified number of days after recognizable events. Whereas fairly clearly Revelation's talk of horses and dragons is symbolic. The kind of 'end' or 'day of the Lord' which some prophets are predicting is often of a lesser kind than the end of the world.[7] The description of chaos in Jeremiah 4: 23–6 is simply a prophecy of the fall of Jerusalem—bad enough, but only a kind of 'end', not the 'end of the world'. On the other hand the final chapters of Revelation, though not necessarily some of the earliest ones, do predict the end of the world. But unfortunately the exact conventions for reading apocalyptic are very unclear to the modern scholar.

A crucial issue of understanding many biblical books concerns the statements of purported authorship contained in them. The 'Screwtape Letters' were not written by Screwtape, although in a sense they purport to be. Our assessment of any truth-value which they contain will have no tendency to rule them out as containing falsity when it is discovered that they were written by C. S. Lewis. This is because they are what I shall call manifest pseudepigraphs, that is, works which in the cultural context of their production would not have been thought by their readers to have been written by their alleged 'author', nor would their real author have thought that the readers would think that they had been; the works belong to a genre in which attribution of authorship is fictional and so has no truth-value. Are any biblical books manifest pseudepigraphs? I do not know, but 2 Esdras and Tobit are to my mind candidates for being manifest pseudepigraphs. There is however clearly another convention at work in the attribution of authorship in many biblical books. If some of a work is literally written or dictated by an original author, then other material written by disciples

[7] See the discussion of this ibid. 256–60.

applying his teaching to new situations may be tacked on to the original material and attributed to the original author. Such attributions would be regarded as true if the teaching was in the spirit of and inspired by the original author. Hence oracles not pronounced by the original Isaiah were tacked on to his oracles. More generally there grew up an Israelite tradition that as the Law began with Moses, who first transmitted the ten commandments from God to Israel in the wilderness, and psalm writing began with David, and 'wisdom' writing began with Solomon, that all law was to be attributed to Moses, all psalms to David, and all wisdom literature to Solomon. At an early stage what was going on was clearly understood: 1 Samuel 30: 25 reports the promulgation by David (*not* Moses) of a new law.[8] But the conventions were thoroughly misunderstood by many in later centuries, who came to suppose that Moses, as the author of Deuteronomy, the 'fifth book of Moses', wrote in the last chapter thereof the description of his own burial. Books or parts thereof attributed correctly in accordance with these conventions to an original inspiring author, although not literally written or dictated by him, I will call traditional pseudepigraphs.

What is unclear is just what are the limits of traditional pseudepigraphy at different Old and New Testament times. Does the new writing in some sense have to be tacked on to a writing of the original author in order to be ascribed to him? Or do there have to be writings of an original author at all? Is it enough that some original teacher provided the inspiration? One piece of evidence which we have from the first decade of the third century AD is Tertullian's comment, in discussing the authorship of the four Gospels, that 'it may well seem that the works which disciples publish belong to their masters'.[9] For example, even if St Matthew did not write a word of St Matthew's Gospel, it can still be truly attributed to him, so long as it was indirectly inspired by him. There is no reason to suppose that conventions were different in the first century. What is unclear is whether the incorporation of historical details which make it look as though the work was not merely inspired by, but actually, literally written or dictated by, the original teacher is the incorporation of false material; or whether that is permissible (i.e. such material does not have

---

[8] See ibid. 205–6. Likewise within the Book of Proverbs, whose opening verse describes them as proverbs of Solomon, are to be found subheadings indicating that proverbs from other sources have been tacked on—e.g. Prov. 30: 1 and 31: 1.

[9] *Against Marcion*, 4. 5.

a truth-value any more than do any personal details about Screwtape contained in his 'letters') because what the disciple is doing is writing not merely in the tradition of the original teacher but in his style and so writing what he would have written if he had been alive at the new time. I do not know the answer to this question, and I do not think that most experts do either. If the incorporation of historical material of this type was not permissible, then St Paul's second Epistle to Timothy and his Epistle to Titus *may* contain false material. These letters were probably not written by St Paul in the literal sense or dictated by him; yet, unlike the first Epistle to Timothy or the Epistle to the Ephesians, they contain personal material which implies that St Paul was the literal author or dictator. This personal material may however be fragments of some other letter written by St Paul. In saying that the letters contain falsity I mean that they do so as letters on their own, not necessarily as parts of a whole Bible; I shall come to that issue in due course. And I do not imply that the author was seeking to deceive; he may have understood the conventions of traditional pseudepigraphy more widely than did his culture. But it is the public conventions which determine how a public document is to be understood. And my main point is the fairly clear one that the work of disciples in biblical times could without falsity be attributed to the original teacher—so long as it was inspired by him and accorded with his teaching.[10]

It is for biblical scholars to explain to us the conventions (including the conventions for attribution of authorship) for interpreting the books at the time they were written, and thereby to analyse their truth-conditions. Those conditions are sometimes far from clear, yet crucial for understanding the works.

Because the Book of Jonah is, it seems to me, an easy case, it is worth spelling out exactly what it did mean, as originally written and circulated on its own. It was probably written and circulated in the fifth or fourth century BC, soon after some of those Jews exiled to Babylon had returned to Palestine and the state of Judah had been reconstituted. The book is anonymous; no author is stated. Its story concerns Jonah, an Israelite prophet of the pre-exilic age (referred to in 2 Kgs. 14: 25)

---

[10] E. Schillebeecx (*Ministry*, trans. J. Bowden (SCM Press, 1981), 12) claims that this was the way in which the leaders of a church, after the death of its apostolic founder, emphasized the continuity of their teaching with his—by publishing it in gospels and epistles attributed to him. The most recent full-length treatment of the whole issue of pseudepigraphy in the Bible is David G. Meade, *Pseudepigraphy and Canon* (Eerdmans, 1987).

whom God told to go to preach to Nineveh, an enormous city, capital of the then superpower Assyria, but who, on receiving this command, fled instead in the opposite direction, taking a boat to Tarshish. A storm at sea led to Jonah being thrown overboard and swallowed by a whale; which, after Jonah in misery had called on God, vomited him up on to dry land. The call to preach to Nineveh however came again and this time Jonah heard it. He preached that Nineveh would be destroyed because of its sins. 'Yet forty days and Nineveh shall be overthrown' (3: 4). But all Nineveh repented genuinely, and God did not destroy it. Jonah however was very bitter that his prophecy had not been fulfilled, and he sulked. But God reminded him of the goodness of pity—Jonah became sorry on behalf of a gourd which had provided shadow for him, but was destroyed by an east wind—and so God said to him, 'Should I not spare Nineveh, that great city, wherein are more than sixscore thousand persons that cannot discern between their left hand and their right hand; and also much cattle?' (4: 11).

Now the ancient world was hardly unfamiliar with fictional stories, nor in particular was Israel unfamiliar with parables—we have already noted Isaiah 5: 1–7. The story of Jonah has obviously legendary elements, it picks up on no known traditions, and contains several very clear moral messages. In its original context it must be a parable. That being clear some of its moral messages become obvious to any reader with a minimum knowledge of the context in which it was written. At least these moral messages are very clearly there: do not try to run away from your vocation; Israel has a vocation to preach to the Gentile world; God may tell prophets to preach immediate destruction, but God is only too willing to rescind threatened destruction if hearers repent; and the proper response to repentance by others is joy, not sulking that they have not been made to suffer. And there are, I think, also one or two other less obvious messages.

I have written that the Book of Jonah is a parable and that this is an easy case for assignment of genre. I have a suspicion however that one reason why it is difficult to assign many other Old Testament books to modern genres, such as the genre of parable, is that biblical writers and their immediate readers do not always make the kind of sharp literal/metaphorical distinctions which we try to make today. Did the Yahwist (the compiler of the J-strand of the first five books of the Old Testament), or even the compiler of the Book of Genesis, see himself as producing a book saying that Genesis 11: 1–9 (the story of the Tower of Babel) was literally true? I am inclined to think that the Yahwist made no sharp division between historical and metaphorical accounts of the human condition. He thought that the divisions among men, symbolized by the divisions of language, were caused by humans exalting themselves above their status (possibly symbolized by towers which the Babylonians built) and so he incorporated in his book an account of roughly how this came about. But, I suspect, he never asked himself the question of just how rough 'roughly' was: namely did humans once have literally the same language or similar languages or was it merely that they got on with each other without quarrelling? Was their pride manifested literally in tower-building or was his talk of towers just the author's way of representing pomp and big temples? The compiler and his audience did not, I suspect, even ask these questions, or at any rate attempt to answer them. My reason for this suspicion is that while the compiler sets his various sections including this one in somewhat of a historical sequence (suggesting a concern with literal history), he makes no attempt to make the separate stories fit together: Genesis 11: 1 assumes that the human race is living together in one place whereas the previous chapter (some of which belongs to the J-strand) had given an account of how the descendants of Noah had given rise to various different races living in different places.[11] This treatment suggests that the compiler regarded the different bits as it were as describing in a rough and picturesque way different aspects of history. Now my account may be quite mistaken. Fortunately not a great deal turns on this. There are other biblical books whose genre is far more obvious—for example Jonah or 2 Samuel (simple history) —and so we can get a general picture of the progress of thought in ancient Israel. And how Genesis 11 is to be understood in the context of a Christian Bible will turn out to depend on very different considerations from that of its original genre.

The Whole Bible

So much for the truth-conditions of individual books of the Bible, considered on their own. In analysing these, I made a crucial assumption that the authors of these books were the ordinary human individuals or groups who compiled the books. But what the Church proclaimed as Holy Scripture were not individual books, let alone the

---

[11] On all this see Von Rad, *Genesis*, 147–55.

units out of which they were made, but the whole collection. Putting the books together into a whole Bible involved giving them a change of context and, in consequence, by processes similar to those involved in the formation of an individual book, a change of meaning.

The process produced a change of literary context: what were before books on their own became parts of a big book. And it also produced a change of social and cultural context, but just what the change was depends on who we suppose to be the author of the whole Bible and who was its intended audience. For, as we have seen, it is the social context and the cultural presuppositions of the author and his audience which dictate how the book is to be interpreted. The Church put the Bible together, but it did so by selecting books deriving from prophets or apostles in which were recorded what in its view was God's revelation through them to man. God, in the Church's view, was the ultimate author of the Bible—working, no doubt, through human writers with their own idiosyncrasies of style, but all the same inspiring the individual books. What the Church proclaimed with respect to the Bible was not just 'here is a book which we have found and recognized as true', but 'here is a book which we have found and recognized as inspired by God and so as true'.

This view of God as the 'ultimate author' of the Bible divides, of course, into various views, from one which sees his contribution as the sole author through one which sees him as the coauthor along with the human authors to one which sees him as merely providing background inspiration which sometimes was and sometimes was not followed.[12] However, in order to explore the consequences of a simple position, I shall work, to begin with, with the strong view that God was the author of the Bible in the sense that he was the sole author. He ensured that the message of each of its sentences was as it was, while allowing it to be expressed in the styles of its various human authors and compilers. I shall not make any assumption about the way in which that inspiration was exerted—whether by midnight vision to authors, a feeling of guidance to compilers, or an indirect and almost unfelt influence in the

[12] On different modern Protestant ways of understanding the 'inspiration' of the Bible, and defence of a preferred such way (a moderately weak one), see W. J. Abraham, *The Divine Inspiration of Holy Scripture* (Oxford University Press, 1981). For the understanding of 'inspiration' in the Fathers, see J. N. D. Kelly, *Early Christian Doctrines* (A. & C. Black, 5th ed., 1977), 60–4. The First Vatican Council affirmed that the Church recognized books as Scripture in virtue of their prior inspiration; the inspiration existed prior to its recognition (Denzinger 3006).

community which formed the views of authors and compilers.[13] Fathers, scholastics, and reformers did tend to assume that each biblical book had only one human author, and that the method of inspiration was a fairly direct one.

After exploring this strong view, I shall then comment on the consequences of modifying that view. We shall see that the view would have to be modified a great deal before it made any very great difference to the way in which the text is to be interpreted.

We need to know, in order to know a book's social context, as well as who was the author, who was the intended audience of the book. For, among other things, it is the cultural context of beliefs which he and they share which normally determine which sentences are to be taken metaphorically and which literally. So for whom was the Bible written? In the end for the whole world, no doubt. But which group was its most immediate audience, best able to understand its allusions and see the point of its stories? If God was its author, he would presumably ensure that the intended audience was the actual audience. Those who immediately received the Bible would be those for whom it was immediately intended. Hence the audience was the Church to whom the Bible came and through whom its message was proclaimed. But not, presumably, the Church of the fourth century AD alone, who finally assembled it, but the Church of earlier centuries as well, who used most of its books, and the old Israel who used some of its books. And the process of refining biblical texts and of enquiring whether the books of the Apocrypha belong to the Bible never having stopped, there is point in saying that the process of canonization has never quite stopped. Further, in some ways which I shall examine shortly, the fourth-century Church held and, as we shall see, had to hold that the Church of later centuries would sometimes be able better to interpret its message than it could itself. So the answer which I suggest is that, if God is the Bible's author, the Bible's audience was the Church of many centuries, including our own and yet future centuries.

I therefore proceed to investigate the question of the tests for what the Bible does mean if God is its author in the strong sense and the Church of many centuries is its intended audience. This social and cultural context, together with the literary context of each book being

---

[13] For various writers, Catholic and Protestant, who have recently championed a 'social theory' of inspiration, i.e. inspiration of the community in which a work was generated and compiled, see Meade, *Pseudepigraphy*, 209 nn. 21 and 22.

part of the whole Bible, provides a framework making possible disambiguation of what, as it stands, is a very ambiguous text. As it stands, it is a collection of separate books, each having its own unity. There are no connecting verses between the separate books nor any preface which explains the relation of one book to another. There are many obvious inner conflicts—for example, between Israelite leaders (apparently on God's behalf) commending some pretty simple and rough justice in the early books of the Bible, such as the Book of Judges; and Jesus (apparently on God's behalf) commending non-violence in the Gospels. Is the Old Testament with its ritual law and (in parts) rough justice of equal authority with the New? Or is the Old Testament simply the record of man seeing some partial truth, more fully revealed in the New? Or, alternatively, is the New the record of man losing a vision grasped by the Old Testament?

The slogan of Protestant confessions, 'the infallible rule of interpretation of Scripture is the Scripture itself',[14] is quite hopeless. The Bible does not belong to an obvious genre which provides rules for how overall meaning is a function of meaning of individual books. We must have a preface. And if not a preface in the same volume, a short guide by the same author issued in the same way as the Bible, providing disambiguation and publicly seen by the intended audience to do so. Such a guide would be an extension of the original work. And that said, there is of course such a guide. It is the Church's creeds and other tradition of public teaching of items treated as central to the Gospel message. While the Church did not use the phrase of God that he was the 'author' of creeds it certainly taught that God through Christ was the author of the tradition of teaching in the Church deriving from Christ by which Scripture was to be interpreted, and that much of that was encapsulated in short and rigorous form in the creeds and other official Church documents. Allegiance to creeds was regarded as far more important at a far earlier stage of the Church's history than acknowledgement of the authority of Scripture. The Bible as promulgated by the Church must therefore be interpreted in the light of the Church's central teaching as a Christian document.

It was with that understanding that Irenaeus commended and got accepted the Bible as a Christian document. 'Every word' of Scripture 'shall seem consistent' to someone, wrote Irenaeus, 'if he for his part diligently read the Scriptures, in company with those who are

---

[14] See (e.g.) art. 1 of the Westminster Confession.

presbyters in the Church, among whom is the apostolic doctrine'.[15] Tertullian comments that disputes between orthodox and heretics could not be settled by appeal to Scripture, since its limits and meaning were uncertain. The Scriptures belong to the Church. Its teaching must first be identified and that will determine how Scripture is to be interpreted. 'Wherever it shall be manifest that the true Christian rule and faith shall be, there will likewise be the true Scripture and expositions thereof.'[16] And the famous rule of Vincent of Lerins, quoted in Chapter 8, that the faith was what was believed 'always, everywhere and by everyone' was given by him in answer to the question how Scripture should be interpreted. So diverse were the interpretations of Scripture that his rule was a guide as to which should be adopted. Scripture consists of what is approved as such by the universal Church, he wrote elsewhere, and it should be interpreted in accordance with 'Catholic dogma'.[17] And later in Christian history in the same tradition, the Council of Trent spoke of the Church, 'to whom it belongs to judge of the Holy Scriptures'.[18]

The idea that the Bible could be interpreted naked, without a tradition of interpretation which clarified its meaning, is not intrinsically plausible and would not have appealed to many before the fifteenth century. Theology from without always dictated which sentences of the Bible were benchmarks by which other sentences were interpreted.[19] (Of course, as I noted in Chapter 7, one ground for affirming some of the statements in the creeds is some passages of the Bible. But for this purpose these passages are simply regarded as historical records, and do not have authority deriving from their place in the Bible.)

A crucial consequence of this rule was, in view of what Christian teaching said about the superiority of the manifestation of God in Christ to all that had gone before, that in any apparent clash between Old and New Testaments, the New took priority. Passages in the Old Testament in apparent conflict with the New were either to be interpreted as God's temporary and limited revelation superseded by the fuller revelation, or to be interpreted metaphorically.

Thus the Pentateuch, the first five books of the Old Testament, contains many detailed laws about justice and sacrifice, said to have

---

[15] *Adversus Haereses*, 4. 32. 1.   [16] Tertullian, *On Prescription against Heretics*, 19.
[17] *Commonitorium*, 27.   [18] Denzinger 1507.
[19] This is one of the themes of James Barr, *Holy Scripture: Canon, Authority, Criticism* (Clarendon Press, 1983). See e.g. 39–41.

been laid down by God himself. The Christian Church taught that much of this was no longer binding. So how were these laws to be taken now; why include them at all in the Bible? Christian apologetic of the early centuries gave one or other of two answers, both of which are to be found in Irenaeus.

The first approach represents the Old Testament Law as a minimum standard of behaviour, consisting in detailed rules and backed up by precise punishments and rewards, useful for educating simple human beings, lacking in much natural love for God and their fellows, and issued by God for a chosen group of such humans. This approach takes its beginning from the words of Christ in St Matthew about divorce; Christ forbade divorce and in response to a question as to why Moses had allowed it stated that this was because of man's hardness of heart.[20] Irenaeus describes the rules of the Law as 'the laws of bondage',[21] suited for the instruction or punishment of the people, and cancelled now by the law of liberty. The ritual provisions of the Pentateuch, which might well be regarded as imperatives before, were now seen as firmly enclosed within quotation marks, reporting an original promulgation which the New Testament showed to be no longer binding.

The other and more prominent approach in Irenaeus is that the law has metaphorical significance; and since the metaphors are developed and integrated, it forms an allegory. Its sacrificial regulations symbolized deeper realities. This particular approach to the ritual law derives its most obvious Christian inspiration from the Epistle to the Hebrews. 'The Tabernacle and all the vessels of the ministry'[22] were commanded by Moses to be 'sprinkled with blood' on occasions of solemn sacrifice. But 'it is impossible that the blood of bulls and goats should take away sins';[23] a voluntary sacrifice of a pure agent is needed for that. The ritual provisions tell us of the need for sacrifice, and they represent by allegory the kind of sacrifice which would be efficacious. Blood represents life, and the tabernacle and vessels represent sacred things, perhaps human beings. 'It was necessary that the copies of the things in the heavens should be cleansed' with the blood of bulls and goats, 'but the heavenly things with better sacrifices than these',[24] namely with the life of the perfect human Jesus Christ. As I noted in Chapter 4, it is a view deeply embedded in Hebrew and early Christian thought, that ancient acts of importance are 'types' of deeper (and often

---

[20] Matt. 19: 7–8, commented on by Irenaeus in *Adversus haereses*, 4. 15. 2.
[21] *Adversus haereses*, 4. 16. 5.   [22] Heb. 9: 22.   [23] Ibid. 10: 4.   [24] Ibid. 9: 23.

future) realities. Sometimes a prophet performs acts deliberately
with symbolic gestures (e.g. Ezek. 37: 15–28). Sometimes those who
performed the ancient acts did so without considering any symbolic
significance which they might have, but the Judaeo-Christian tradition expected to find in the Old Testament many 'types' of later
developments, and above all of the events of the New Testament. So
Irenaeus claims that the 'first Testament' 'exhibited a type of heavenly
things'.[25]

The Revelation to the Old Israel

Irenaeus' general approach can be extended to the Old Testament as a
whole, and leads us to make two separate claims about it, which the
Church of early centuries also wished to make. The first is that much of
it (though not all of it) is the record of God's interactions with Israel,
and his gradual education of his people. The Epistle to the Hebrews
writes of 'God who at sundry times and in divers manners spoke in
times past to our fathers by the prophets',[26] and the Nicene Creed
captures this in its expression of belief in the Holy Spirit who 'spoke by
the prophets' (using, I suspect, 'prophets' in a wide sense to include
Law and prophets and possibly the rest of the Old Testament as well).

In the absence of any clash with Christian doctrine, a biblical book is
to be read in accordance with the rules for the genre to which the book
belongs. Thus the story of David and Jonathan in 2 Samuel is a simple
historical narrative without many implications about the character of
God or any other point of Christian doctrine. But, as I argued earlier,
the Book of Jonah is a parable; and one with a content clearly in line
with Christian doctrine, and thus also to be read in its original sense.
But if what is written suggests a rather limited view of God's nature
and commands the passage must be read as belonging to a wider
context than that of a single Old Testament book; the reader must
consider that it has a place in the Old Testament as a whole, which
according to Christian teaching is, as I wrote above, a record of God's
interactions with Israel, and his gradual education of his people. God
might give them commands (e.g. about divorce) or hymns (psalms
praying for victory over worldly enemies) of limited application in time
and place to a particular people ill formed spiritually. He might instruct
them in very simple principles of justice (such as that victims have

---

[25] *Adversus haereses*, 4. 32. 2.   [26] Heb. 1: 1.

the right to secure the punishment of their oppressors) without going into the deeper principles of mercy (that it is often supererogatorily good that they should not seek to exercise that right).[27] Whole books of teaching can be seen, as it were, as enclosed in quotation marks, as announcements of this kind, made through some prophet or writer (and, of course, exclamations, such as are the content of many verses of the psalms, can only have a truth-value if enclosed in quotation marks).

God would be expected, by the argument of Chapter 2, to cast his message within the presuppositions (theological and scientific) of the culture of those whom he was addressing, and his doing so would not render that message false (see p. 28 and p. 31). Thus many Old Testament passages treating of God's attitude to particular actions of men seem to represent God as embodied or subject to emotion, as 'striking people down' or as 'angry'. Christian doctrine taught that God was not like this. However we can plausibly suppose that God spoke to the people of Israel in terms of their presuppositions (which sometimes, though not generally, included thinking of God as embodied and subject to emotion). This point was common currency of the Fathers. Thus Novatian:

The prophet was speaking about God at that point in symbolic language, fitted to that stage of belief, not as God was, but as the people were able to understand...God, therefore is not finite, but the people's understanding is finite; God is not limited, but the intellectual capacity of the people's mind is limited.[28]

Similarly the scientific presuppositions, such as those of Psalm 104 or Genesis 8: 4 on which I commented earlier, are the ones in terms of which God would have inspired primitive Israel to think of him. That

[27] On punishment as a right and mercy as a work of supererogation which goes beyond rights, see my *Responsibility and Atonement* (Clarendon Press, 1989) esp. 99.

[28] Novatian, *De Trinitate*, 6. For Origen's use of this 'principle of accommodation', as it has been called, see R. P. C. Hanson, *Allegory and Event* (SCM Press, 1959), 224–31. Aquinas writes with respect to such cases that 'Holy Scripture is intended for us all in common without distinction of persons ... and fitly puts forward spiritual things under bodily likenesses; at all events, the uneducated may then lay hold of them, those, that is to say, who are not ready to take intellectual truths neat with nothing else' (*Summa theologiae*, 1a. 1. 9, trans. Thomas Gilby OP (Blackfriars, 1964)). Interestingly, the issue about anthropomorphism in scriptural talk of God arose early in the development of Islam. Here whether God literally had a body was the subject of considerable controversy. (See A. J. Arberry, *Revelation and Reason in Islam* (Allen & Unwin, 1957), 21–2.) However, the metaphorical interpretation of such talk eventually won: Al Ghazzali, who led the 'back to the Quran' movement (AD *c.*1100), allowed that such talk was metaphorical, but claimed that 'the philosophers' had wrongly allegorized too much else in the Quran, e.g. descriptions of Heaven and Hell. (See Arberry, *Revelation and Reason*, 63.)

the message of Genesis was expressed in terms of a false and primitive science was common currency among the Fathers and scholastics who believed that the Greeks had discovered the truth—or something a lot nearer to the truth than ancient Israel had known—about physics and astronomy. Thus Aquinas doubted whether there were in a literal sense 'waters above the firmament' (Gen. 1: 7) on the scientific grounds that any water in such parts would be compelled by its weight to fall down to the Earth. He therefore interprets the text in accord with the principle that 'Moses was speaking to ignorant people and out of condescension to their simpleness presented to them only those things immediately obvious to the senses.'[29]

Most passages of books of the Old Testament can be treated thus either on their own (with the rules for its own genre of book)—which I shall call treating them straight—and/or historically (as God's message at the time to Israel). Treating a passage straight is not the same as treating it literally. The context of publication of the book as a book and the genre to which it belongs may involve treating many of the sentences in it metaphorically. It is simply a matter of treating the passage as a passage of a book written by a human author, inspired by God, addressed to Israelites at the time of its publication. Treating a passage historically is treating it as enclosed within a statement that God through a human author announced certain things or encouraged meditation or reflection on certain things (e.g. psalms) to Israelites at the time of the publication of the book; the enclosed passage is to be interpreted on its own in accord with the rules for its genre. If passages can be treated either straight or historically, this is the way (according to the Christian doctrine that God the Holy Spirit 'spoke through the prophets') it ought to be done. The record of the later 'historical' books (such as 2 Samuel), taken on their own, is, I suspect, in general true—by the rough and ready standards of historical truth by which such matters would then be judged.[30] (See Chapter 4 for the relevance of different standards of accuracy for the truth-value.) Although, as I have stressed, there is much uncertainty about the nature of biblical genres, and cultural and social contexts, a vague general picture does however begin to emerge from this way of treating the Old Testament.

---

[29] *Summa theologiae*, 1a. 68. 3, trans. William Wallace OP (Blackfriars, 1967), x.

[30] Augustine recognized that minor discrepancies of historical detail between biblical passages do not rule out the historical truth of the main claims' of the passages, which is all that is relevant (see *De cons. Evang.* 12. 29 and 21. 51, cited in G. Bonner, 'Augustine as Biblical Scholar', in P. R. Ackroyd and C. F. Evans (eds.), *The Cambridge History of the Bible*, viii (Cambridge University Press, 1979), 556).

A primitive nomadic people became conscious of a god who had chosen them to be his own people, a god more powerful than the gods of neighbouring peoples. So great a God was he that to worship anything less was a sin worthy of death. He commanded from them high standards of personal conduct, of honesty, and respect of persons in their dealings with one another; he was prepared to deny them if they did not keep his commandments, and to allow them to suffer for their own good. He provided them with detailed ways of showing respect to him, to each other, and to those who lived among them. God minded about what happened to each Israelite, and historical narrative is important because what happened to individual Israelites is important and the recorded events symbolize the unrecorded ones. Right conduct mattered enormously, and even an unintended sin against God needed atonement; but God was often a God merciful to a genuine penitent even for an intended sin. Gradually he led Israel to see deeper insights about right conduct than they had originally had: that women had many rights equal to those of men, that slaves could not be kept as such permanently and still had many rights while temporarily enslaved, and finally that God was the only god, the God of all peoples of the Earth, who had chosen Israel as his special people to be a vehicle of his revelation to all peoples, who were equally worthy of respect.

Such, I believe, is the core of many of the books of the Old Testament, taken in their historical order and treated in the ways stated; and much of the final form of teaching is contained in the Book of Jonah, one of the latest books. What I write would not, I think, be greatly disputed in its most general tone—though of course any more detailed filling out would be more contestable. What however the modern world has become far more conscious of is that some parts of the Old Testament cannot be treated in this way; for they state (and not merely presuppose) historical falsities, or they represent God as behaving immorally. It has therefore tended to say that the Old Testament contains a mixture of truth and falsity, revelation and misunderstanding; and that attitude of course leads to a fairly low view of the sacredness of Scripture. And if one reads the books of the Old Testament straight or historically on their own, one must certainly say that, if God was inspiring the development of Israel and its recording in the Old Testament, his inspiration got mixed with much error. But what the modern world has forgotten is that the Church which proclaimed the Old Testament proclaimed it as part of a whole Bible, subject to interpretation by Christian doctrine, an interpretation which the

Fathers of the early Church considered to have the consequence that any parts of the Old Testament which could not be taken straight or historically had to be taken in a purely metaphorical sense, a sense forced on the book, not by considerations of the need to make sense of the biblical book taken on its own, but by the need to make sense of it as part of a Christian Scripture. I have already pointed out that some passages of biblical books may need to be taken metaphorically in view of the former considerations. For the rest of this chapter, however, for the sake of brevity of exposition I shall ignore that point, and refer to metaphorical interpretation forced on the text by taking it as part of a Christian Scripture simply as metaphorical interpretation; and so contrast taking a passage straight or historically on the one hand with taking it metaphorically on the other.

Metaphorical Interpretation of the Old Testament

The rules for recognizing metaphor elucidated in Chapter 3 suggest that normally (i.e. unless the genre suggests otherwise) you only take metaphorically a sentence which taken literally would be obviously false or inappropriate in the context. If God is the author of the Bible and the Church of many centuries its intended audience, then that context will include central Christian doctrines, including those developed in the New Testament. Right to the centre of those doctrines will be Christian moral doctrines about how it is good to treat other humans. The vengeful sentiments of Psalm 137 which says of the Babylon which held Jews in captivity, 'Happy shall he be, that taketh and dasheth thy little ones against the Rock',[31] cannot be regarded as inspired by the God of the Christians. (The early Church saw 'bless them that persecute you, bless and curse not'—Rom. 12: 14—as very central to Christian teaching.) Indeed the sentiments of Psalm 137 are quite contrary to those of the contemporary letter of Jeremiah to the Jews in Babylon, telling them to pray for their captors[32]—also part of Scripture. Hence metaphorical interpretation must be adopted. Metaphorical interpretation was the utilization, in a culture expecting to find allegories and types in religious documents in a way in which we do not, of the techniques naturally and readily available for interpreting passages which could not be taken literally, of a kind with our own rules for recognizing metaphor.

[31] Ps. 137: 9.   [32] Jer. 29: 7.

The beliefs shared by God and the Church of many centuries which force metaphorical interpretation on the text will be not only those of Christian doctrine, but those of science and history, provided by normal secular enquiry. God knows all truths in these fields; so if the Bible is addressed to the Church of many centuries, then truths of which that Church also becomes aware may force metaphorical interpretation on biblical passages which, taken literally, contradict them. I noted in Chapter 4 that it suffices to force metaphorical meaning on a passage if many, even if not all, of an intended audience recognize the obvious falsity or irrelevance of what is said, if taken literally. Hence the falsity evident to God and much of the later Church of passages of science or history, even if not to all the early Church, forces reinterpretation on the text. This point was not a modern discovery but well recognized in the centuries which preceded the final canonization of Scripture, and is therefore among the understandings with which it was canonized, as I shall emphasize more fully in due course.

Take Genesis 1. Suppose we treat it not as a hymn, but wrongly (I suspect) as a document intended to be true sentence by sentence (i.e., whose total truth depends on the truth of each of its constituent sentences). Then, science suggests to us and suggested to the Church of the fourth century AD, it cannot be taken either straight or historically. Augustine thought this, though our reasons were not all his. He taught (in his commentary *De Genesi ad litteram*) that the 'days' of creation could not be taken literally, because (in his view) there could only be 'days' when there was a sun, and the narrative recorded the creation of the sun on only the fourth day. Our (somewhat different) reasons for denying the literal truth of Genesis 1 need no spelling out by me.

When the passage is to be taken metaphorically, what are the rules for how it is to be taken? For metaphor in all contexts, as we saw in Chapter 3, the rules are: take the words of the passage (apart from words which link it to its context) in their literal senses. Consider the objects or properties normally designated by these words, and objects or properties commonly associated with them. Interpret the words as designating some of these latter objects or properties instead. Take as the true interpretation that which interprets the words as designating objects or properties closely rather than remotely connected with their normal designata, in so far as can be done in a way which makes the sentence appropriate to the context. In so far as there is no one obvious such interpretation, the passage will be ambiguous. As the history of biblical interpretation suggests, these rules do yield the result that many biblical passages are ambiguous; but perhaps not as ambiguous as that history suggests. For the interpreter should take for first consideration objects or properties *closely* connected with those normally designated by the words at stake. And so interpretations which are not too far distant from the literal are to be preferred to more remote ones.

To my mind the metaphorical interpretation nearest to the literal under which Genesis 1 comes out as plausibly true, and so the preferred metaphorical interpretation, is derived by treating 'days' as long periods of time and the detailed order of creation as not to be taken as too important. Then the passage tells us that gradually God brought about the various facets of creation over long periods of time, no doubt through 'secondary causes' (i.e. the normal operations of scientific laws which God sustains), as Genesis 2 suggests. Augustine also took the passage metaphorically, but his interpretation is by comparison a very far-fetched one. He claimed that all things described in Genesis 1 were created simultaneously, and that talk about 'days' is to be interpreted as talk about stages in the knowledge of creation possessed by the angels.[33] But 'days' are more like billenniums than they are like logical stages in the growth of knowledge. My metaphorical interpretation is, therefore, by normal criteria for metaphorical interpretation, better than his.

I argued in Chapter 4 from the example of a secular poem that in some cases a double interpretation—both literal and metaphorical—is correct. I claimed there that a double interpretation of passages of works of biblical genres is more obviously often appropriate than such interpretation of passages of more modern works. Biblical writers had available to them a wealth of terms with standard symbolic meanings which they used to describe events which they were clearly also asserting to be historical, which force a metaphorical interpretation on the text in addition to the literal one. I shall say a little more about these standard symbols shortly. But any reader of St John's Gospel familiar with these standard symbols will ascribe to many of its passages, as passages just of that book, a double meaning. I pointed out in Chapter 7 that the story of the pool of Bethesda may have a double meaning. But one much simpler example which clearly has a double meaning is the answer which St John attributes to Jesus in response to

[33] 'That day which God has made recurs in connection with his works not by a material passage of time but by spiritual knowledge, when the blessed company of angels contemplate from the beginning in the Word of God the divine decree to create' (*De Genesi ad literam*, 4. 26, trans. J. H. Taylor (Newman Press, 1982)).

the soldiers who came to arrest him. Jesus asked them, 'Whom seek ye?' They replied, 'Jesus of Nazareth', and Jesus responded (in Greek), ἐγώ εἰμι.[34] This is translated in English bibles 'I am he', that is, 'I am Jesus of Nazareth', and that is clearly one thing which St John sees Jesus as saying. But a word-by-word translation yields only 'I am', and that is the name of God as revealed to Moses,[35] and St John also sees Jesus as affirming his divinity before people who did not recognize it—for the first chapter of the Gospel clearly reveals that St John thought that Jesus was God and manifested his divinity to a world which did not recognize it. The response which St John attributes to Jesus must therefore be construed not merely in its literal sense, but as making this claim that Jesus claimed to be God, not especially at the moment of his arrest but in his whole life. Now if biblical books, taken on their own, are, in cases where available symbols so suggest, to be interpreted as having a double meaning, the same should apply to passages in the context of the whole Bible. Where a straight or histori- cal reading is not ruled out, but the understanding of the symbolic conventions of the first few centuries AD and the way of applying them in the context of the whole Bible then customary suggest a plausible metaphorical meaning, that also should be read. And of course the context of the whole Bible as a Christian document reinforces rather than diminishes the need for the double interpretation of ἐγώ εἰμι.

In the case of the ritual provisions of the Law, we can adopt both a historical interpretation and a metaphorical interpretation, which, being a developed and integrated one, then gives allegorical significance to the historical events. An 'allegorical' or 'symbolical' interpretation of Old Testament events is often natural in the light of New Testament and later Church teaching claiming (explicitly or implicitly) that the needs which Old Testament people, rituals, and events met were met more fully in the Christian dispensation; and in such cases a metaphorical as well as a historical interpretation seems appropriate. Whether the story of Jonah was taken by Jesus as history or parable we do not know, but he used the story of Jonah in the whale's belly, according to St Matthew, as a metaphorical prediction of his own death and resurrec- tion.[36] Likewise certain ethical or metaphysical teaching can be given a historical interpretation—as the conveying within the narrow pre- suppositions of the culture of an important message—as well as a meta- phorical interpretation, when later Church teaching is taken into

---

[34] John 18: 5. [35] Exod. 3: 14. [36] Matt. 12: 39–40.

account. To the extent to which this can be done, the Old Testament appears as the record of a limited revelation, which Christian teaching has always taught it to be, which is given deeper significance in the light of specifically Christian doctrines.

Still, the normal public rules for recognizing metaphor do not in general force metaphorical meaning on passages which can be taken non-metaphorically, and the Fathers who resisted excessive allegorizing recognized that, for meaning is something determined by public criteria and once you interpret metaphorically when public considerations do not force you to, there is a danger that 'anything goes'. Many of the Fathers, belonging to what is known as the Antiochene as opposed to the Alexandrian tradition of exegesis, held that allegorizing often went too far. As St Basil wrote: 'When I hear "grass", I understand by it grass, and likewise with "plant", "fish", "beast" and "property", all these words, in the sense in which they are spoken, thus I understand them. For I am not ashamed of the Gospel.'[37] This, however, clashes with a tradition developing in patristic times but strong in the Middle Ages, that *all* passages have one or more than one metaphorical sense.[38] This tradition must be given some weight by the modern investigator seeking to discover 'the meaning' of a passage in the Christian Bible, because of its early and sustained place in the teaching of the Church which promulgated that Bible.

The Genesis 1 example of metaphorical interpretation was of a passage interpreted in a way fairly close to the literal. There clearly are scriptural passages which cannot be interpreted in ways at all close to the straight or historical ways. In such cases the Old and New Testaments, together with early Church tradition, have a wealth of ready interpretations provided by typology and allegory. The Church which recognized the books of the Old and New Testament as divinely inspired Scripture recognized them as such while having ready a whole set of ready interpretations of the people, places, and actions referred to in Scripture, when passages which referred to them could not be taken literally. This set came from a number of sources. There was a Palestinian rabbinic tradition; there was an Alexandrian tradition,

---

[37] St Basil, *In hexaemeron*, 188.

[38] Origen recognized three different senses of Scripture (*De principiis*, 4. 2. 4—see commentary thereon in Kelly, *Early Christian Doctrines*, 75). Augustine recognized four different senses of Scripture (*De utilitate credendi*, 5–8). Both writers however held that not all passages could be interpreted literally. The 'fourfold' scheme of interpretation was common in the Middle Ages.

centred on Philo, which in turn derived from the Hellenistic tradition of treating the writings of Homer and the legends of the Greek gods metaphorically. Then there were the acts of Jesus: for instance his feeding the 5,000 clearly patterned after Elijah feeding the 100 made his claim to be a new and greater Elijah. And finally the New Testament writings themselves provided in some passages explicit typologies and allegories, available for interpreting other passages.[39] We noted earlier how the Epistle to the Hebrews drew explicit attention to the Old Testament sacrificial regulations which were the type of various central New Testament events. The rabbinic tradition seldom denied the straight or historical reading, but the Philonic tradition did so much more often while continuing of course to affirm that every sentence of Scripture was true, if correctly interpreted—and that often meant metaphorically. But all traditions had learnt to interpret one piece of Scripture in a metaphorical way, justified by regarding it not as a book on its own but as part of the revelation to Israel—the Song of Songs. The Song, which, taken straight, expresses the sexual love of a man for a woman, owed its incorporation into the Jewish canon to the understanding that it was to be read metaphorically as expressing God's agapeistic love for Israel.[40]

I give but three simple examples of how the wealth of standard typology and allegory belonging to the world of the early Church forces upon passages which cannot be taken straight or historically a natural metaphorical interpretation. I have already quoted Psalm 137: 9. The blessing conferred on any who 'dasheth the little ones' of 'Babylon' against 'the rock' cannot be taken literally. 'Babylon' however is a standard type in the Bible. Since the period of the exile, it came to represent any big evil power—sometimes Rome in New Testament times, but more generally the power of evil. Once one thinks of it as a power, its 'little ones' are naturally interpreted as the particular evil inclinations of humans. So there is a very natural interpretation of the verse as a command addressed to humans to destroy their evil inclinations. Traditionally too Christ is the 'rock': so the command can

---

[39] For description of these traditions, see Hanson, *Allegory and event*, pt. I. On Philo's method of exegesis see also *Cambridge History of the Bible*, i. 379–83, 429f., and 434f. Hanson's most valuable book goes on to describe the use made by Origen of the available typologies and allegories.

[40] 'The Song of Songs owed its final acceptance to allegorical interpretation' (G. W. Anderson, 'The Old Testament: Canonical and Non-canonical', in *Cambridge History of the Bible*, i. 134).

be read as 'let Christ destroy your evil inclinations'. But that carries the text a little further from the most obvious interpretation.

Then there is the command to the Israelites invading Canaan to exterminate the Canaanites.[41] This command was fulfilled by Joshua, according to the Book of Joshua. Joshua is the Hebrew form of the name Jesus. Joshua took the old Israel to the earthly promised land, Canaan. The Church believed of Jesus that he was taking the new Israel to the heavenly promised land. The Canaanites are the evil which is to be conquered if Israel is to occupy the promised land; to occupy an earthly land its human inhabitants must be exterminated. No extermination of other humans is necessary if a given human is to become a member of the Kingdom of Heaven, but he does need to exterminate his evil inclinations.[42] The typology is therefore readily and naturally available for interpreting any narrative passages in the Book of Joshua which cannot be taken historically, in a metaphorical sense as predictions. And the command to exterminate can be interpreted, *if* we do not wish to take it historically,[43] as the command to exterminate evil inclinations.

My third example is one for which the interpretation is provided in the New Testament itself. St Paul in his Epistle to the Galatians[44] recalls that 'Abraham had two sons, the one [Ishmael] by a bondmaid [Hagar] the other [Isaac] by a free woman [Sarah]', and that Scripture tells us, 'Cast out the bondwoman and her son: for the son of the bondwoman shall not be heir with the son of the freewoman.' St Paul finds the basis for his allegorical interpretation that 'he who was of the bondwoman was born after the flesh; but he of the freewoman was by promise'. And the interpretation is that 'these women are two covenants; one from Mount Sinai bearing children unto bondage, which is Hagar. Now this Hagar is Mount Sinai in Arabia, and answereth to the Jerusalem that now is; for she is in bondage with her children. But the Jerusalem which is above is free.' There is a genuine similarity here: the relation with a bondwoman of the type which Abraham had is a relation with a concubine based simply on the desire for sexual satisfaction and

---

[41] Deut. 20: 17.

[42] Origen interpreted the story of Joshua's execution of the five kings in Josh. 10: 15–27 allegorically. See the comparison of his treatment of this story with that of others in Hanson, *Allegory and Event*, ch. 5.

[43] I myself believe that a God who gives life has the right to take it away; and in that case he has the right to command someóne else to take it away for him. So a historical interpretation of such passages seems in order.

[44] Gal. 4: 21–31.

so 'after the flesh'; whereas the relation with a freewoman of the type which Abraham had is a relation with a wife, Sarah, who shares with the husband the other aspects of his life as well and above all the nurture of children within a family, the greatest of all human relationships. And this particular marriage was the object of a promise by God that Abraham and Sarah, though both old, would have a child and through that all nations would be blessed. The bondage to slavery giving rise to a child as a result of mere sexual lust is not inappropriately compared to the bondage to the letter of a law, the keeping of which is a formal and servile matter; while a marriage with a free person involving a generous and deep relationship which is the object of God's promise of blessing is the nearest mundane comparison to a Christian's free, spontaneous, and generous relationship with God, which is indeed the object of God's unmerited promise of abundant blessing.

That keeping the Jewish law is a servile relationship and serving God freely without its narrow constraints is the better way was a very deeply embedded part of the Christian message. Paul's interpretation of the passage as part of a Christian Scripture is therefore highly natural. The passage should be read as a commendation to us of the free relationship with God in the Church of the New Jerusalem rather than the relation of bondage under the old Law. St Paul no doubt thinks the passage to be historically accurate, though he does not say so. The allegorical interpretation is a second meaning which it has, but for St Paul by far the more important one. And for the later Church, of course, that latter interpretation is unavoidable in view of its commendation by St Paul's letter, now part of Scripture itself—whether or not it thinks that there is a straight interpretation as well.

The New Testament

The Church proclaimed the New Testament as the record of what Jesus Christ had said and done and how it was to be interpreted. As we saw in Chapter 7, mere ordinary historical investigation may give a fairly blurred picture of what Jesus taught. But if, as I have urged, Jesus founded a Church and God gave his signature to the teaching of Jesus by raising him from the dead, then the Church becomes authoritative on what Jesus taught. He said what it said he said, and that was to be understood in the way it said it was. The Gospels therefore contain a true record of what Jesus did and said—true by the rough and ready standards of historical truth then applied (e.g. the exact temporal order of the teaching and geographical location where it was given were not relevant.[45] Likewise the further elements of revelation given immediately after the Resurrection (e.g. concerning the admission of Gentiles to the Church) and the record and interpretation of the teaching in St Paul's letters are a true record and interpretation.

However it follows that since the books of the New Testament, as well as the Old, gain their status as canonical documents through the Church's recognition of their inspiration by God, they too must be interpreted in the light of central Christian doctrines proclaimed by the Church as codifying in precise and clear form the essence of the Christian revelation. Thus clearly some New Testament passages say or imply that Jesus Christ was God and had existed from all eternity: clearly the opening passage of St John's Gospel for example carries this implication. Other New Testament passages do not seem to think of Christ in such exalted terms and seem to imply that his exalted status (possible lower than that of God himself) was only his subsequently to the Resurrection. Romans 1: 4 seems to have this lower Christology, when it speaks of Christ as 'declared (ὁρισθέντος) to be the son of God with power, according to the spirit of holiness, by the resurrection of the dead'. 'Declared to be' might mean 'recognized as' but is more naturally interpreted as 'made'. 'Son of God' may mean simply a holy person, not necessarily divine. If we take St John's Gospel and the Epistle to the Romans as two separate works written by two separate authors, the most plausible historical interpretation of the latter suggests that those authors had different views about the status of Christ. But if we think of them as having the same author, God, who also guided the Church to produce the creeds, the initially less natural interpretation of Romans must be the true one. These works have no authority for Christians unless they see them as deriving their authority

---

[45] Eusebius quotes a passage from a lost work of Papias (AD *c.*140) of what he learnt from 'John the presbyter' concerning the composition of St Mark's Gospel: 'And John the presbyter also said this: Mark being the interpreter of Peter, whatsoever he recorded he wrote with great accuracy, but not, however, in the order in which it was spoken or done by our Lord, for he neither heard nor followed our Lord, but, as before said, he was in company with Peter, who gave him such instruction as was necessary, but not to give a history of our Lord's discourses: wherefore Mark has not erred in any thing, but writing some things as he has recorded them; for he was carefully attentive to one thing, not to pass by anything that he heard, or to state anything falsely in the accounts' (Eusebius, *Ecclesiastical History*, 3. 39). See too the remarks of Augustine referred to in n. 30.

from the Church's recognition of their inspiration by God, and in that case all the rules of textual interpretation force upon them, as their true meaning, a meaning compatible with central Christian doctrine, as formulated by the Church—which includes the divinity of Christ. If you translate ὁρισθέντος as 'recognized as' such a meaning emerges, however the phrase 'Son of God' be taken.[46] Saying this is quite compatible with claiming that St Paul himself, at any rate while writing the Epistle to the Romans, had a lower Christology; if he did, he was inspired by God to write things whose meaning was a little different from what he supposed.

Wider Christian doctrine too is needed in order to see which commands addressed in the Gospels and Epistles to various individuals are of universal application and which are of application only to the individuals to whom they are addressed. Commands in the Epistles concerned with the obedience of slaves to their masters, wives to their husbands, and all people to the state must have applied to them wider Christian doctrine to determine the scope of their application.

Meaning Determined by Future Context

If God is the author of Scripture, and also the author of the central claims of Christian doctrine embodied in the creeds, then, we have seen, the latter constrain the interpretation of the former for the reason that creeds are designed to encapsulate the central claims of the faith in as precise a way as possible. But any truth evident to the speaker and his audience which shows some sentence taken literally to be false also forces a metaphorical interpretation on the sentence, whether that evident truth is contained in some other work of the same author or not. We have seen how Augustine allowed that scientific discovery forced metaphorical interpretation on a text; for it was scientific 'discovery' which suggested that in a literal sense there were not separate 'days' of creation. And Augustine belonged to the century which promulgated a canonized Scripture. But if the intended audience of Scripture is the Church, not only of the first century (many of whom,

---

[46] For a brief survey of the Christologies implicit in various parts of the New Testament, see Harold Attridge's 'Calling Jesus Christ', in T. P. Flint and E. Stump (eds.), *Philosophical Theology and Biblical Exegesis* (University of Notre Dame Press, 1992). The paper brings out the differences in the Christologies. My views in the text at this place were originally delivered in a reply to Attridge's paper at a conference.

presumably, Augustine would have regarded as scientifically backward) or the first four centuries, but of later centuries and millenniums, then, I have argued, truth evident to the latter (especially as the Church of later centuries is by numbers of members much larger than the earlier Church) must also be allowed to force a reinterpretation on the text in the way that truth evident to Augustine forced that. New scientific and historical discoveries may force that kind of reinterpretation. Now we know that the world began a lot longer ago than 4,000 BC, and Methuselah did not really live 969 years. So take passages which state or entail that the world began about 4,000 BC or that Methuselah lived 969 years in senses nearest to the literal in which they come out as consistent with other truth evident to the later Church and with the credal framework which constrains all interpretations.

Historical and scientific knowledge may also force metaphorical readings on the text of the New Testament books. The most obvious example of this concerns the Book of Revelation. A careful study of the text in the light of the contemporary history suggests that its human author was predicting the end of the world around the beginning of the second century AD. But the Church which gave it canonical status in the fourth century AD obviously did not understand it that way. Dionysius of Alexandria in the middle of the third century confesses that he does not understand it and suspects that it should be allegorized;[47] and there was a considerable tradition of treating it allegorically over the next millennium.

That the sense of some passages can be seen only in a 'future context' follows from my earlier point that if a social context is known only to a speaker and not some of his audience, the latter may not understand the meaning of a passage unless they become familiar with that context. Scientific understanding may reveal the meaning of a passage; and so may new historical understanding, both of past and future. It follows also that predictions (and we have seen that not all prophecies are predictions) may be understood only when the time comes about which the prediction was made. God could foresee the 'future context' of his prediction in advance, and express his prediction in terms of that context, whose meaning would only become clear to those without foreknowledge when the time arrived. Biblical writers were not unaware that he to whom a prediction was given could not always understand it;[48] and Augustine taught that the Spirit often inspires people to utter

---

[47] See *Cambridge History of the Bible*, i. 434–5.

[48] The purported author of the Book of Daniel claimed not to understand his prophecies—'I heard, but I understood not' (Dan. 12: 8).

or see a message which they do not understand.[49] And some of the Fathers and scholastics taught about predictions, as I have done, that their meaning and truth would become evident at the same time. That is, our understanding some oracle and seeing its fulfilment will be simultaneous; when we see certain things to be so, we will also see that that was what the mysterious passage was getting at. Irenaeus writes, 'every prophecy is to men [full of] enigmas and ambiguities. But when the time has arrived, and the prediction has come to pass, then the prophecies have a clear and certain exposition.'[50] And nearly a millennium later Hugh of St Victor wrote about the prophecies of the Old Testament that no one could understand them 'before they were fulfilled. They were sealed and none could loose their seals but the Lion of the tribe of Judah' (namely Christ).[51]

The tradition of reinterpretation of biblical prophecy in the light of history is itself a biblical tradition. Daniel 9 reinterprets Jeremiah's talk of 'seventy years' (Jer. 25: 12) as seventy 'weeks of years'; and 2 Esdras 12: 11 reinterprets Daniel 7: 17. Those in that tradition would not have been unduly disconcerted to discover that in its original context the Book of Daniel prophesied an 'end' in the second century BC or the Book of Revelation prophesied an 'end' in the second century AD. They would have reflected that the meaning of the prophecies was something other than the original understanding of them; and that time would show what that meaning was. Perhaps too the literal 'failure' of the prophecy makes clear that all prophecy is warning, not prediction; and maybe that warning was heeded by someone.

Historical investigation may also reveal how the attributions of human authorship in the Bible are to be understood. If Moses is not the literal author or dictator of the first five books of the Bible, then their attribution to him must be understood in a much more liberal way. I have argued that the attribution of 'authorship' was so understood by the then secular criteria in biblical times. My point here is that even if it was not, the view that God was the ultimate author of the Bible in a strong sense and so the presuppositions which he shares with the Church of many centuries, including such historical knowledge as the

---

[49] *De diversis quaestionibus*, 2. 1. 1. The examples which he gives are of those who see visions and utter words, recorded in the Bible; not of biblical authors themselves. But application of his thesis to the biblical authors seems to result from his teaching about what inspiration amounts to.

[50] Irenaeus, *Adversus haereses*, 4. 26.

[51] Hugh of St Victor, *Didascalion*, trans. J. Taylor (Columbia University Press, 1961), 6. 6.

latter comes to acquire, dictate how it is to be understood; this understanding forces on the text the more liberal understanding of attribution
of human authorship.

The account which I have now given of how Scripture is to be interpreted if God is supposed to be its author and the Church of future
centuries its intended audience follows from the general rules for
interpreting texts which I described in Part I. Investigate who is the
author, who the intended audience, what is the genre, and what are the
conventions for interpreting works of that genre, interpret a work in
terms of a preface or other guide, take as metaphorical what the author
cannot have intended as literal, and so on, are all very general rules for
understanding works in no way peculiar to the Bible. It's just that they
give results far from obvious to modern men when applied to this case.
Treating the Bible 'like any other book' in the way you interpret it has
the consequence that it turns out to be very unlike any other book in its
pattern and structure.

Inspiration

So far I have been investigating the meaning of the biblical text on the
assumption that God is its author in the strong sense that he was its
sole author who inspired its human authors and compilers to record
his message. Holy Scripture, said Gregory the Great, is 'a letter of God
almighty to his creature', from which its followed that it was not
important who was the human author of its various books.[52] This
assumption has the consequence, in view of what we know about the
process by which the Bible was composed, that what God inspired its
human authors and compilers to do was to put together material whose
meaning would depend on which other material was eventually incorporated into a Bible promulgated as Christian Scripture. Its human
authors and compilers would often have understood much, but would
not have understood all, and would sometimes have misunderstood
some of what they were inspired to produce. Progressively more explicit
understanding of aspects of a tradition not previously drawn out is a
phenomenon known to traditions, literary, scientific, and philosophical;
if God is the author of that tradition and knows where it is going, what
comes first is to be understood in the light of what comes later.

[52] *Epistolae*, 4. 31 (PL 77: 706); and *Moralium*, Praefatio, 2 and 3. (PL 75: 517).

A more detailed example will illustrate more fully the strong view of God's authorship. The first human authors of the early parts of the Old Testament saw God as concerned to exterminate those who worshipped other gods (as in the Book of Joshua) and those who had wronged God's chosen people, and their families too (as in Psalm 137). Now it is *not* good that anyone should worship lesser gods, and those who have done wrong *do* deserve punishment. The human authors of the early parts of the Old Testament correctly captured these insights—and they are insights, perhaps ones so obvious that we do not notice them. But they failed to realize that it is not always good to punish those who do wrong (to show mercy is often better); those who do wrong in ignorance do not deserve much (if any) punishment, children must not be punished for the wrongdoing of parents, and all of us, who do wrong and suffer wrong of obvious kinds from each other, are guilty of so much wrong to God in consequence of yielding to our bad inclinations. God inspired the human authors to see things which had quite a bit of truth in them; but what they wrote down, taken on its own, had quite a lot of falsity too. However what they wrote down was ambiguous in the sense that a fuller context could give it a different meaning from what it would have on its own. God did provide a later context which made what they wrote down have meanings such as I have illustrated on pp. 189–91, and thus to express statements which were entirely true. This account thus brings out the continuity between the two ways of interpreting Scripture (historical or straight, versus metaphorical). The human authors grasped much of God's nature and purposes. But where they misunderstood that, what they wrote down had sufficient truth to it that, in a larger context, it came to have a sense which it would not have on its own, in which it was altogether true.

Again, as we saw earlier, the human authors of the early chapters of Genesis clothed their message in the scientific presuppositions of their culture. Their (this time) true but limited understanding led them to write down a message susceptible of a deeper metaphorical meaning.

This strong view is perfectly compatible with the view that God inspired the writing of many other non-biblical books. But the Church gave its authority to those which form our Bible (with whatever qualifications on the extent of the Bible arise from uncertainties about the limits of the canon, discussed in Chapter 8); that is, it recognized them as inspired in the course of its proclamations as to the content of Christian doctrine. And, by the argument of Chapter 8, its authority to expound Christian doctrine derives from God himself.

However the considerations of Chapter 8 for determining what is true doctrine may lead us to hold that there is only sufficient historical warrant for a somewhat weaker view of the divine inspiration of the Bible (i.e. the twin criteria of continuity of organization and doctrine developed there lead only to such a view). This is the view that God is the author of the Bible only in the sense that he 'inspired' the human authors to write and compilers to compile the books they did; yet not merely did those human authors have their own style and presuppositions and God sought only to breathe his message through those (as the strong view allowed), but also the human authors and compilers were less than fully pliable. They were not fully open to divine truth,[53] and allowed some small amount of falsity on important matters to infect Scripture. Analogously we may come to hold that the canonizers were not fully open to divine guidance with respect to which books they canonized. The Bible then is like a symphony written and conducted by a genius, but played by an orchestra of wilful amateurs.

But that is not going to make much difference to how we are going to understand the Bible's message—so long as basically God is the inspirer and guide of Scripture—with respect to those passages whose literal falsity can be detected. For how are we to recognize the aberrations which human authors have introduced into the biblical message? In the same way as we would recognize errors of transmission in any other work of art or literature: by their discrepancy with the main message and with other known beliefs of the author. Hence we do not take as literal truth anything at odds with the central message of the Bible—and that, if God is its author, is, by previous arguments, the message of the Church's creeds—and other known scientific and historical truth. Yet by earlier arguments, we do not take such passages as literally true anyway, even if God is the sole author of every word of the Bible. The only difference is that if God is the sole author, we regard all passages at odds with the Bible's central message as having metaphorical truth; whereas if he is only an 'inspirer' whose inspiration

---

[53] Clearly this view must be taken in so far as there was any deliberate deceit as opposed to mere lack of understanding, in the production of biblical books—in the way discussed on 172 with respect to two letters attributed to St Paul. If the human author was other than St Paul, and he attributed these letters to St Paul and filled them with personal Pauline details, not simply in accord with the current conventions of manifest or traditional pseudepigraphy, but going beyond them in order to deceive his readers into supposing they were written by St Paul, we cannot suppose the author to be open fully to divine inspiration. For a perfectly good God cannot inspire a human author to write something which he recognizes as deceptive.

may not always be followed, we must regard some such passages as false, since they have been written contrary to his inspiration and so have only human authors as their authors and so different criteria of meaning, which may often pick them out as having a literal meaning and so a false one. But there will be no way of distinguishing among those passages which are recognizably literally false those which are just false and those which have metaphorical truth. Either way, Psalm 137: 9 must be assessed in the light of central Christian doctrine; and the assessment may take the form either of metaphorical interpretation or of attributing it to a human author inserting a vengeful sentiment contrary to divine inspiration. And the metaphorical interpretation will be one to which we are committed anyway by central Christian doctrine.

The only difference will concern passages compatible with but not entailed by central Christian doctrines and other known scientific and historical truth. They will need to be read straight or historically, if God is the author of the Bible in the strong sense, as a true message from God or maybe an account of what he said to Israel at a particular stage of its history. But if God is only the author of the Bible in a somewhat weaker sense, some falsity may have crept into such passages. Take for example the teaching in two passages of Pauline letters about the role of women in the Church—1 Corinthians 14: 34–6 and 1 Timothy 2: 8–15—that they were not to lead and teach in the congregation. The way these passages are phrased suggests that this teaching is of general application, and not merely of application to the situation of the immediate recipients of the letter.

Now this teaching is hardly entailed by central Christian doctrine or other evident truth. One might hold that it was incompatible with central Christian doctrine—for example St Paul's own teaching in Galatians 3: 8 about the equality of men and women before God, or a strand of Christian teaching which holds that the greatest of ordinary human saints was a woman Mary, 'Queen of Heaven', and so forth—or with evident moral truth. In that case, on the somewhat weaker understanding of divine inspiration, the passages must be regarded as ones in which St Paul was not fully open to divine inspiration and so wrote what was false. On the strong understanding of divine inspiration they will have to be interpreted either historically or metaphorically; and a historical reading would be a lot more natural than a metaphorical one. Reading the passages historically involves interpreting them as St Paul's commands (on behalf of God) to particular churches, local instructions

not to let women preach in those churches—for which there might be
many good Christian reasons (e.g. it would lead to some particular
misunderstanding or schism).[54] And I re-emphasize that reading the
passages in such a way is *not* saying that that is what St Paul meant by
what he wrote. People sometimes write what they do not mean; what
they mean is determined by the context, and if the context is the whole
Bible as a Christian document inspired by God, the meaning of these
passages may be quite other than St Paul meant them to have.

However it is not unreasonable to suppose that these passages
are compatible with central Christian doctrines or other evident moral
truths. It may well be compatible with holding that men and women
are equally precious to God and equally to be rewarded in the unending
life of the world to come, also to hold that they have slightly different
roles for their very short life in this world, and that for women does
not involve leading the congregation in church. (After all, Christ
taught that 'whosoever would become great among you shall be your
minister',[55] i.e. wait on others in a humble capacity.) In that case, on the
strong view of inspiration, these passages are to be read straight as true
messages from God. On the somewhat weaker view of inspiration, some
falsity may have crept in. But if that view of inspiration entails that
such falsity is a rare occurrence, then probably this passage is a true
message from God; and should be treated as such in the absence of
other considerations.

Such uncertainty about what is the Bible's message can however
affect our assessment only of those passages concerned with matters
about which central Christian doctrines have nothing to say and there is
no other evident extra-doctrinal truth. On the somewhat weaker view,
as on the strong view of inspiration, it remains the case that taking
seriously the notion of God as the inspirer via authors and compilers of
the whole text forces a consistent interpretation on the text in central
respects—just as inserting a few verses at the end of Ecclesiastes forces
upon the text of earlier chapters a meaning which they would lack without it. It is only if one came to have so weak a doctrine of biblical inspiration that one regarded the books of the Bible as basically of human
origin that one would cease to regard it as having a message at all,
whether or not one which was occasionally corrupted in detail.

---

[54] One of Augustine's rules for interpreting Scripture is: 'to recognize that some
commands are given to all in common, others to particular classes of persons' (*De doctrina
Christiana*, 3. 17. 25.)

[55] Matt. 20: 26.

But given a strong or moderate doctrine of biblical inspiration, whereby biblical passages are interpreted in the light of basic Christian doctrines, it will follow that the Bible can be shown false only in so far as the creeds and central doctrines can be shown false; for they constrain its interpretation. If it were shown false, in this way, it would of course follow that God was not its author in the strong sense or in any other sense. Otherwise it will amplify but not deny those doctrines.

But why a Bible with such complicated rules of interpretation? Why not instead a 500-page creed (namely a Denzinger)? For the kind of reasons outlined in Chapter 5. There is point in lesser revelations before a final one; we find those in the Old Testament, mixed with human confusions. The particular is sacred, and a record of how God interacted with men and helped them, within the presuppositions of a culture but one with more understanding of God than other cultures and one chosen to be the vehicle of his fullest revelation, to understand yet more about himself brings this out. Then a Bible allows children and the uneducated who cannot understand the subtleties of creeds to get some very simple messages from very simple stories: for example to get from the story of the Golden Calf (Exod. 32) the message that the only God worthy of worship is a God too great to be represented by images. In the Bible God provides a book from which the simple can get simple true messages; but when the simple stories suggest false messages (e.g. the Book of Judges might suggest to some that God wants Christians to exterminate non-Christians), then there are available the other parts of the Bible and the Church's tradition of teaching to correct the misunderstanding. It is good that humans should work out their understanding of revelation in co-operation with each other, trying to get into focus various Christian documents through a developing understanding of science and history, and wrestling with the biblical text with the help of others who have done the same under the guidance of basic Christian doctrine is a profound way of doing this. Just because it is initially unclear whether a passage is to be taken literally or metaphorically, we need to work out whether it is consistent with basic Christian doctrine and other evident truth, and that helps us to deepen religious understanding and hand on a deeper faith to the next generation. The framework of Church and creeds guarantees that any misunderstanding of the Bible on central matters will not be too long lasting. And finally, because we do not have the words to express many deep Christian truths, we need metaphor, and we need many metaphors developing a point at length if we are to get it home; and a developed parable may well sometimes get the point home better than a 500-page creed. And thus this complicated way of expressing doctrine reminds us of what a 500-page creed would hide from us, that divine truth is often far too profound to be captured adequately by any human sentences. We thus get in the Bible, as interpreted by the Church via the creeds, the advantages described in Chapter 5 of both culture-relative and culturally independent revelation.

The Tradition of Biblical Interpretation

Since the way of understanding the Bible which I have derived from basic philosophical principles, with its consequence that many a passage has to be interpreted in metaphorical ways, to yield a meaning which is not that of the passage taken in the context of its biblical book by itself, will seem very strange to many modern readers, I will end this chapter by emphasizing just how normal it was in the early Church. Origen, Gregory of Nyssa, and Augustine, three of the greatest doctors of the Church, all adopted metaphorical interpretation explicitly.

Origen gives his account of the rules for biblical interpretation at some length in *De principiis*, 4. 3. The chapter begins with a long list of passages of Scripture which, our general knowledge of the world shows us, cannot possibly be taken literally. They do include passages which the human author of the biblical book probably did not so intend, but in general they are ones which we must judge to have been intended literally by the author of the book. They include passages from both Old Testament (e.g. Genesis) and New Testament (the devil taking Jesus up 'into a high mountain' to show him 'the kingdoms of the whole world'). Origen says we must take literally what we can take literally, and he emphasizes that he is far from denying that there is much literal truth in the Bible. But he claims that 'the whole of divine scripture' has 'a spiritual meaning, but not all a bodily meaning'.[56] The key to scriptural meaning is the New Testament teaching of the Kingdom of God as the New Jerusalem (roughly, Heaven), the Church as the New Israel, and other explicitly recognized New Testament fulfilments of Old Testament types. Then all Old Testament talk about 'Jerusalem', whether or not it can be taken literally about Jerusalem in

---

[56] *De principiis*, 4. 3. 5.

Palestine, must be held to have a spiritual content concerning the heavenly Jerusalem:

If therefore the prophecies relating to Judaea, to Jerusalem, and to Israel, Judah, and Jacob, suggest to us because we do not interpret them in a fleshly sense, mysteries such as these, it will follow that the prophecies which relate to Egypt and the Egyptians, to Babylon and the Babylonians, to Tyre and the Tyrians, to Sidon and the Sidonians, or to any of the other nations, are not spoken solely of the bodily Egyptians, Babylonians, Tyrians, and Sidonians. If the Israelites are spiritual, it follows that the Egyptians and Babylonians are also spiritual.[57]

And so on. Origen's principles of interpretation had immense influence on the subsequent interpretation of Scripture. Beryl Smalley has written that 'to write a history of Origenist influence on the West would be tantamount to writing a history of Western exegesis'.[58]

Teaching very similar to Origen's is given by Gregory of Nyssa in the prologue to his commentary on the Song of Songs. There is much immoral conduct apparently commended in the Old Testament, Gregory points out: 'What benefit to virtuous living can we obtain from the prophet Hosea [Hos. 1: 2], or from Isaiah having intercourse with a prophetess [Isa. 8: 3], unless something else lies beyond the mere letter.'[59]

But the 'mere letter' is only 'the apparent reprehensible sense'; allegory turns it 'into something having a divine meaning'. And he goes on to illustrate that with his interpretation of all the literature attributed to Solomon: Proverbs, Ecclesiastes, and above all the Song of Songs. The Solomon to whom (1 Kgs. 3: 12 claims) God gave 'a wise and an understanding heart; so that there hath been none like thee before thee, nor after thee shall any arise like unto thee' is not however the historical Solomon who was not so wise or holy, but 'another Solomon' 'whose wisdom is infinite', namely Christ. Christ 'used Solomon as an instrument and speaks to us through his voice'.[60] The highest point of the Solomonic literature is the Song of Songs: 'What is described there is a marriage; but what is understood is the union of the human soul with God.'[61]

---

[57] Ibid. 4. 3. 9.
[58] Beryl Smalley, *The Study of the Bible in the Middle Ages* (Basil Blackwell, 1952), 14.
[59] St Gregory of Nyssa, *Commentary on the Song of Songs*, trans. C. McCambley (Hellenic College Press, 1987), 36–7.
[60] Ibid. 44.   [61] Ibid. 47.

Thirdly Augustine, whose basic rule is the same as that of Origen and Gregory, and that suggested by general principles of meaning:

We must show the way to find out whether a phrase is literal or figurative. And the way is certainly as follows: whatever there is in the word of God that cannot, when taken literally, be referred either to purity of life or soundness of doctrine, you may set down as figurative.[62]

And among the things which constrain us to interpret certain passages figuratively are, as we saw earlier, the discoveries of physical science: so Augustine taught at length in *De Genesi ad litteram*. On the whole Augustine seems to think that the figurative meaning which his rules enable him to detect is that of the biblical writer, though he does in principle grant the point that the Holy Spirit may inspire humans to say things whose deep meaning is hidden from them.[63] Gregory (see his claim about Solomon) seems to thinks of Christ, and Origen of the Holy Spirit, as the authors of the Bible, and the human writer to be irrelevant. In view of the way the Bible was composed, one cannot think of any biblical passage as having just one human author; and the logic of my argument and that of Origen, Gregory, and Augustine certainly does not lead us to suppose that any human author always fully understood the meaning of any passage he wrote, when its meaning was given only by the larger whole into which it was inserted.

Not all the early Fathers made explicit acknowledgement of the rule for distinguishing the literal and the figurative (given e.g. by Augustine), let alone used it to yield as much by way of figurative meaning as Origen did, yet they all allowed that metaphor and parable have their role in the Bible, and others had little by way of explicit rival doctrine to that of the three great Church Fathers whom I have cited. They all too had a standard apparatus of 'types' ready to provide metaphorical interpretations. They distinguished between those passages which could and those passages which could not be taken literally—even though they often wished to claim for the former senses additional to the literal. And on the whole their metaphorical interpretations were, given the armoury of explicit typology available from the earliest period of the Church, in my view sensible ones. But subsequently to New Testament times and the time of the formation of the canon of Scripture, it cannot be denied that allegorizing often went wild. Passages which there was no reason to take in other than their literal sense were

---

[62] *De doctrina Christiana*, 3. 10. 14.   [63] See n. 49.

supposed to have a clear metaphorical sense, and sometimes not a literal sense at all; and the metaphorical sense was generated by quite new armouries of typology unknown to the Scripture's first Christian expositors.

Consider Maximus the Confessor, the dominant theologian in the Eastern Church in the post-patristic centuries. In his *Quaestiones ad Thalassium* he answers many questions about the meaning of scriptural passages. Although he thinks that many of the passages which he discusses are literally true, he thinks that in the case of many of the Old Testament passages the literal meaning is spiritually worthless and we should seek the important deep figurative meaning. Some historical incident which Scripture records may indeed have occurred, but it has no importance: what matters is the figurative meaning of the text. His treatment can be illustrated by just one passage which he reasonably does not think should be construed as a literal prophecy: Zechariah 4: 10a. The text of this passage may well be corrupt, and its meaning is certainly obscure. It is part of Zechariah's vision of the seven-branched lampstand. In the Authorized Version, whose text is nearer to that of Maximus than some more modern versions, it reads: 'They shall rejoice and shall see the plummet in the hand of Zerubbabel with those seven; they are the eyes of the Lord which run to and fro through the whole Earth.' Maximus[64] reads it as saying that the plummet is decorated with the seven eyes of the Lord, which look over the whole Earth. He claims that this makes no sense literally. But Zerubbabel represents Christ: a plausible interpretation as he was the governor of Judaea in the immediate post-exilic period, for whom Haggai prophesied greater things, presumably kingship;[65] he was to be the restored David. The plummet or 'stone' of lead as he reads it, he interprets as 'faith in Christ'. New Testament talk of Christ as the rock or stone, on which we can build securely, suggests that—although not too naturally. But then the interpretation becomes less plausible. Maximus reads the text as saying that Zerubbabel holds the plummet; and holding, he says, is an active thing, a work. Hence faith is manifested by the active process of works; and he quotes St James's saying that 'faith without works is dead'.[66] The seven eyes of faith are the 'seven' gifts of the Spirit or virtues, described by Isaiah.[67] So Christ by actively grasping the stone

---

[64] PG 90: 521. For exposition of St Maximus' treatment of Scripture generally, see J. Pelikan, *The Christian Tradition*, ii: *The Spirit of Eastern Christendom* (University of Chicago) Press, 1974, ch. 1.

[65] Hag. 2: 23.   [66] Jas. 1: 26.   [67] Isa. 11: 2.

of faith shows that faith is manifested by the work of practising the virtues, and the verse says that men will see that and rejoice. A tortuous interpretation, and one which others could easily recognize as going far beyond the 'typological' interpretation of Hebrews or the Song of Songs quoted earlier. But it serves as an example of just how deeply rooted in the Church's tradition is metaphorical interpretation of Scripture. Better and less frequent metaphorical interpretations belong to the tradition; to avoid them altogether would be to abandon it.

So there was a wide tradition in the early Church of reading the Bible metaphorically and not always literally; it was the Church of the centuries which established the canon of Scripture which taught that this was the way in which it ought to be read. It was the Bible understood in that way which they declared to be true. The rebirth of learning in the West in the twelfth century led to considerable scriptural study, the most famous centre for which was the Abbey of St Victor at Paris. About the year AD 1127 Hugh of St Victor wrote his *Didascalion*, the latter part of which was concerned with the principles of scriptural exegesis; it proved a work widely influential in the Middle Ages. His basic principles were those of Origen and Augustine; and he advised against too quick a resort to non-literal interpretation.

'Sacred Scripture has three ways of conveying meaning-namely history, allegory, and tropology.' By 'allegory' in the narrow sense in which he uses the term in this paragraph, Hugh understands a metaphorical interpretation conveying Christian doctrine; by 'tropology' he understands a metaphorical interpretation conveying moral instruction. 'To be sure', he continues, 'all things in the divine utterance must not be wrenched to an interpretation such that each of them is held to contain history, allegory, and tropology all at once', as some had taught.

Even if a triple meaning can appropriately be assigned in many passages, nevertheless it is either difficult or impossible to see it everywhere ... In the divine utterances are placed certain things which are intended to be understood spiritually only, certain things that emphasize the importance of moral conduct, and certain things said according to the simple sense of history.[68]

There are, he repeats, 'certain places in the divine page which cannot be read literally'.[69] But care has to be exercised in construing a passage allegorically. You need to know the rest of your Bible; he does not

[68] *Didascation*, 5. 2.   [69] Ibid. 6. 4.

'think that you will be able to become perfectly sensitive to allegory unless you have first been grounded in history'.[70] But above all passages have to be read in such a way as to be consonant with the Christian faith: 'The very bases of your spiritual structure are certain principles of the faith, principles which form your starting point.'[71] And he commends those who 'know how to bend all Scriptural passages whatever into fitting interpretation and to judge both what is out of keeping with sound faith and what is consonant with it'.

By and large this general spirit of interpretation continued, despite much more emphasis on the literal meaning, during the later Middle Ages and even the period of classical Reformers.[72] But in the nineteenth century the Bible came to be interpreted by many Anglo-Saxon Protestants in perhaps the most literal and insensitive way in which it has ever been interpreted in Christian history. This literalism was encouraged by the basic philosophical mistake of equating the 'original meaning' of the text, gradually being probed by historical enquiry, with the meaning of the text in the context of a Christian document. We may hanker after the 'original meaning' in the sense of the meaning of the separate units before they were used to form a Bible, but that sense is *not* relevant to assessing its truth; for the Bible is a patchwork and context changes meaning.

In the end, for someone who longs to interpret the Bible in terms of the 'original meaning' of its books, there is always one acid test of whether this is a reasonable construal of the Bible as canonized and promulgated as a Christian book by the Church of early centuries: how do you interpret the Song of Songs? It is ludicrous to suppose that any Church Father, even the most 'literal-minded' one, would have

[70] Ibid. 6. 3.   [71] Ibid. 6. 4.

[72] See A. E. McGrath, *Intellectual Origins of the European Reformation* (Basil Blackwell, 1987), ch. 6, for the hermeneutics of the immediate pre- and post-Reformation period. A pre-Reformation distinction developed between two 'literal' senses of the Old Testament, the 'carnal' 'rabbinical' sense, and the 'prophetic' sense in which the Old Testament was read as concerned with Christ. The 'prophetic literal' sense was in no way the reading which would be yielded by taking the text straight or historically, in my terminology. It involved reading the Old Testament in the light of the New Testament, as interpreted by Christian doctrine; and so, in my terminology, metaphorically. The 'David' of the Psalms was read as 'Christ' for example. So while both Luther and Zwingli did not go along with the medieval fourfold interpretation of Scripture (see my n. 38), and advocated the 'literal sense' alone, this is misleading if we do not take into account that that often meant the 'literal prophetic' sense. See McGrath, *Intellectual Origins*, 157, 159, and 169. However not all the Reformers had the same canons of interpretation.

supposed that its meaning was its meaning as a book on its own. On its own it is an erotic love poem. They would all[73] have said that its meaning was to be understood in terms of its place in a Christian Bible. Just as the rabbis had interpreted it as concerned with God's agapeistic love for the old Israel, so now the Church Fathers normally interpreted it as concerned with God's (or perhaps Christ's) love for Israel, new (the Church) as well as old. Even those Church Fathers who protested against the allegorical interpretations of other passages interpreted allegorically here and no doubt in some other places as well. There is no justification whatever for them or us to regard the Song as a special case; whatever rules apply to it apply generally. The genetic fallacy that origins determine present operation leads us to suppose that we understand the meaning of a text when we understand its literary history. But we do not; what we need to know is its literary context, not its literary history.

Of course if we are misguided enough to interpret the Bible in terms of the 'original meaning' of the text, that original meaning is often false:[74] there is scientific, historical, moral, and theological falsity in the Bible, if it is so interpreted. This evident fact led many liberal-minded theologians of the twentieth century to cease to talk of the Bible being 'true', but to speak rather of it being 'useful' or 'insightful' if read in accord with some rule or other of interpretation; and there have evolved as many ways of interpreting as there have been theologians to do the interpreting. And saying this sort of thing about the Bible hardly gives it a special status—the same could be said of any great work of literature. A general fog settled over 'hermeneutics'.[75] And yet the rules are there, sanctified by centuries of use by those who claimed in accord with Christian tradition that the Bible was 'true'. If we wish to take seriously claims for the truth of the Bible, we must understand it in the way that both philosophical rules for interpreting other texts, and so many of those who interpreted the Bible or laid down the rules for

[73] All those who accepted it as canonical Scripture, that is. The firmest opponents of any allegorizing were the followers of Marcion who, as we have noted, denied scriptural status to any of the Old Testament.

[74] This seems to be the moral of Hans Frei's influential book *The Eclipse of Biblical Narrative* (Yale University Press, 1974), pleading for much of the Bible 'to be read as simple narrative whether or not the narrative corresponds to historical fact'.

[75] For descriptions of different contemporary methods of interpreting the Old Testament, see Barton, *Reading the Old Testament*, and D. H. Kelsey, *The Uses of Scripture in Recent Theology* (SCM Press, 1975). Barton defends explicitly the thesis that there is no privileged method of interpretation.

doing so in previous centuries, suggest; and that includes their admission that it contains deeper truths which future generations wiser than themselves might detect by using their rules.[76]

[76] The declaration of the Second Vatican Council on revelation, *Dei Verbum*, emphasized the crucial points that for understanding a passage we must understand the genre of the book to which it belongs, and that we must consider it as an element in the whole Bible: 'Those who search out the intention of the sacred writers must, among other things, have regard for literary forms ... But since Holy Scripture must be read and interpreted according to the same Spirit by whom it was written no less serious attention must be given to the content and unity of the whole of Scripture, if the meaning of the sacred texts is to be correctly brought to light' (*Dei Verbum*, 12).

11

Conclusion

Weighing the Evidence

I argued in Chapter 5 that God might be expected to reveal to humans truths of central importance to the conduct of their life on Earth—including truths about what God is like and has done for humans, which have consequences for the way in which he is to be approached and worshipped. However clever humans were, they could not reach true conclusions on some of the relevant matters without help; and in fact humans are not clever enough to reach true conclusions on any of those matters without help. Nevertheless there is great value in humans reaching their own conclusions on these matters; and so the kind of revelation which we might well expect to be given would have enough content to provide something for humans to get to grips with, but not enough detail for humans not to need to sort things out for themselves. An original revelation would need an interpreting community in which its content could be preserved, developed, corrected, and reinterpreted to answer new questions and meet new needs.

I argued in Chapter 6 that there would be evidence that a purported revelation was indeed a revelation from God in so far as it had somewhat of the above character, was backed by a powerful divine miracle, and in so far as we could judge by independent criteria that quite a lot of it was likely to be true and none of it was probably false. Then we would have good reason for believing the rest of the revelation, and additional reasons for believing those parts which we had some prior reason for believing true anyway.

In the light of these general considerations, I began to investigate the purported Christian revelation—after commenting that it alone of the great religions could present a serious candidate for a miraculous foundation event. It seems fairly clear that Jesus Christ claimed to have a revelation from God, and the early Church saw his resurrection as authenticating that. So there is a crucial question for the historian of how strong is the evidence that the Resurrection took place, as regards its physical aspects, roughly as reported in the Gospels. The stronger that evidence, the better authorized as revelatory is the teaching which flowed from it. I argued that the detailed evidence (from reports of witnesses and sources) of historical sources must always be weighed in the light of background evidence of how likely that event is to occur anyway. On a theistic view on which God has the power to intervene miraculously in history and reason for doing so, such an event is not unlikely and other things being equal, the witnesses should be believed. I argued in Chapter 5 that God has reason for thus intervening in order to authenticate a revelation. He may have other reasons also for manifestly bringing to life again Jesus Christ: for example if thereby he symbolized his acceptance of Christ's sacrifice on the Cross.[1] So there are questions for the historian, of just how strong the detailed historical evidence is; and for the philosopher of religion, of how strong is the evidence for that sort of God.

Then there is the issue of which present-day community is the 'best continuer' of the Church of the apostles, whether there is one such, or whether that Church is now divided. The issue here turns again on historical issues as to which line of descent from the apostles best preserves organization and continuity of teaching with them. I emphasized that one would expect the later Church to draw out things which were not on the surface in the original revelation, to formulate doctrines to make sense of that revelation, which would otherwise have little justification; but not of course to add new content or to contradict the original revelation. This line is difficult to draw, but I tried to illustrate the principles involved in Chapter 8. However, what does 'draw out' correctly the original revelation will be far from clear, and hence the need for an authorized body to do it; whose interpretation is to be accepted in so far as there is some reason for supposing that it is doing it correctly and as much reason to believe that it is doing it correctly as that any other body is, as well as for reasons of continuity of organization.

Once we reach the 'best continuer' today, with respect to doctrine and organization, we must consider the probability, on grounds other than that the 'best continuer' is teaching it, that what it is teaching is a true revelation from God. Such probability I shall call the prior prob-

---

[1] As I have argued elsewhere—see *Responsibility and Atonement* (Clarendon Press, 1989), 160.

ability of a purported revelation. This will involve considering whether what it is teaching, true or not, is relevant to human needs in the way which I described in Chapter 5. If an ecclesiastical body is insisting on doctrines as revealed and important for belief, whether probably true or not, which seem to have no connection with deep truths about the universe or important aspects of conduct, that must count against the claim of that body to be a vehicle of revelation. Clearly it must be a charge for the Roman Catholic Church to meet that it demands too much for its adherents to believe; or more accurately, for its adherents to put their trust in; and that some of those doctrines, for instance those connected with Mary, her supposed immaculate conception and bodily assumption, do not at first sight seem to have the kind of relevance needed. Of course 'first sight' may mislead; my only point is that there is a case to be met.

The prior probability of a purported revelation is, however, more centrally, a matter of whether it is probably true—on grounds other than that a 'church' is teaching it. Undoubtedly the most central doctrines of the Christian religion are the Christian moral ideal of love and the doctrines contained in the early creeds of the Church; so much is agreed by Roman Catholics, Orthodox, and Protestants. Among those, the most central specifically Christian doctrines are those of the Trinity, the Incarnation, and the Atonement—three doctrines concerned with who Christ was, and what he did. The two former doctrines received a canonical form in the fourth and fifth centuries AD; and have been proclaimed by almost all bodies deriving from the Church of the apostles (with some relatively small exceptions). If these doctrines are basically false, then there is no Christian revelation, in my sense of revelation of a body of statements to be believed on authority. I stress 'basically'; there might be scope for slight rephrasing of those doctrines. The doctrine of the Atonement never received a 'canonical form' in the way that the other two doctrines did. Yet Christians always held as a central belief that Jesus Christ came down from Heaven, in the words of the Nicene Creed, 'for us men and for our salvation'; but just how he effected our salvation is something over which Christians have differed. However, if in no sense did Jesus Christ effect our salvation, then there is no Christian revelation.

Any evidence (other than their centrality in a Christian tradition) concerned with the truth or falsity of these doctrines will be evidence for or against there having been a Christian revelation. This evidence again must involve historical components: for example evidence that

Christ was crucified for a crime he did not commit is relevant to the view that in some sense he saved us from our sins. On this I cannot think that there is any serious doubt that the Crucifixion took place, nor very much doubt that Jesus Christ had done nothing which by any true standards deserved that sort of punishment. Also relevant is historical evidence to show that Jesus allowed himself to be crucified and intended his death as a sacrificial offering. I have described in Chapter 7 evidence of Jesus' acts which suggests just that. But philosophical argument is again also crucially relevant: to show the plausibility of the moral ideal and the internal coherence of the doctrines of the Trinity and the Incarnation, and the coherence of supposing that one person can in some sense atone for the sins of another; and to show the prior probability (i.e. probability apart from evidence that it has been revealed) that God is three persons in one substance or likely to become incarnate. One major argument for the latter is that there is considerable prior probability that he will seek, by an incarnate life of supererogatory goodness, to make available atonement for our sins.[2]

If the result of all such enquiries was decisively against traditional Christian doctrines having any significant prior probability, then even if there was a clear 'closest continuer' of a church founded on a well-established miraculous resurrection, the rational enquirer must conclude all the same that it is unlikely that there has been a Christian revelation. But if traditional doctrines have some, perhaps not very great, prior probability then the evidence of the Church founded on the Resurrection teaching them may well increase their probability until they become more probable than not (i.e. have posterior probability on that evidence of more than $1/2$).

Outside this central core are other doctrines well established in Christian tradition, such as the other doctrines expressed in the creeds. I have claimed that there is scope in a revelation for some error and so for some correction of error, given a basic framework of doctrine within which implications can be drawn out to make the correction. Hence any intrinsic improbability of less central doctrines, although it cuts somewhat against there having been a Christian revelation, does not cut

---

[2] I have given argument for those of these philosophical points which concern the Atonement in *Responsibility and Atonement*. I hope to give argument on those philosophical points which concern the Trinity and the Incarnation in the next volume of the present tetralogy. There is also an argument why one might expect God to become incarnate, arising from the problem of evil, which I hope to discuss in the last volume of this tetralogy.

nearly so much. If the prior probability of the most central doctrines makes it, together with evidence of a church founded on miracle, probable that the Church is the vehicle of revelation, that has the consequence that it raises the probability of other doctrines which are initially very improbable. If some of the things in a letter are quite probable, and that in turn makes it probable that the letter had a certain reliable source, then that greatly adds to the probability that the other things in the letter are true, even if initially they seemed most unlikely to be true.

Among doctrines near to the centre, but not right at the centre, of Christian teaching have been doctrines such as that after death the good enjoy the vision of God and the bad are permanently deprived of it; that Jesus was born of a Virgin and had no human father; and that he instituted within the Church the sacraments of baptism and the eucharist.

Outside these fairly central doctrines, there lie doctrines which are more and more peripheral—either in the sense that they have only been taught at certain periods of the Church's history or by certain ecclesiastical bodies, or in the sense that the Church itself has seen them as dependent for their truth on the more central doctrines and to be less important in the Christian scheme. The further away we get from the core, the more successor bodies have disputed the truth of doctrines; and it has been, I have urged, part of the point of revelation that there should be such dispute within a basically Christian scheme.

It is with doctrines well outside the central core, I suggest, that the secular world has found its strongest objections to the teaching of the Christian churches. Of course the secular world has not found the central doctrines of Christian theism very plausible, but its fire has burnt hottest against certain teaching which can hardly be regarded as other than fairly peripheral. It must however be acknowledged that at the times of most acute controversy about some of these issues, some Christian bodies have often claimed for the doctrines under attack a fairly central, and even an essential, place in the scheme of revelation. I suggest that the history of Christianity indicates that they have been quite wrong to make that claim.

Let me illustrate by two examples. First of course there have been the famous controversies between 'science and religion', especially the Copernican controversy over the Earth's centrality in the universe, and the Darwinian controversy about man's evolution over hundreds of millions of years from primitive animals. I have already argued in

Chapters 9 and 10 that the great theologians of the past did not see the Christian revelation as containing the sort of scientific teaching in dispute in these controversies, controversies arising from taking the presuppositions or statements about scientific or historical matters in the Bible as statements of Christian doctrine, where these have no implications one way or the other for central Christian doctrines.[3] What you think man is now like is unaffected by what you think about his bodily ancestry.

Secondly, one must mention with shame the practice, sometimes backed up by formal teaching, of the persecution and coercion of non-Christians and heretics. Now the Church has never claimed in this or any other matter that individual Christians or even Church authorities are always faithful in their practice, and the practice which they inspire, to the Church's revelation. And Christians persecuting or doing anything else contrary to the Church's teaching would not be evidence against the revealed character of that teaching. But there is no doubt that formal doctrinal pronouncements have sometimes legitimized this conduct, even though the conduct has been far more widespread than the pronouncements which legitimized it permitted.

For example, churches have occasionally used formal pronouncements of a detailed administrative character, not statements of purported timeless doctrine, encouraging the limitation of the civil rights of Jews and other non-Christians. The Fourth Lateran Council, AD 1215, issued pronouncements of this kind against Jews: thus Christian princes were forbidden to give any government appointment to a Jew on pain of excommunication. Clearly too anti-Semitic conduct by Christians has far outpaced even any administrative pronouncements which legitimized it. There have been from time to time formal Church declarations forbidding the forcible conversion to Christianity of adult individuals or their young children and declaring that the practice of other religions must be tolerated.[4] Yet there have been places and periods when forcible conversion was widespread.

Supposed heretics (i.e. baptized Christians who have adopted supposedly heretical beliefs) and apostates have been often shamefully

---

[3] I repeat that I am *not* saying that *all* scientific or historical claims are irrelevant to Christian doctrine. To give another example: a scientific proof that man does not have free will—which is possible, though I believe unlikely (see my *The Evolution of the Soul* (Clarendon Press, 1986), ch. 13)—would be crucially relevant to doctrines concerned with man (human sin and destiny); as I argue in several places in *Responsibility and Atonement*.

[4] See (e.g.) the Letter of Gregory the Great (Denzinger 480).

treated. There are teachings of influential (mainly medieval) theologians[5] and one pronouncement of a Pope[6] which legitimized the execution of heretics in order to compel them to repent of their heresy, for the sake of their souls' well-being. The different treatment of heretics from infidels was justified on the grounds that at their baptism they accepted an allegiance to Christ: 'heresy is a species of infidelity, attaching to those who profess faith of Christ yet corrupt his dogmas',[7] whereas Jews and Muslims have acquired no such allegiance. The civil power has the right to punish those who so wrong God, the argument went.

These are terrible things. But the very few doctrinal pronouncements on these matters are quite clearly on the periphery of Christian teaching, and equally clearly they are out of line with the few remarks the New Testament makes on these matters,[8] and they have no basis in the practice and doctrine of the Church of the first three centuries, as a body which sought to win and keep converts by persuasion and not by force.[9] Hence, given an understanding of revelation as a body of doctrine which may contain minor error which it is the responsibility of the Church to sort out, pronouncements on such peripheral matters cannot count very heavily against the occurrence of a revelation. The Roman Catholic Church finally gave its final formal doctrinal seal on the right of every human to practise whatever religion he or she chose in the declaration of the Second Vatican Council, *Dignitatis humanae*.

I have argued that we need to approach the question of whether there has been a revelation having sorted out beforehand two crucial issues. The first is: what sort of a revelation are we looking for? A

---

[5] Aquinas holds that heretics may be justly put to death *Summa theologiae*, 2a. 2ae. 11. 3.

[6] In his Bull of 1520 Pope Leo X listed among the errors of Martin Luther the view that 'the burning of heretics is contrary to the will of the Holy Spirit' (Denzinger 1483).

[7] Aquinas, *Summa theologiae*, 2a. 2ae. 11. 1.

[8] See Luke 9: 49–55 or John 12: 47–8.

[9] After the establishment of Christianity as a state religion of the Roman Empire, the emperors developed an interest for the sake of the unity of the Empire in preventing Church divisions, and Church authorities began to use the state as a tool for putting pressure on those deemed heretics or schismatics. The Church first appealed to the state to secure its buildings for its exclusive use; but advanced from there to supporting the use of fines against heretics and schismatics, and then more severe penalties. For some of the first moves along this downhill path, see S. L. Greenslade, *Schism in the Early Church* (SCM Press, 1953), ch. 7. The first execution of someone apparently for heresy was the execution of Priscillian in AD 385, by Magnus Maximus (although the crime was nominally magic). This drew considerable protest in the Church, including from the Pope himself. Augustine at first opposed any coercion of Donatists by the state, but eventually supported fines on them.

golden tablet thrown down from the sky, preserved in a sealed glass case from all interference, including radioactivity? Or a whole way of looking at things, embedded in documents and in a community and continually being worked out by them? And the second is: which general theory of the world (e.g. theism or materialism) do we think is best supported by other evidence? For general theory is crucial for assessing particular claims. Within this framework we must weigh up detailed philosophical arguments about the extent of prior probability of Christian doctrines and detailed historical arguments about the acts and teaching of Jesus and which is the 'closest continuer' of the Church of the apostles. Weakness in some parts of this web of evidence may be compensated by strength in other parts.

That evidence for the truth of revelation comes from many sources, weakness in one being compensated by strength in another, and that the cumulative force of the total evidence makes it probable that the Christian revelation is a true one has been in effect the view of most Christian writers since Christianity began—apart from those writers of the last two centuries whose theological thinking derives from the philosophies of Kant and Kierkegaard and who seem to hold that faith in the Christian Revelation can in some sense be 'rational' without there being any evidence for it. Yet, while this cumulative force has in general been stressed, not all apologists have given quite such a central place in their scheme to the evidence of eye-witnesses about the Resurrection as I have done in my scheme and, as I claim, the first-century writers did in theirs. One reason for their greater emphasis on other kinds of evidence is, I believe, the fact that, in ages lacking sophisticated historical research, it was a lot more difficult than in our age to sort out legend from genuine history after more than a hundred years. We are in a much better position than investigators between the second and the sixteenth centuries to analyse what happened in Jerusalem around AD 30. The other reason is that opponents of Christianity might well allow that big 'miracles' sometimes occur—Celsus was prepared to allow to Origen, for the sake of argument, that the Resurrection occurred[10]—and yet deny that that showed very much about revelation. Aquinas, however, in his section in the *Summa theologiae* on the Resurrection, emphasized the importance of eye-witness testimony (to the empty tomb and Resurrection appearances) in giving us knowledge of the faith.[11] And the centrality of miracle in a cumulative case was

[10] Origen, *Contra Celsum*, 1. 68.   [11] *Summa theologiae*, 3. 53. 1.

restressed by British empiricist philosophers of the seventeenth and eighteenth centuries. Paley asked the rhetorical question: 'Now in what way can a revelation be made but by miracles?', and answered, 'In none which we are able to conceive.'[12]

Although the later patristic and the medieval period did not in general place great emphasis on the Resurrection or miracles as such in their cumulative case statements of evidence for revelation, these things had their place; and it is worthwhile setting out one systematic account, among others of the period, of the evidence for revelation from those periods, given by one of Christianity's greatest thinkers, in order to show the similarity of my account to his, despite its different emphases. Duns Scotus sets out at the beginning of his systematic theology, the *Ordinatio*, ten separate reasons for the credibility of Holy Scripture, and thus of the doctrines which can be derived from it: (1) *Praenuntiatio prophetica* (the fulfilment of Old Testament prophecy in the New), (2) *Scripturarum concordia* (Scriptures have a common message, and that includes the common witness of the New Testament writers to the teaching and deeds of Jesus), (3) *Auctoritas Scribentium* (the human authors' conviction that they spoke with God's authority), (4) *Diligentia recipientium* (the careful way in which the Church formed the canon of Scripture), (5) *Rationabilitas contentarum* (the prior probability of its doctrines), (6) *Irrationabilitas errorum* (the inadequacy of objections), (7) *Ecclesiae stabilitas* (the long and constant witness of the Church), (8) *Miraculorum limpiditas* (biblical and later miracles, including the great miracle of the conversion of the Western world), (9) *Testimonia non fidelium* (alleged prophecies of pagan writers), (10) *Promissorum efficacia* (the sanctifying power of the Church's teaching in the lives of the faithful).[13]

(2), (3), and (4) all include aspects of historical eye-witness (2), confident (3), well-tested (4) evidence for historical events. Although Scotus does not single out the Resurrection in this context, miraculous foundation events are included under (8). Although other religions and philosophies as well as Christianity have had great success, and so the mere fact of success is not much of an argument for truth, I have

---

[12] W. Paley, *A View of the Evidences of Christianity* (1st pub. 1794), Prefatory Considerations. See too John Locke's defence of the crucial importance of the miracles of the New Testament as evidence for Christianity, in his *A Third Letter Concerning Toleration*, ch. 10. (See the selection therefrom in John Locke, *The Reasonableness of Christianity*, ed. I. T. Ramsey (A. & C. Black, 1958).)

[13] *Ordinatio*, Prologus, 2. 100–19.

argued that if a super-miracle such as a resurrection had the effect of promulgating a religion that would be evidence of its truth. While allowing some scope for it, I have downplayed any role for Old Testament prophecy (1) in the cumulative case. (9) may have a small place, but only if it is seen as showing that pagan writers uninfluenced by Christianity saw the need for a Christian-type revelation. I have given an important place to any independent grounds for supposing central Christian doctrines to be true (5), (6), and (10), and to the continuity in the teaching of these doctrines in the Church (7).

Weighing different evidence and different kinds of evidence against each other is always a delicate and difficult matter, but it is something that historians and scientists have to do all the time, and the situation in this regard in theology is no different in principle, only in scale, from what it is in science[14] and history. Again, in all such matters, there is no end to the enquiries which can be pursued, and it is always possible that each new stage of an enquiry might throw up new evidence which might point in a quite different direction from evidence obtained so far. But, as I have argued elsewhere,[15] each of us should pursue such enquiry as we have time and capacity to do and act on its results. Most of us will have to make do with some pretty limited historical investigation filtered down to us from the works of experts. But as we move from the very general issues of whether there is a God to the very detailed issues of just what the Church of the second century believed about the papacy, clearly the results, although they matter, matter less. For while belief in a Christian God leads to quite a different course of conduct on the part of one who seeks to do good (e.g. it will lead to worship and prayer in a Christian community, for forgiveness and for others), differences of belief within Christianity will lead to less difference of conduct (e.g. in respect of the method of worship and the way in which forgiveness is sought—always privately or sometimes from a priest in the confessional, etc.). As I stressed earlier, among mainstream Christian bodies similarity of doctrine vastly outweighs differences.

---

[14] It is sometimes suggested that scientific hypotheses are different from those of history or theology because they are open to fresh testing by new observations. But such testing is not necessary for a theory to be rendered probable by current evidence, and scientific hypotheses may well be rendered probable by evidence even when fresh testing is not possible—see my *The Existence of God* (Clarendon Press, 1979), 66–7. And further enquiries which may always yield new observations are relevant to history, and so to theology in so far as it depends on history.

[15] *Faith and Reason* (Clarendon Press, 1981), esp. ch. 3.

The Final Picture

If the evidence described above finally supports a Christian revelation, the following is the picture of it which it supports. First of course that something was made known before Christ. Humans all over the world and long ago had, by their experience of the world and their use of reason, much knowledge of right and wrong and of God as their creator to whom they owed worship. But God gave a deeper knowledge of himself to a particular community, Israel; and the Old Testament contains a record of a people who unlike their neighbours came to know that there was only one supreme and holy God, so different from us and so uncontrollable by us that no images of him could be formed; who had given special commands to Israel by obeying which they would be themselves made holy. And the Old Testament contains also the record of their failure to obey those commands. Much of the revelation given to Israel was however a revelation embedded in its presuppositions about history and science, and much was directed to particular needs: its commandments had little to say about the morality of nuclear de-terrence. Further the division between history and parable was not always very sharp or obvious—to original writers, let alone to later interpreters.

In the teaching of Jesus Christ a more complete revelation was given. He gave men and women an ideal of total goodness and a hope of eter-nal life (including life after death) in which the good would enjoy the vision of God. If my account of his 'actions' in Chapter 7 is anywhere near correct, he taught that we need divine forgiveness for our sins, and that that is freely available through the Passion of Christ, in the Church which he founded. What else he taught is not so clear from the Gospel record taken on its own; but if he was indeed the divine messenger, and founded a Church to proclaim that message, then what the Church subsequently taught was what he explicitly or implicitly taught. Its teaching included its proclamation of the New Testament itself, and the Gospels as basically reliable records of Christ. It subsequently taught that Jesus Christ was God Incarnate, the second person of the Holy Trinity. How far Jesus Christ taught that explicitly, I am unsure. The 'proof texts' for these doctrines in the New Testament can be construed in different ways. But certainly these doctrines are implicit in certain New Testament passages, and especially St John's Gospel. I suggested in Chapters 8 and 10 that the process of making them explicit was a reasonable one.

The process of refining Christianity has been going on for 2,000 years. It has involved removing the presuppositions of the original message, and applying it to new circumstances and spelling it out so as to answer new questions. It has involved, for example, discovering the scope of various commandments, such as whether what St Paul had to say about the role of women in the Church is to be read historically, as applicable only to Corinth in the first century AD, or straight, as applicable to all communities at all times. It has involved discovering which Old and New Testament passages are to be read metaphorically—for instance, which passages of the Book of Revelation are to be so read—and trying to spell them out more literally. It has involved 'interpretation' but an 'interpretation' which the interpreting Church has always seen need to justify as an extrapolation from an original revelation. It could never appeal to new data of revelation. It rejected the late second-century 'heresy' Montanism with its claim of further major divine revelation,[16] and it has rejected similar claims ever since.

But growth of understanding there has been. Vincent of Lerins wrote:

But perhaps someone may object: Does this mean that in the Church of Christ, religion can never make any advances? No, there can be the greatest progress. Who is so envious of his fellow human beings, so hated by God that he would try to stop it? The important point to watch is this: that it is real progress of the faith, not a change in the faith. Progress means that each thing grows within itself; change, on the other hand, means that one thing is changed into something else. So, by all means, there must be growth.[17]

This passage was quoted with approval by the First Vatican Council.[18] And the Second Vatican Council wrote: 'The tradition which comes from the apostles develops in the Church with the help of the Holy Spirit. For there is a growth in the understanding of the realities and the words which have been handed down.'[19]

Gregory Nazianzen's explanation of this growth is that the Church could not swallow too much at once:

---

[16] Montanism was a charismatic movement, claiming that the Spirit had given new teaching to prophets, whose deliverances were additional to those of Scripture and ecclesiastical tradition. See (e.g.) J. Tixeront, *History of Dogmas*, i (B. Herder, 1930), 192–9.

[17] *Commonitorium*, 1. 23. Translated in Robert B. Eno, *Teaching Authority in the Early Church* (Michael Glazier Inc., 1984), 146.

[18] Denzinger 3020.　　[19] *Dei Verbum*, 8.

You will reach perfection only by continuing to expand. For example, the Old Testament proclaimed the Father openly, the Son more obscurely. The New Testament has clearly shown the Son but only suggested the divinity of the Spirit. In our day the Spirit lives among us and gives us a clear indication of himself. For it was not without danger—when the divinity of the Father was not yet confessed, to proclaim the Son openly; nor when the divinity of the Son was not yet admitted, to add on the Holy Spirit as a burden, to use a somewhat audacious term. Otherwise, weighed down, so to speak, by a nourishment that was too much for them and looking up into the sun with eyes still too weak, men risked losing even what they had. On the contrary, by gradual steps, and as David said, by 'going from strength to strength' [Ps. 84: 6], by moving 'from glory to glory' [2 Cor. 3: 18], the light of the Trinity will shine out with greater brilliance.[20]

That is clearly so only if one of the purposes of a revelation is to give people enough to work out more for themselves; and that by co-operative and diligent enquiry and honest pursuit of truth. I have suggested that it is. If people are thus to pursue truth, they will need alternative theories: for example that Christ is fully God, or that he is almost God. And one way of pursuing truth honestly is to cleave to what you see as true despite the eminence of those who advocate the opposite viewpoint. Vincent of Lerins sees this as the reason why heresy is allowed to flourish in the Church.

So now you see clearly the reason why Divine Providence sometimes allows certain teachers in the Church to put forward some new ideas. 'The Lord your God is testing you.' And the great test is when someone you considered to be a prophet, a follower of prophets, a teacher of and fighter for the truth, someone whom you have embraced with great veneration and love, this very person has subtly brought in dangerous errors which you have not been able immediately to detect because you are under the spell of this man and you cannot easily bring yourself to condemn him while affection for your teacher holds you.[21]

Metaphor abounds in the Old Testament, whether because the original human authors wrote metaphorically or because passages originally intended literally have to be taken metaphorically in the context of a Christian document. In the process of doctrinal clarification the Church has tried to produce credal statements as near to literal as it could; though sometimes, and above all when talking of the divine nature, it has to make do with analogy. Because of this process of historical devel-

---

[20] Gregory Nazianzen, *Oration*, 31. 26. Translated in Eno, *Teaching Authority*, 115.
[21] *Commonitorium*, 1. 10. Translated in Eno, *Teaching Authority*, 144.

opment, I have subtitled this book on revelation 'From Metaphor to Analogy'.

That revelation is something whose interpretation is to be worked out within a continuing organization is, I believe, a considerable theme of the teaching of the New Testament itself, which I now illustrate in general terms. The revelation which God provides will not be that evident, it will need searching out: such is the teaching of the parables of the pearl of great price (Matt. 13: 45–6) or the treasure hid in the field (Matt. 13: 44). Indeed, so much of Jesus' teaching was by parable, and by showing what he did, in order to get others to see things which he did not state: 'But who say ye that I am?' (Matt. 16: 15). His answer to the question of the disciples of John, 'Art thou he that cometh, or look we for another?', was, 'Go your way and tell John the things which ye do hear and see' (Matt. 11: 3–4). The revelation is to be spread by some telling others about it: 'The harvest truly is great, but the labourers are few; pray ye therefore the Lord of the harvest that he would send forth labourers into his vineyard' (Matt. 9: 38). The presence of Christ to later disciples is associated with a grouping of them: 'where two or three are gathered together in my name, there am I in the midst of them' (Matt. 18: 20); which suggests (though it certainly does not state) that the understanding of Christian truth will be a communal activity. Even after we have learnt what we can of the Gospel, we shall not be certain of it: 'we walk by faith, not by sight' (2 Cor. 5: 7). And we have a vague and confused vision: 'Now we see in a mirror darkly; but then face to face: now I know in part; but then shall I know even as also I have been known' (1 Cor. 13: 12).

And no one better than the human author of the Fourth Gospel expounded the view that understanding of revelation grows in the community through reflection. Christ had spoken to his disciples the message of the Father. 'The words that I say unto you I speak not from myself' (John 14: 10); 'all things that I have heard from my Father I have made known unto you' (John 15: 15). And not merely had Christ given the orders of the Father, he had lived to explain the point of them: 'The servant knoweth not what his Lord doeth; but I have called you friends' (John 15: 15). To quite an extent the message had been received: 'The words which thou gavest me I have given unto them; and they received them, and knew of a truth that I came forth from thee, and they believed that thou didst send me' (John 17: 8). Yet even then the message had been imperfectly understood: 'Have I been so long time with you, and dost thou not know me, Philip?' (John 14: 9).

And indeed, there was more to come, which simply could not be understood at that time and place: 'I have yet many things to say unto you, but ye cannot bear them now' (John 16: 12). There was a need of future guidance: 'When he, the Spirit of truth, is come, he shall guide you into all truth' (John 16: 13). But the Spirit's witness will be combined with the historical witness of the disciples: 'The Comforter ... shall bear witness of me; and ye also bear witness, because ye have been with me from the beginning' (John 15: 26–7). The Spirit will reinforce the disciples' witness to Christ. And he will help them to remember and understand what Christ did: 'He shall teach you all things and bring to your remembrance all that I said unto you' (John 14: 26). However, the Spirit's witness will not be public: 'The world cannot receive' the Spirit of Truth (John 14: 17). The manifestation of Christ through the Spirit is for those who love Christ and keep his commandments: 'He that hath my commandments, and keepeth them, he it is that loveth me: and he that loveth me shall be loved of my Father, and I will love him and will manifest myself to him' (John 14: 21). In other words, that is in my words, the revelation spoken by and the deeds acted by Christ will be interpreted by human witnesses who keep the commandments of God under the guidance of the Spirit of God. The revelation goes on; it is their witness and yet their witness to an original source which forms the revelation.

Additional Notes

1. I derive my terminology of statement and proposition from Lemmon. See E. J. Lemmon, 'Sentences, Statements and Propositions', in Bernard Williams and Alan Montefiore (eds.) *British Analytical Philosophy*, (Routledge & Kegan Paul, 1966). My definitions differ from his in that his criterion of property identity is that of coextensionality. My 'statement' is Russell's 'proposition'. The Fregean concept of a 'thought' seems to be such that the same thought is expressed if and only if both the same statement and the same proposition are expressed, except in the respect that moments of time have to be picked out non-indexically if a definite thought is to be expressed, and thus Fregean thoughts have a timeless truth-value. (See G. Frege, 'Thoughts', in G. Frege, *Collected Papers on Mathematics, Logic, and Philosophy*, trans. P. Geach and R. H. Stoothoff (Basil Blackwell, 1984). Note: 'the words "this tree is covered with green leaves" are not sufficient by themselves to constitute the expression of thought, for the time of utterance is involved as well. Without the time specification thus given we have not a complete thought, that is we have no thought at all' (370). For a brief account of Frege's concept see C. Peacocke, *Thoughts: An Essay on Content* (Basil Blackwell, 1986), 1–2.) My 'proposition' is Perry's 'relativized proposition'. (John Perry, 'The Problem of the Essential Indexical', *Nous*, 13 (1979), 3–21, see 12–15.) It has some similarity to Kaplan's 'character', with, if I understand Kaplan correctly, the crucial difference that a 'character' does not have a truth-value; it is rather what (together with context) gives truth-value to a sentence (David Kaplan, 'On the Logic of Demonstratives', in P. A. French *et al.* (eds.), *Contemporary Perspectives in the Philosophy of Language* (University of Minnesota Press, 1979)).

2. This view is associated with Donnellan (Keith S. Donnellan, 'Reference and Definite Descriptions', *Philosophical Review*, 75 (1966), 281–304; and 'Speaker Reference, Descriptions, and Anaphora', in French *et al.* (eds.), *Contemporary Perspectives in the Philosophy of Language*). However, what Donnellan actually claims is that, so long as by the description 'the man drinking Martini' I was intending my hearers to pick out a certain man, then the man to whom I refer is the man to whom I am intending to refer. My intention suffices, whatever the indications or lack of them provided by the context, to secure reference. At least this is so, claims Donnellan, of definite descriptions used referentially. Donnellan distinguishes the attributive from the referring use of definite descriptions. 'The *A*' used attributively in 'The *A* is *B*' says merely, 'Whoever is the *A* is *B*,' 'The *A*' used referentially is simply a device for picking out an object which could be picked out in other ways; the

fact that the description 'the *A*' applies to it is not of importance for what is being said. Donnellan's cited claim concerns only definite descriptions used referentially. However, it must only hold when the context makes clear to whom the speaker was intending to refer; for meaning is a public matter and a mere intention to refer to some individual cannot ensure that the speaker does so refer. For if Donnellan was right one could never say in such cases, 'Even if what you meant to say was true, what you actually said was false'; and that surely is a comment which must always have application to all public assertions. Unless the context does make clear that the intended reference (speaker's reference) is other than the object picked out by the description (semantic reference), then the reference is the semantic reference. This account must be extended to proper names, as when I say, 'John looks tired', but the context reveals that I mean that George looks tired (as Kripke pointed out—see S. A. Kripke, 'Speaker's Reference and Semantic Reference', in French *et al.* (eds.), *Contemporary Perspectives in the Philosophy of Language*). For full-length discussion of the criteria for determining to which (if any) object a referring expression refers, see Gareth Evans, *The Varieties of Reference* (Clarendon Press, 1982), esp. ch. 9.

3. There is another argument which can be derived from recent writing in the philosophy of science which has some force in supporting my conclusion that true statements may be made about objects picked out by means of descriptions which are not true of them. This argument is often implicit in some passage rather than explicit but one place where it is fairly near to the surface is pp. 272–82 of H. Putnam, 'Language and Reality', in his *Mind, Language and Reality*, vol. ii of *Philosophical Papers* (Cambridge University Press, 1975). The argument is that science has made gradual progress over the past three millenniums; and that this can only be if earlier science achieved some correct results, formulated in true sentences, and, in the course of time, science achieved more and more such correct results. Yet the sentences which record the correct results will often have picked out entities by means of false descriptions. If you suppose that something is known about an object (e.g. electricity) only when you have a fully true description of its nature or effects by which to pick it out, little would have been discovered by scientists, the argument goes, until the last century and a half. The argument does however assume that progress consists in adding to the stock of true sentences; and an objector might suggest that on the contrary it consists in replacing false sentences by other false sentences which are more nearly true. I think that this objection can be met; but I prefer the argument in the text which is not open to an objection of this kind.

4. Some of these distinctive features may only be believed to belong to the objects, or are suggested by them, as a result of immediately previous conversation. If a speaker in a conversation has been complaining about the exorbitant price paid for a cord of wood, 'That refrigerator is my cord of wood' will then

mean in that context that the refrigerator was very expensive. I take this point and example from Marie Bergmann, 'Metaphorical Assertions', *Philosophical Review* (1982), 239–45. That we *seek to make sense* of the sentence by taking it as making a comparison between *distinctive* features of the objects mentioned is, I think, the major point at which Fogelin is getting when he asserts that metaphors make figurative rather than literal comparisons. '*S* is *O*' is indeed to be read as '*S* is like *O*'. But if overall *S* is not like *O*, the comparison must be read figuratively. If *S* is the subject of conversation, we take first the salient features of *O*, and in a feature space dominated by them look for the similar features of *S* which would justify the comparison. See Robert J. Fogelin, *Figuratively Speaking* (Yale University Press, 1986), 88–9. The salient features of the object of comparison introduced into the discussion are the crucial ones for assessing the truth of the comparison. '*S* is like *O*' is true if there are features of *S* similar to the salient features of *O*. This account of course needs elaboration to deal with sentences other than subject-predicate sentences.

5. There was an interesting recent debate between Mary Hesse, advocating the view that metaphorical claims are cognitive and thus have truth-value, and Richard Rorty who follows Davidson in claiming that they don't have truth-value. Rorty claims that, like the logical positivists, Mary Hesse overvalues the importance of 'meaning' and undervalues the importance of 'non-cognitive genius'. Metaphor works (e.g. causes us to think useful thoughts) when it lacks a meaning, not when it becomes dead and acquires one. Mary Hesse points out that there is a continuity between the metaphorical and the non-metaphorical, and hence that there is little justification for drawing the sharp line represented by the distinction between sentences that do and sentences that do not have a truth-value—whatever view one takes about the nature of meaning. (I would add that the continuity between the metaphorical and the non-metaphorical shows in the increasing vagueness of the statements expressed, which, unlike having a truth-value, is a matter of degree.) However, Mary Hesse goes on to point out that Rorty and Davidson hold the view that talk about the cognitive 'meaning' of normal sentences is just talk about regular linguistic behaviour. Sentences have cognitive meaning in so far as we can predict what other sentences the utterers of one sentence will utter in different circumstances. Talk of meaning is talk of rule-governed use. There is no 'principle of charity' involved in interpreting sentences; because there is nothing behind the sentences to interpret. Like Hesse, I find this implausible. Humans, unlike computers, try to express mental thoughts in public sentences; and they can be quite wrongly interpreted—on occasion. Given that, a thought may still be clear and possess truth-value, even if the public language allows it to be expressed only via a metaphorical utterance, which gives the hearer little scope for subsequent prediction. See Richard Rorty, 'Hesse and Davidson on Metaphor', and Mary Hesse, 'Tropical Talk: The Myth of the Literal', *Proceedings of the Aristotelian Society*, Supplementary Volume, 61 (1987), 283–311. For

commentary on this debate see also Susan Haack, 'Surprising Noises: Rorty and Hesse on Metaphor', *Proceedings of the Aristotelian Society*, 88 (1987–8), 293–301.

6. This group of acts must also include the naming of Simon as Peter, or (in Aramaic) Cephas. Names stick, and all the New Testament documents know him by his new name and ascribe importance to him. The giving of a name with meaning is, for the writers of the Old Testament and so for those learned in it, an act of great significance—it is not the casual attribution of a nickname, which it might be for us. Peter was obviously named by Jesus as the rock on which the apostles formed the Church, the leader of the Church. Though hesitant, E. P. Sanders is inclined to agree with this, pointing out that 'When the name passed into Greek, sometimes the Aramaic was retained... but often the word was translated rather than transliterated, thus putting the emphasis on meaning' (*Jesus and Judaism* (SCM Press, 1985), 146). It is of course a matter of acute controversy as to the kind of leadership which Jesus entrusted to Peter (e.g. whether it included any infallibility on faith and morals) and to how, if at all, it was to be continued in the later Church, a controversy of a kind which I must avoid if I am to get across the main message of this book.

7. There was an occasional custom in the ancient world of a person instituting a 'memorial meal' to be held annually (normally on the person's birthday) after his death. Jeremias has shown that the eucharist was not in this sense a memorial meal. The sacred ceremony was what 'do this in remembrance of me' referred to; the meal was separable from that. He argues that the command to 'remember' was a 'command to remind God' (i.e. plead the Passion before him), not to remind disciples. See J. Jeremias, *The Eucharistic Words of Jesus* (SCM Press, 1966), 237–55. An all-important point to my mind is that the meal was celebrated weekly—on the first day of the week from early times (see Acts 20: 7)—which could only be in order to celebrate the victorious ending to the Passion, the Resurrection. If it was a birthday celebration, it was Christ's heavenly birthday, not his earthly one, which was being celebrated; and of course the Church's saints' days are normally the days of their 'heavenly birthday', in their case the days of their earthly death. The celebration of the eucharist on Sundays in an important piece of evidence that the very early Church believed the Resurrection to have been an event which happened on a particular day.

8. Barth seems to allow this. The Bible, he claims, is not itself the Christian revelation, but is the unique witness thereto. It does not provide a series of infallible propositions, but rather a matrix to which the preacher responds in preaching the Gospel. The men whom in it 'we hear as witnesses speak as fallible, erring men like ourselves' (*Church Dogmatics*, ed. G. W. Bromley and T. F. Torrance, (T. & T. Clark, 1956), I. 2. 507). If the prophets and apostles are to act as signs of the eternal word, 'there is a constant need of that continuing work of the Holy Spirit in the Church' (ibid. 513). Dogmatics begins with

the hearing of the word of God 'in the proclamation of the Church' (775). Dogmatics will find itself 'in conversation not only with the Church of its own generation, but also with that of all previous "presents" which have now become "past". Dogmatics can be properly understood only when viewed as part of a single movement, of which it forms the most recent stage' (779). In other words, he seems to be saying, the Bible must be interpreted in the light of the record of Church doctrine. But Barth does not seem to carry this programme, at which he hints, through thoroughly. Asked, 'What gives the present canon of Scripture its authority?', he replied, 'the canon is the canon just because it is so' (quoted from his 'Table Talk' in J. Bowden, *Karl Barth* (SCM Press, 1971), 113–14.)

9. There is in Rahner the extraordinary claim that 'within the last hundred years we have arrived at a situation in which a new definition can no longer be false because in any such new definition the *legitimate* range of interpretation is so wide that it no longer leaves any room for error outside it' (K. Rahner, *Theological Investigations*, xiv, trans. D. Bourke (Darton, Longman, & Todd, 1976), 80. He thinks that this arises because old definitions already fix the framework of what must be believed as firmly as the analogical use of language allows it to be fixed. But no argument is given to show that the definitions of the early Church ruled out certain propositions, whereas later definitions could not rule out any further propositions. If 'analogy' could render later definitions empty of clear content, I cannot see why it cannot wreak equal havoc with earlier definitions; and if it did, the Church could not be a vehicle of revelation. Analogical use of words does not, I have claimed, as such prevent sentences from having significant content. Rahner's next sentence suggests his awareness of the unargued nature of his claim: 'A question which we may leave open at this point is whether the impossibility we have declared to exist is capable of absolute proof at the theoretical level, or merely a practical one.'

Index

Index